connect the shapes
CROCHET MOTIFS

connect the shapes
CROCHET MOTIFS

CREATIVE TECHNIQUES FOR
JOINING MOTIFS OF ALL SHAPES

EDIE ECKMAN

Storey Publishing

To Ann with love

The mission of Storey Publishing is to serve our customers by publishing practical information that encourages personal independence in harmony with the environment.

Edited by **Gwen Steege** and **Pam Thompson**
Art direction and book design by **Carolyn Eckert**
Text production by **Jennifer Jepson Smith**

Cover photography by © **John Polak Photography**, except for author's photograph by **Charles Eckman**
Interior photography by © **John Polak Photography**, except for pages 19 top right, 222, 226, 230, 231, 234, 238 top, 242, 245, 246, 251, 257, and 259 by © **Chattman Photography**, pages 25 bottom, 27 middle, 97 bottom, 101 left, 211 left, 228, and 263 row 4, center by **Mars Vilaubi**, page 27 bottom by © **Myra Wood** and page 27 top courtesy of the author.
Charts by **Karen Manthey**

Indexed by **Christine R. Lindemer**, Boston Road Communications
Tech edited by **Karen Manthey**

The information in this book is true and complete to the best of our knowledge. All recommendations are made without guarantee on the part of the author or Storey Publishing. The author and publisher disclaim any liability in connection with the use of this information.

Storey books are available for special premium and promotional uses and for customized editions. For further information, please call 1-800-793-9396.

Storey Publishing
210 MASS MoCA Way
North Adams, MA 01247
www.storey.com

Printed in China by Toppan Leefung Printing Limited
10 9 8 7 6 5 4 3 2 1

Library of Congress Cataloging-in-Publication Data

Eckman, Edie.
  Connect the shapes crochet motifs / by Edie Eckman.
    pages cm
  Includes index.
  ISBN 978-1-60342-973-3 (hardcover with concealed
    wire-o : alk. paper)
  1. Crocheting—Patterns. I. Title.
  TT820.E349 2012
  746.43'4—dc23
                                              2012013934

contents

introduction

CROCHETED MOTIFS CONTINUE TO FASCINATE US. They can be used on their own for embellishments, or repeated and combined to create larger projects. They are usually (but not always) worked in the round from the center out. The most common crochet motif is the granny square (see page 46). Indeed, the term "granny square" is often used to mean *any* square crocheted unit worked in the round. Here, I use the word "motif" instead, because they can be so many more shapes than square, and they certainly aren't confined to grannies!

What is it about the use of color, shape, and texture that grabs our interest and makes us willing to stitch the same motif over and over again? Perhaps it is the repetition itself that is so soothing, or the almost instant gratification that we get from seeing a project (or at least part of a project) begun and ended in such a short amount of time. Perhaps it is the ability to play with color, without fear of wasting too much time or yarn if the results are not what we would like. Or perhaps it is the construction of a whole from individual units that appeals to us, evoking the puzzles and blocks of our childhoods.

Many crocheters love to stitch motifs but dread the process of joining them. Connecting one motif to another — or many motifs to each other — doesn't have to be the most-feared and least-looked-forward-to aspect of a crochet project. In fact, it can be as exhilarating as the stitching! And because crochet is so versatile, we don't have to stick to joining pieces only at their points or edges. We can layer motifs or add filler motifs. We can connect motifs on more than one round or join them internally, creating entire fabrics that are joined together as part of their essential structure.

connected
with a filler motif

connected
in layers

In *Connect the Shapes Crochet Motifs*, I build on what I started in my first book about motifs. In *Beyond the Square Crochet Motifs*, I explored a variety of shapes, colors, and textures, and experimented with techniques to improve the look of the motif. In *Connect the Shapes*, I gather motifs in families and explore ways of joining them to each other. The families usually begin with a motif originally designed for this book. From this starting point, I vary stitches and colors, add corners, textures, and layers, and otherwise morph the original into new motifs. These may resemble each other in the way of close siblings — or somewhat distant cousins. Joining the motifs in new and surprising ways carries them even further from their origins, and in this book I delve into many methods of joining, exploring both the design and technical aspects of creating a whole fabric from individual units. And finally, I include projects that demonstrate some practical uses for these connection methods.

Connect the Shapes is meant to be a jumping-off point for your own creativity. Make the projects in the book, by all means, but more importantly, study the techniques, examine the samples, and try your own variations in order to fashion your own beautiful one-of-a-kind creations!

Join the fun!

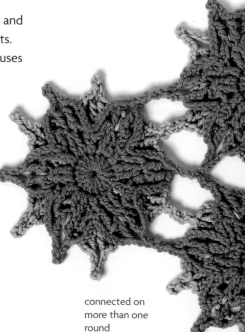

connected on
more than one
round

quick-start guide

Getting started. Unless otherwise stated, all motifs begin with a sliding loop (see page 12).

How to make the stitches. See Glossary (page 264) for descriptions of crochet stitches and the stitch key on the inside back cover.

Understanding rounds. Symbol charts are shown in two (or more) colors, indicating alternate rounds (or sometimes rows). Round (or row) numbers appear at the beginning of each one.

Multicolor motifs. Most motifs are written as if they are to be stitched using one color, using techniques familiar to American crocheters. Many of the samples, however, have been stitched using multiple colors. Refer to the accompanying notes to see what colors were used on which rounds.

Absence of build-up chains. In some instances, a new round begins without the typical build-up chain. Instead, the stitch is started with the yarn unconnected to the current working piece. See page 14 for an explanation of these *standing stitches*.

Special techniques. As you study the photographs of the motifs, you'll notice that many were stitched using one or more of the special tips and tricks covered in Get Started and Get It Together. For best results, incorporate these techniques into your crocheting repertoire.

American crochet terms are used throughout the book.

US	UK
slip stitch	single crochet
single crochet	double crochet
half double crochet	half treble crochet
double crochet	treble crochet
double treble crochet	triple treble crochet

PART I

TECHNIQUES

The motifs and patterns in this book are meant to be accessible to all skill levels. Inexperienced crocheters will want to take time to explore Get Started in depth. More experienced crocheters may just take a look at the Quick-Start Guide opposite and jump into the rest of the book. Get It Together examines the range of possibilities for connecting motifs, including exciting ways to join motifs to each other as you go.

get started

LET'S FACE IT: looking at line after line of crochet instructions can be pretty mind-blowing. If you don't understand the terminology, it is difficult, if not impossible, to see what is supposed to happen on each round. But reading a line of crochet text is like reading a recipe. If you take time to understand the abbreviations (c = cup, T = tablespoon, t = teaspoon; ch = chain, dc = double crochet) and common techniques (sauté, dice; join, fasten off), you will get a sense of the construction without actually cooking (or stitching).

Like computer code, crochet instructions are meant to be interpreted bit by bit, line by line. (Or so I'm told. I have no clue about computer code.) What this means in our world of crochet is that crochet instructions use more-or-less standardized abbreviations for common terms, with punctuation marks to tell us when to pause, repeat, and continue, where to put each stitch, and what to do at the end of each round.

In this book, all standard stitches are defined in the glossary (page 264), and for ease of use, any special stitches or techniques are included at the beginning of each pattern.

Reading Charts

For many crocheters, charts are the perfect alternative to line-by-line instructions. Crochet charts offer a visual representation of the crocheted fabric; the chart *looks like* what you are stitching. It shows the shape of the finished item, which stitches are used, and the relationship of stitches to each other.

Each stitch or group of stitches has its own symbol, and each symbol bears a resemblance to the stitch itself. Once you learn the symbol for the common stitches, it's like reading a book. If you know ┃ stands for "double crochet," and ⌒ stands for "chain," when you see ⋀⋀⋀, you'll know it means "make 5 double crochet stitches in the chain-3 space." Using charts and text together can usually clear up any ambiguity about where or how to create a stitch.

It is worth learning to read charts as your primary means of understanding a pattern, or at the very least as an adjunct to understanding line-by-line instructions.

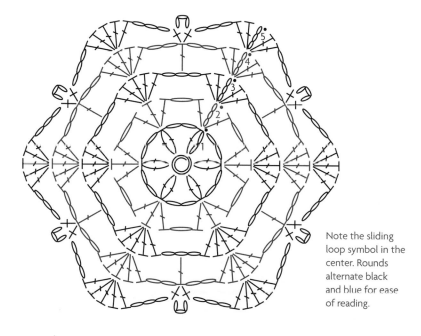

Note the sliding loop symbol in the center. Rounds alternate black and blue for ease of reading.

Poke, Wrap, Pull: You Can Do It!

Relax. You can do this! If you can hold the hook in one hand and yarn in the other, insert the hook somewhere, wrap the yarn over the hook, and pull it through whatever is on your hook, you can crochet anything.

Poke, wrap, and pull: It's the combination of these three moves, in infinite variations, that creates crochet. Turn to the glossary (page 264) for basic stitch instructions. Start with some of the simpler motifs (labeled Quick & Easy), and take your time. Remember to breathe. Relax your shoulders. Ask experienced crocheters for help when you get stuck. Soon you'll be crocheting anything you choose!

[LEFTIES ARE SPECIAL]

Ah, the trials and tribulations of being left-handed! Scissors don't cut, the ergonomic computer mouse at work doesn't fit your hand, and crochet patterns assume you crochet with your right hand. It's lucky you are smart enough to know that usually when a crochet pattern says "right," you think "left," and vice versa. If you need to flip the images in the book for a better perspective, look at them in a mirror or scan the page and flip it on the vertical axis. You'll do just fine!

In the Beginning

While there are several different ways to begin a flat piece in the round, only two methods are needed for these patterns.

CHAIN RING

The chain ring, which most crocheters are familiar with, creates a sturdy, small circle with a set diameter around which to stitch your motif. The circle can be made as large as necessary to create an open center and to accommodate many stitches. On the other hand, it may not be a good choice if you want to have a very tight, closed center; there's a limit to how small it can be.

 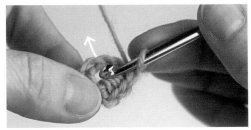

1. Beginning with a slip knot on your hook, chain the number of times indicated. Slip stitch into the first chain to form a ring.

2. Work the first round's stitches into the ring, rather than into the individual chain stitches that form the ring.

SLIDING LOOP

An alternative to the chain ring is the sliding loop. Some crocheters are familiar with the magic loop method of beginning a round; the sliding loop offers an extra measure of security for the tail. The sliding loop offers a variable diameter for the center ring, and it can accommodate quite a few stitches while still allowing the center to be closed tightly. It may take a few tries before the sliding loop becomes second nature, but it's well worth the effort.

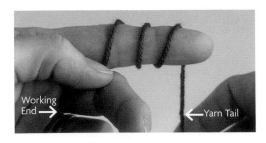 

1. Wrap yarn clockwise around the non-dominant index finger two times to form a ring. (That's the left index finger for right-handers and the right index finger for left-handers.)

2. Holding the yarn tail between thumb and middle finger, insert the hook into the ring, grab the working end of the yarn, and pull it through the ring.

3. Chain the number of times required to begin the first round. Drop ring from finger.

4. Work additional stitches into the ring to complete the first round.

5. Before joining the first round, gently pull the beginning tail to partially cinch up the ring. You'll find that one of the ring's two strands tightens, while the other does not.

6. Now gently tug the tightened ring until you see the other strand getting smaller.

7. When that second strand is as tight as you want it, pull the tail again to close the ring. Some yarns stick more than others, but if you take care not to pull too hard on the tail at first, you can easily tighten both strands, one at a time. For some more slippery yarns, you may find that your initial tug on the tail tightens both loops.

Starting a Round

When beginning a new round, most patterns instruct you to chain the appropriate number and then work the next stitch. Because crochet stitches are formed below the hook, this *build-up chain* (sometimes referred to as a *turning chain*, even when no turning is involved) allows the hook to reach the right height to work the first stitch of the next round.

BUILD-UP CHAIN

The number of chains needed depends on the height of the stitch: 1 chain stitch for single crochet, 2 chain stitches for half double crochet, 3 chain stitches for double crochet, and so on. Many times, this chain replaces the actual stitch; the pattern will indicate if this is so.

STANDING STITCHES

If the new round begins with the yarn not already tethered to the current work, such as when you are starting a new color, there is no real reason to start the round with a chain. Because the hook can be held at any height you choose, you can just finish off the old color and begin stitching the round with the new yarn. While there's no universally accepted name for this type of stitch — because, after all, it's just a plain stitch — I think of it as a *standing stitch*. Standing stitches have the benefit of creating a perfectly invisible start to a new round.

With slip knot

Beginning with a slip knot on the hook and, treating that knot as an existing stitch, work the first stitch of the round in the regular way.

SINGLE CROCHET

Insert the hook into the first stitch and pull up a loop, yarn over, and pull through 2 loops on hook.

DOUBLE CROCHET

Make a yarn over before inserting the hook, and then proceed as you would for an ordinary double crochet stitch.

With this method, you'll end up with a small knot just to the side of the first stitch; either hide it on the wrong side when weaving in your ends, or unknot it after you've joined the round.

Without slip knot

Wrap the yarn around the hook from back to front to simulate a slip knot and any initial yarn-overs: two times for single crochet, three for double crochet, and four for treble. In all cases, the first wrap will be dropped.

SINGLE CROCHET

Insert the hook into the first stitch and pull up a loop, *yarn over and pull through 2 loops on hook.

DOUBLE CROCHET

For double crochet, repeat from *. Note that the extra wrap you made in the first step serves as the yarn over you're accustomed to making for a double crochet stitch.

Let go of the remaining tail and unwrap it from around the hook, allowing it to hang loose at the back of the work. The top of the first crochet will be incomplete at this point.

Ending a Round

When one round is complete, the last stitch must be joined to the first stitch to connect the stitches before beginning the next round. There are three types of end-of-round joins used in this book.

SLIP-STITCH JOIN

This is the most common join used in crochet. Simply insert the hook into the first stitch, yarn over, and pull through all the loops on the hook.

SHIFTING-END-OF-ROUND JOIN

A single, half double, or double crochet is sometimes used as a joining stitch to move the end of the round to the right (or to the left, for left-handed crocheters). The joining stitch is used in place of a chain or chains to allow the new round to begin in the center of that space.

INVISIBLE (OR TAPESTRY NEEDLE) JOIN

Since this join creates a completely invisible end to the round, it's the best choice for the final join of the last round of the shape.

1. Complete the last stitch, but do not join it to the first stitch.

2. Cut the yarn, leaving at least a 4" (10 cm) tail, and pull up the loop on the hook until the yarn tail comes through the stitch.

3. Thread the tail onto a tapestry needle, and insert under both loops of the V at

the top of the first stitch of the round; pull the yarn tail through. If you begin the round with a slip knot, you'll be working over it.

4. Insert the needle from top to bottom back down into the V at the top of the last stitch of the round, and weave in the end.

WITH SLIP KNOT

Weaving in Ends

Logic dictates that for every piece of yarn used, two ends need to be secured. The best methods are invisible on the right side of the fabric, yet secure enough to ensure that the ends don't work themselves out with handling. The ends may be worked in as the piece is stitched or woven in after it is complete, using a variety of methods. It's fine to use a combination of methods, depending on what works best with the crocheted fabric. If you work over the tail while you are stitching, leave a bit of loose tail so you can go back later and weave it in the opposite direction for greater security.

Working over a tail as part of the stitching

[HIDING THOSE ENDS]

- Don't skimp on tail length — leave at least 4 inches (10 cm) to work with. Thicker yarn needs even longer tails.

- Weave in more than one direction — clockwise, counterclockwise, diagonally, horizontally, vertically.

- Weave in on the wrong side of the same color as the tail whenever possible.

Attitude Adjustment

Admittedly, this is not exactly a technique, but it might be the most important tip for weaving in ends. Instead of letting the Fear and Dread of Multiple Ends keep you from using all the colors of yarn you desire, think of the task as just another important step in making the best possible project you can. Consider the satisfaction you get from a just-mown lawn. The mowing itself might not be exciting, but the joy of turning a shaggy patch of grass into a tidy yard is worth the work. Play a mental game to see how many different and inventive ways you can hide the tail. Take pride in the tidiness and colorfulness of your amazing work!

Choosing Yarn

Keep in mind the structure of the motifs and the fabric they will create when put together. Some motifs are lacy, while others are fairly solid, and yet others are three-dimensional. Many motifs have multiple characteristics. A fabric made of very thick, solid pieces might not be comfortable made into a garment because of its weight and lack of drape, though the same fabric might make a very comfy afghan. Just be sure that afghan is not too heavy to lift!

A motif with large open areas might work as a lovely lacy scarf, but it might be too holey and unstructured when combined with other similar motifs in a heavy yarn. In addition to the fiber used, the weight and diameter of the yarn and the hook used can create quite diverse looks for the same motif. Here is Motif 17 (see page 70) stitched in an assortment of yarns, beginning for comparison's sake with the Shelridge Farm double-knitting-weight wool used to stitch all the book's motifs.

| Dk weight: wool | Worsted weight: slubbed cotton/acrylic/nylon/elastic | Dk weight: kid mohair/ silk/metallic | Size 10 crochet thread: cotton |

You will be happiest with your finished work if you choose a yarn that is well suited to your project. Natural fibers like wool, cotton, and alpaca — and blends using those fibers — work well for motif-based crochet because they can be blocked to hold their shape. Soft, flowing yarns like silk and bamboo may not hold their shape as well as wool. Acrylic and other fibers will work also, although care must be taken when blocking to avoid ruining the fabric. Generally speaking, use the best-quality yarn you can afford. If you are spending hours stitching, it's worth the expense to be happy with the result!

Why Gauge Matters

Gauge **is the number of stitches and rounds** over a specified length. With motifs worked in the round, the gauge is most often given as the finished measurement of the motif over all rounds. Many crocheters simply ignore gauge and stick to projects where fit doesn't matter. Nevertheless, gauge is an important piece of information. Of course, matching gauge in a pattern is important in order to make sure the project comes out to be the desired size. Matching gauge with a particular yarn ensures that the fabric you are making is similar in drape and appearance to the sample project. It is also a way to know that you will have enough yarn to finish the project.

VARIEGATED YARNS

Multicolored yarns may present a challenge when working motifs. Since part of the beauty of the motif is the way the combinations of stitches form shapes, any color shading that interferes with our ability to see those patterns will be less than successful. This interference is more likely to occur with yarns that have sudden color changes and relatively short stretches of color.

Short color-change yarn can obscure the motif.

The Poet Vest (page 245)

Before committing to a variegated yarn, study the yarn and make several swatches to ensure that the results will be intended. When working with a new ball of multicolored yarn, hand-wind the yarn into a center-pull ball, even if it already comes in a center-pull hank. That way, you can see how the colors progress: in what order the color changes and the lengths.

You may even discover a color hidden in the middle of the ball that wasn't apparent before you went exploring!

The Poet Vest uses a yarn that has long lengths of color that shade gradually from one color to the next. The size of the motifs was kept small to allow each motif to remain a single color. Careful attention to the order of stitching the blocks and their arrangement yields a fabric that optimizes the beautiful colorwork inherent in the yarn.

[TIP]

Hand-wind balls to see how the yarn's color progresses before you stitch (see next page).

Hand-Winding Center-Pull Balls

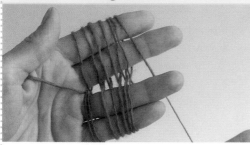

Hold the tail of the yarn in the crook of your thumb so that it rests on the back of your hand. Wrap the yarn several times in a figure 8 around your fingers, taking care that the strands lie parallel on your fingers.

With your other hand, pinch the yarn where it crosses itself and then pull it from your fingers.

Keeping the tail free throughout, fold this little skein of yarn in half and begin wrapping additional yarn around it, taking care not to wrap too tightly. Continue wrapping yarn in various directions to create a ball; wrapping over the fingers prevents the yarn from getting too tight.

Yarns with longer color changes have design potential.

An alternative to optimizing the shading feature of a yarn is to create intentional randomness in the color arrangement. Even this seeming randomness, though, may take some planning to prevent unwanted pooling of colors. In the example below, the motifs were worked up to the last round, then a sufficient amount of yarn was pulled out to complete the motif.

The partial motifs were then placed in the desired arrangement and the final rounds worked with a join-as-you-go (JAYGo) method (see page 35) to complete the fabric.

Working with Color

Color is a major component — perhaps *the* major component — in the success of a motif-based project. Color is powerful. Perhaps the colors on the cover of this book were the first thing to catch your eye and make you want to pick it up. Color is also very personal; we each perceive color differently and have different emotional responses to certain colors.

Volumes have been written on color theory; they are much more complete and in-depth than I need be. If you like, take time to study the tenets and terminology of color theory. Whether you follow the "rules" or go with your instincts, the most important thing to understand is that there is no "right" or "wrong" in choosing colors. Nevertheless, a few basic guidelines might help you select an appealing mix of colors for your project.

Choosing Colors without Theory

> **Go outside.** If you pay attention, you'll see that Mother Nature has a plethora of beautiful color combinations.

> **Look at projects** others have made and choose colorways that appeal to you. Browse the Internet for a huge selection!

> **Select a painting** you like, and choose yarn colors based on that painting.

> **Use online tools,** such as Adobe's Kuler or myPantone.

> **Visit the paint section** of your local home improvement store to see what color combinations are popular.

Experimenting with analogous colors . . .

dark and light . . .

complementary colors . . .

and the golden mean (see Classic Grannies, page 46).

CHOOSING COLORWAYS

The success of a colorway depends not just on hue (color) but on the value (darkness/lightness) and saturation (how much color or dye it has) of the colors, and on the proportions of the colors used.

Lighter values pop relative to darker values, but it is not always easy to determine color value just by looking. One way to determine value is to make a gray-scale photocopy (or a gray-scale scan or digital picture) of the yarns. Colors with lighter values will show up as light gray, while the darker values will appear black. If the yarns seem to be the same color on the gray-scale image, they are the same value.

Colors may be chosen to appear in equal amounts or in different proportions. You can test your ideas before stitching by wrapping the yarn around a piece of white cardboard. Wrap each color several times around a small piece of white cardboard, trying different color combinations and using more or less of some colors. See how different colors look when they are placed next to each other.

Nothing beats swatching to work out the best colorway for your project.

[**TIP**] Try stitching the same motif over and over again, changing colors in different rounds, and in different orders.

The golden mean refers to a mathematical concept, which in this context says there is a universally appealing proportion of about two-thirds to one-third. If you are using two colors for your project, make about two-thirds of it in one color and the remaining third in the other color.

For a three-color piece, make about one-third of the total in the first color, then divide the remaining two-thirds in three again, using the second color for one-third of that two-thirds (that is, ⅔), and the remaining color for the final two-thirds of the two-thirds (⅔). To use even more colors, make further subdivisions of that last two-thirds, using increasingly smaller amounts of the additional colors.

Creating Shapes

You may follow the directions in this book to re-create the motifs shown exactly, but chances are that you will find yourself wanting to expand on these offerings. You may add rounds to make a shape bigger, or use elements of a design to go in a different direction to create your own custom-designed motif. Along the way, you'll need to know a few things about creating shapes.

Circles, triangles, squares, hexagons, and octagons are formed by placing increases at equidistant points to create corners around a center point. A circle, of course, has no corners. Thus, its increases are evenly spaced around the center ring. Increases for triangles are made in three evenly spaced locations, for squares in four locations, and so on. The more corners or points a shape has, the closer to circular it appears, so an octagonal piece with rounded corners may appear more round than octagonal. Even hexagonal pieces may appear round. It's just a matter of semantics and how you choose to attach that shape to others around it.

The number of stitches you need to increase on each round to keep the piece flat — not ruffled with too many stitches nor cupped with too few — depends on the height of the stitches in each round. It all has something to do with geometry, circumference, and π, but you really don't have to know the details. What you do need to know is this: if all the stitches are the same height, follow these rules of thumb to determine how many total stitches need to be increased on each round:

stitch	increases per round
single	6
half double	8
double	12
treble	18

If the rounds contain stitches of different heights, or special stitches like popcorns and bobbles, you may need to play with the guidelines somewhat to figure out the correct proportions for your situation.

Not all motifs maintain the same shape throughout. A piece that begins as a circle can become a square. Hexagons can become circles. It's all a matter of what the stitches are and how they are grouped. Even color can be used to make a motif appear a different shape than it really is.

SUPERSIZE MOTIFS

It can be tempting to make a motif bigger by adding more rounds. This is a fine thought, but beware of a pitfall: as motifs grow beyond six rounds or so, the corners may not seem as crisp as they did on the first few rounds and may actually skew. This happens because each stitch is not always placed directly in line with the stitch below it. If skewing is a problem, it may be ameliorated by adjusting the corners to make them asymmetrical and thus get the sides of the shape back on track.

SKEWED
On this large square the corners appear to be twisting to the left.

NOT SKEWED
The problem was solved by substituting (4 dc, ch 2, 2 dc) for the called-for (3 dc, ch 2, 3 dc) corners. This substitution may not be required for every round; you'll have to experiment.

[WAVES AND CURLS]

Although most shapes are designed to lie flat, sometimes they start to misbehave. Try any combination of the following on one or more rounds to solve the problem.

to correct waviness

Use fewer increases on one or more rounds.

Use fewer chains between stitches.

Make the center opening larger.

Use extended stitches in place of standard stitches (see glossary, page 264).

Use a smaller hook.

to correct cupping

Use additional increases on one or more rounds.

Use more chains between stitches.

Make the center opening smaller.

Use a bigger hook.

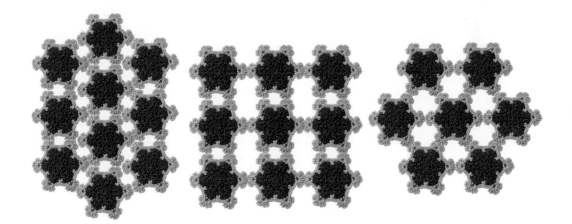

Arranging Shapes

Arranging pieces to create a fabric can be as much fun as the stitching and as easy as placing squares next to each other. Chances are, however, that you will want an arrangement that is a bit more interesting than that! The shape of the individual motifs and the type of finished product you are trying to create will help determine the arrangement and attachment of motifs. Think of all the different ways mosaic tiles can be arranged to create a picture, and you'll start to imagine some of the possibilities for motif-based crochet.

Pieces can be joined along all adjacent sides, at the corners only, or with some combination of the two, as these pictures show. Motifs may touch at the corners, be aligned in straight rows and columns, or be offset by a half-drop or some other arrangement. Different sizes and styles of motifs can be used together.

Try mixing geometric shapes like triangles, squares, and hexagons. Consider using half or quarter motifs to fill in spaces. And don't forget to use negative space — open air or the absence of a motif — as an effective design element.

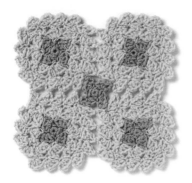

This join uses the first two rounds of Motif 73 as a filler.

Filler Motifs

Some motif arrangements make use of *filler motifs*, smaller motifs that join to existing motifs and fill in empty spaces left between larger motifs. These fillers are both decorative and functional, adding stability to the larger fabric.

The design of the filler motif should complement the motifs they join. Often a filler is made from the first round or two of the main motif, perhaps with additional chain corners added to reach out to the main motifs.

Other times a fraction of a motif is what you need. A half hexagon can fit into the edges of a hexagonal afghan to create straight sides. You'll find examples of partial motifs in Motifs and Joins, but you can make your own partial motif to fit your needs.

To do so, you will work back and forth in rows, and these stitches will not be squeezed into place, as they are when worked in the round. They'll try to spread out and you

might find yourself wondering why you have five-eighths of a circle instead of a true half circle. To correct this tendency, create your partial motif with 1 to 3 stitches *fewer* per round than you might expect.

Planning Pays

Plan a pleasing design ahead of time so that you don't have to stitch all the pieces, rip out, and rearrange.

Think of the motifs as puzzle pieces that can be colored and arranged as you choose. Use graph paper and colored pencils to sketch color arrangements, or use a black-and-white photocopier to play with shape arrangements. You can make photocopies of the motif stitch charts, cut them out, and color them with markers or colored pencils. If you don't have access to a printer or photocopier, just trace a motif, then cut out multiple copies and color them.

If you are willing to stitch several motifs — one of each colorway and/or shape that you plan to use — you can be even more accurate in your planning. Photograph or scan each motif individually to create a digital image of the motif. Print out one or more color copies of the motif(s), then cut them out to form a paper motif in the shape of the original.

Free-form

Free-form crochet is extremely popular, and for good reason. In free-form, you can follow your every whim, stitch any stitch in any direction, change colors, and allow yourself to break any self-imposed rules about what is right. Motifs are perfect for free-form crochet! Use just a round or two of any motif, or use the whole thing. Add additional rounds, even asymmetrical ones, to get your motif to fit with others. Save your "oops" motifs — those hexagons with only five corners — as free-form fodder. In free-form, it doesn't matter if your square is lopsided!

Even black-and-white photocopies can help you visualize your final piece.

Now that you have colorful puzzle pieces, it's time to play! Experiment with arranging the pieces by shape and color until you have a pleasing arrangement. Make additional paper motifs if necessary to get the number you need of each color. Once you are satisfied with your design, tape the pieces together to form a pattern template, or just take a picture or draw a sketch of the finished paper project.

You can even plan exactly which stitch to join in by looking carefully at your copied image. Can you identify the individual stitches on your paper pattern? You may find it easier to see if you use a black marker to add crochet stitch symbols (see inside back cover) on each pattern piece. Now, use a highlighter or colored pencils to mark the stitches that will be joined. Refer to your template as you work — and join — the motifs.

Irish Crochet

Traditional Irish crochet uses a steel hook, fine thread, and a variety of flower- and leaflike motifs. These motifs are joined with a crocheted mesh created with a combination of slip-stitch, single crochet, and double crochet stitches. You do not need to stitch traditional patterns to borrow these techniques.

For a modern variation of Irish crochet, use cotton crochet thread to make a number of motifs of your choice — they don't have to be flowers or leaves. If you like, you may join some of the motifs to each other using the method of your choice. Cut out a paper or cloth template of the fabric shape you are trying to create. Pin the shapes in place, stretching each motif out to its full size. If you are using a cloth template, you may choose at this point to baste the shapes in place on the fabric. Using the same thread, begin filling the open spaces in the template with a crocheted mesh that joins the shapes to each other; take care to keep the motifs stretched out. When the mesh is complete, remove the pins or basting from the template, and block the finished piece. The Cottage Lamp Shade (page 257) uses this technique.

For an even easier Irish crochet lookalike, simply create a mesh fabric in the size and shape of your choice (using any yarn or thread), then sew completed motifs onto the mesh in whatever design you wish.

Trust Your Gut

You may be looking at this book to find out the Right Way to put crochet motifs together. Learning all you can from books, the Internet, and other crocheters is a good way to supply yourself with the tools you need to tackle any crocheting challenge, but there is no one right way to do anything. Because every project is different, it is really worth thinking for yourself about what technique will work best. Don't hesitate to try more than one way to accomplish something. Better to take a few moments to experiment before settling on a best-way-for-now decision. Remember — you can always R&R (rip and restitch)!

get it together

OH, THE OPTIONS TO CHOOSE FROM when connecting pieces! Learn them all — or create your own — for the perfect join.

The location of the connections is an important decision, as it will affect the overall function and look of the fabric. Too few joins may create an unstable fabric, while pieces that are joined too tightly may stiffen the drape of the fabric. The style of the motif and the finished use of the fabric will be your guide to choosing the location and frequency of the joins.

Corners and points of motifs are obvious and often crucial joining points. Arches or scallops along sides are possible joining points. You may find that you also need to join wherever two motif points approach each other, even if they don't quite touch. Adjacent edges are often joined along the entire edge, but it may not always be necessary or even desirable to join each stitch.

The intersection of three or more motifs may be a challenge, as the corner of one motif needs to be attached to other motifs.

It can be tricky to strike the right balance between too many connections (resulting in a lumpy mess) and too few connections (creating an unwanted hole). Sometimes it is best to keep connecting the pieces in a series, ignoring the motif in the corner diagonally opposite; other times it is best to join *only* the diagonal corners. Now is when experimentation is your friend. Take the time to try several options to determine which one works best.

Be aware that joined motifs may look somewhat different from their unattached siblings, especially at the corners. An unattached shape does not have any outside forces acting on it, so it remains in its original form. Once you add additional shapes, depending on the joining method and how much force it exerts on the motif — pulling it toward other motifs — you may see that the motif changes shape.

For this reason, before embarking on a large project involving many connected motifs, experiment with joining methods and arrangements. Stitch and connect at least five or six motifs, fastening off the final round but leaving the tail longer than usual and not woven in. Study the connected motifs to see if you need adjustments to make the pieces fit more comfortably.

Corners may be made longer with taller stitches or added chains. Sides may be flattened out by placing shorter stitches in the center of the side and taller stitches toward the corners.

Joining methods may be chosen for their height — double crochet join versus flat join, for example — to make the pieces fit together nicely. If necessary, rip out the final round(s) and make modifications until the fit is perfect. Don't forget to make a note of your changes so that you can re-create them for the remainder of the pieces!

The connected motifs here were adapted from Motif 14 (page 66) to fit better alongside each other.

too many → connections

← just right

↑
too few connections

GET IT TOGETHER

A Special Note about Triangles

Joining triangles can be a bit tricky. In order for triangles to fit tightly along an entire edge all the way to the corner, the three corners must be fairly pointy — perhaps more so than would look nice on a motif standing by itself. In some cases, a triangle actually has sides that bow out, creating an even greater challenge for a smooth, flat connection.

You can achieve a corner extension by using taller stitches, chains, or a combination of both.

Sometimes you may not want the piece to lie completely flat. The Pie Wedge Pillow (page 240) takes advantage of the curved edges of Motif 72. When joined, five of these triangles form a slightly convex circle, perfect for covering a round pillow form. Although you might expect a circle to be made of six equilateral triangles, the slightly curved sides of each triangle plump out to fill the extra space.

These triangle motifs are the same through the next-to-last round.

The corners of this version are extended to allow for a better fit with other similar triangles.

Join When You're Done

With join-when-you're-done methods, the project remains in pieces — and wonderfully portable — until the final joining. You may play with the arrangement of colors and the physical placement of motifs until the very last moment.

The main drawback of this approach is that if you are averse to anything that smacks of finishing, you'll be pretty unhappy when it comes time to put all those pieces together. It can be daunting to realize that you have dozens (or hundreds) of individual pieces to put together before you have a finished project!

Arrange your pieces in the finished layout, then take a few moments to decide in what order they should be joined. Obviously, you'll want to try to plan for as few seams (and thus as few yarn tails) as possible. Consider joining them with a Join-As-You-Go (JAYGo) Continuous Round (see page 38).

The various methods of joining pieces of crochet look different depending on where you insert the tapestry needle or crochet hook — try all three ways!

Hook placed under both loops of stitches

Hook placed under the outer loops of stitches

Hook placed under the inner loops of stitches

Motifs held with right sides together and whipstitched through the inside loops, with the diagonal corner left unstitched, creates a small hole that becomes a decorative element.

[**TIP**] As much as possible, try to separate the beginning and ending of rounds from the connecting points. Connections are sometimes under stress, and the end-of-the-round stitch is often not the strongest area of the motif. If it is necessary to have them near each other, take extra care to weave in the ends securely.

SEWING TOGETHER

Sewing motifs together with a tapestry needle is a tried-and-true method of joining motifs. It provides an attractive, flat, strong seam, but it can be quite time-consuming. It is most often done on pieces with adjoining straight edges, with the seam stitches worked into every crochet stitch along the edges. Most crocheters use a color that matches the outside edge of the motifs wherever possible, but careful use of a contrasting color can be a playful surprise.

Pieces are usually sewn from the wrong side, holding the right sides together. But you may want to try sewing pieces together with wrong sides facing, use a contrasting color yarn, or otherwise be creative with your seaming.

Whipstitch is the easiest and most common way of sewing pieces together. Holding pieces with right sides together, whipstitch pieces together, working into each stitch.

There is a slight directionality to whipstitches, meaning that they slant slightly. If you are using a contrasting color yarn to stitch with, you'll want to pay attention to this characteristic when deciding your stitching order, so that the stitches slant the same way.

RS together under both loops

RS together through outside loops

[**TIP**] Count the number of stitches on the last round of each motif as you make it. This will prevent errors and possible frustration later when you try to connect motifs and find they have different numbers of stitches.

CROCHETING TOGETHER

Crocheting pieces together is a much faster method of joining, and it can be decorative as well as functional. This is where joining really gets fun! There are various methods you can use to crochet pieces together after they are complete.

Single crochet together Single crochet through both loops of each stitch along the edge. This creates a raised ridge. If worked while holding right sides of the motifs together, the ridge is on the wrong side; if worked with wrong sides together, the ridge is on the right side, creating a textural design element.

RS together through both loops

WS together through both loops

WS together through inside loops

RS together through inside loops.

Single crochet / slip stitch together Holding wrong sides together, *single crochet in both loops of the front stitch, slip stitch in both loops of the back stitch; repeat from * in every other pair of stitches across. This makes a flatter seam than the plain single crochet method.

WS together through both loops

Slip stitch together Slip stitch the pieces together, going into the loops any way you like. Slip stitching together does not create a ridge, but be careful not to work too tightly, which might ruin the flexibility of the fabric.

WS together through inside loops

RS together through both loops and into ch-space

Zigzag chain With right sides facing, single crochet in 1 stitch or space on one motif, chain 3 (or desired number), then single crochet into a corresponding point on the adjacent motif. Continue working back and forth between motifs, creating a decorative zigzag pattern between the shapes.

Single crochet with chain With right sides or wrong sides together, as desired, single crochet through both motifs, chain 2, skip 2 stitches, then single crochet through the next pair of stitches. Continue connecting pieces with single crochet, placing a short chain over the skipped stitches. This method is highly adaptable for different circumstances.

WS together through both loops

Double crochet two together For more space between the motifs, use this combination: Work a partial double crochet (yarn over, insert hook into joining point and pull up a loop, yarn over and pull through 2 loops) into the joining point of the first motif and another partial double crochet into the corresponding joining point of the second motif; yarn over and pull through all 3 loops on the hook to finish off the 2 partial double crochet stitches together. Continue working along edges to be joined, placing chains and skipped stitches between the joining stitches as necessary to achieve an attractive seam.

Through both loops

Join as You Go (JAYGo)

Join as you go — JAYGo — has particular appeal for those who like to minimize finishing tasks; in other words: everyone. Many crocheters find it exciting to see their project grow motif by motif as they join each new piece. In traditional JAYGo work, you complete the first motif in its entirety, and then work to the place on the second motif where it is to be joined to the first. Most JAYGo is worked on the final round of a motif, though you can also join motifs before the final round or on multiple rounds.

Hybrid methods combine the best features of joining after you stitch with the best features of JAYGo. Working a continuous final round or using connecting motifs allows you to combine the portability and flexibility of the former with the finishing ease of the latter.

While JAYGo offers a number of advantages, it does require that you know ahead of time how your pieces are going to fit together to form the whole. Read Planning Pays (page 26) to see how to decide on an assembly strategy before you stitch. Of course, if you are working free-form, you don't have to plan anything at all. Just stitch and connect wherever you feel like it.

CONNECTING METHODS

No matter what your JAYGo strategy, you'll probably use one or more of these basic connection methods to join your motifs. While the methods described at right indicate inserting your hook from front to back, you may also want to experiment with inserting the hook from back to front.

SLIP-STITCH JOIN

1. Insert the hook from front to back into the joining point on the previous motif, yarn over, and pull through both the joining point and the loop on hook. You may prefer to insert the hook from back to front; see which method looks best to you.

2. Continue working stitches on the current motif until the next joining point.

3. A slip stitch forms a close connection.

FLAT JOIN

1. Drop the loop from the hook and insert the hook from front to back through the joining point on the previous motif then back into the dropped loop. Pull the loop through the joining point on the previous motif.

2. Continue working stitches on the current motif.

3. A flat join is similar to a slip stitch, but it creates a slightly smoother, more braided look.

SINGLE CROCHET JOIN

1. Without dropping the loop from the hook, and working from front to back, single crochet into the joining point on the previous motif.

2. Continue working around the current motif.

3. A single crochet join places the motifs slightly farther apart and forms a sturdy, yet more visible connection.

JAYGO CONTINUOUS ROUND

If all the joined motifs are meant to have a final round of the same color, it may be possible to join all the motifs in one final, continuous round, drastically decreasing the number of yarn tails to be woven in, and keeping the motifs themselves separate (and thus very portable) until the end is near.

Depending on the shape and arrangement of the motifs, you may be able to eliminate starts and stops with a bit of thought. Basically, it's like those brainteaser puzzles that you may have tried: Can you draw a continuous line around all these pieces without lifting your pencil? If the answer is "yes," then you can work a continuous joining round. Luckily for you, you don't have to figure it out all by yourself. I have several options for a continuous path to get you started. The Layered Motif Afghan (page 234) uses this technique, as does the join on page 145.

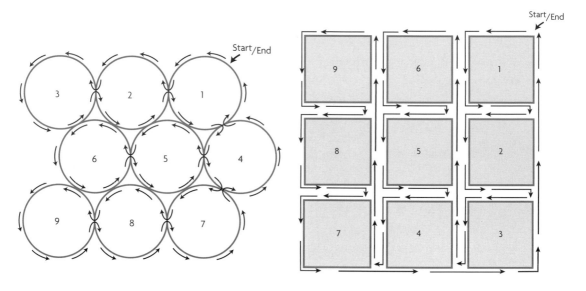

Follow the directional arrows to see how the continuous final round is stitched.

[**TIP**] Choosing one color for the final round of widely disparate motifs helps unify the design and makes seaming easier.

JAYGO HYBRID

What if the final round of the motifs isn't the same color? Consider this afghan plan, in which motifs are joined to each other in the order shown. This is a nice, easy-to-follow layout, but as the piece gets larger, its portability is compromised.

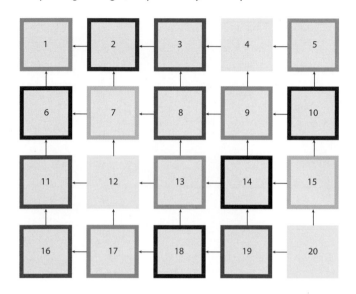

METHOD 1
Last round of every motif may be a different color

Now consider what would happen if you joined the squares in the order shown here. You could make all the odd-numbered squares independently, then join them while working the final round of the even-numbered squares. In effect, each even-numbered square serves as a full-size filler motif or connecting square. If each square is multicolored, you could even work each connecting square to the beginning of the last color, then set it aside until all the connecting squares are ready for their final rounds. Then it's just a matter of working those final rounds and joining all the squares — a couple of night's worth of stitching, and you're all finished!

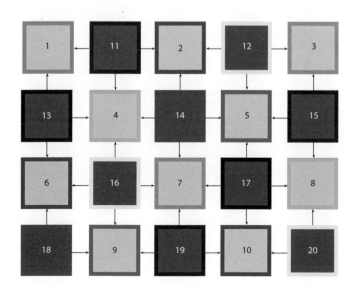

METHOD 2
Last round of each motif may be a different color

INTERNAL CONNECTIONS

Internal joins are less common than the methods already described, but they offer exciting possibilities. With internal joins, individual motifs are joined at some point before the final round; the join is an inherent part of the motif.

IN MOTIF 99
double-crochet rings are joined to each other with the initial chain ring.

MOTIF 94
involves creating separate motifs within the larger motif, creating a Siamese-twin effect.

JOINING MOTIF 36
before the final round makes it three-dimensional.

MOTIF 35
features interlocking layers, another type of internal join.

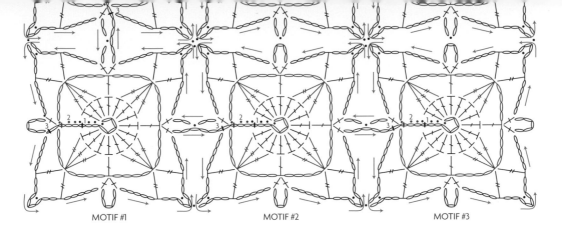

MOTIF #1   MOTIF #2   MOTIF #3

Here's a sample of diagram that shows a continuous motif join of Motif 23. The foundation chain for each motif is shown in red, while green arrows show the direction of work from one motif to another.

Continuous Motifs

Continuously joined motifs are not truly individual, independent pieces that are joined, but rather a way of creating a fabric that only *seems* to be made up of independent units. Sometimes called seamless crochet, you might say that this method takes the JAYGo techniques I've been discussing a bit further. Continuous motif crochet is much easier to show as a diagram than to explain in words — yet another reason to learn to read crochet charts!

We already discussed joining motifs with a final, continuous round. The **continuous motif** method joins not just on the final round, but with a chain that makes a path in to the very center ring of the next motif.

We'll call this chain a **foundation chain**, sometimes called a **starting chain**. The foundation chain serves several functions. It creates a path from the outside edge of one motif into the center of the next and serves as a beginning chain-ring. As the rounds of this motif are worked from the center outward, the foundation chain can act as an independent chain or as the base for a stitch, as needed. For example, slip stitching into each of two chains and then working a **crossover slip stitch** (see next page) mimics a double crochet and stands in for any double crochet called for in your pattern.

All rounds are worked in the regular way — counterclockwise for right-handers and clockwise for left-handers — but because the foundation chain already exists when you finish the round, it has to be crossed at the end of each round. That's not as intimidating as it might seem. Sometimes, instead of making the build-up chain at the round's start, slip stitch into the appropriate number of chains of the foundation chain, making your final slip stitch a crossover slip stitch. This serves as the first stitch and settles the work properly so that you can continue working the new round.

Other times, the foundation chain will stand on its own and serve as an entire stitch or chain-space, with no slip stitches worked into it at all, but with a crossover slip stitch placed as needed to begin working on the other side of the foundation chain.

The final round is not completed on every motif as it is worked. In some cases, part of the final round is worked and then completed later as it is being joined to other motifs. This final step, as indeed all of the steps, will depend on the shape, design, and arrangement of the motifs. But no matter what the arrangement, the tail of the yarn ends up at the same place it began!

Crossover Slip Stitch

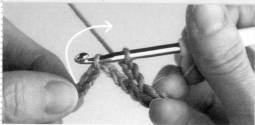

1. This example shows a ch-3 build-up chain and 3 skipped foundation chains. To work a crossover slip stitch, insert the hook into the next chain, then pass the tail of the foundation chain and any previous work-in-progress over the working yarn, or pass the yarn ball under the chain, so that the working yarn is now on the left side of the chain (right side for left-handers).

2. Yarn over and pull through everything on the hook to complete the slip stitch.

3. The slip stitch now crosses over the foundation chain and you are ready to continue working stitches on the left side of the foundation chain.

It is hard to describe the logic in words: It makes much more sense with yarn and hook in hand. Try working the continuous motifs on page 84 to gain a better understanding of the technique.

To convert a single motif into a continuously joined motif fabric, you will need to study the structure of the motif. Examine the stitch chart. Is there an identifiable *path in* and *path out*? In other words, can you figure out a way to begin on the outside edge of the motif, chain a length to create a path into the center, then work your way from the center outward, connecting to the established chain as you work each round? Have you decided how many motifs you need, and how they should be arranged and where they will touch? Now, can you determine a continuous path around the outside of the motifs, as described on page 38?

Clearly, the major benefit of this method is the minimum number of ends to weave in: potentially only two, if your project uses a single ball of yarn. There are, however, some drawbacks. As you may have guessed by the mention of a "single ball," this method is best suited to a single color of yarn. Unlike many motif-based projects where you can go on autopilot for a while, with continuous motifs you must pay attention while stitching to ensure that the motifs are created and joined in the proper order. In other words, you probably want to keep the stitch chart right in front of you!

For examples of this technique, see pages 84 and 251.

Edges and Finishing

Once all your pieces have been joined, they will probably benefit from the addition of a good edging. Edgings add a bit of polish and prevent the edges of the fabric from becoming distorted. The edging can be as simple as a row or round (or two) of single crochet, perhaps finished off with a row or round of Crab Stitch (Reverse single crochet). Or perhaps you want a border that serves as an additional decorative element, one whose design complements the design of the motifs.

Keep in mind that any edging that goes around a shape will need to be adapted to enable it to lie flat as it travels around corners and curves. An interior corner will require some sort of decrease to prevent unhappy bunching. The more acute the angle, the more decreases will be required. Exterior corners, on the other hand, require some sort of increase, depending on the stitch height and the angle of the corner. For example, a 90° right-angle corner on a square will prob-ably require 3 single crochet stitches to lie flat, while a 60° corner on a hexagon may only require 2 single crochet stitches. Refer to page 24 for a discussion of how to keep your pieces smooth and flat, and take a look at my *Around the Corner Crochet Borders*, which offers 150 decorative and functional edgings you can choose from to finish your connected motif project.

Simple Crab Stitch edging

A more elaborate edge that relates to the motif's design

[TIPS FOR CONTINUOUS MOTIFS]

When working continuous motifs, diagrams are much more helpful than written instructions. In any case, these general rules of thumb will help you understand:

> Right-handers always work in a counterclockwise direction around the motif, and left-handers work clockwise.

> At the end of rounds, work up the foundation chain with the corresponding number of slip stitches (generally): 1 for single crochet, 2 for half double, 3 for double crochet, and so forth. In some circumstances, the foundation chain may stand alone and act as a chain-space or stitch.

> Use crossover slip stitches (opposite) to begin working on the other side of the starting chain.

A simple crocheted chain or braid is a quick and flexible way to connect individual motifs.

BLOCKING

Careful blocking of your crochet enhances the fabric, sets the stitches, and makes your work appear neat and tidy. While synthetic yarns may not need much blocking, any natural fibers or fiber blends need to be blocked, and even 100% acrylic projects may benefit from appropriate attention. Blocking should be done for individual motifs for join-after-you-stitch, with another light blocking taking place after assembly. JAYGo fabrics are blocked when complete.

Connecting Crochet in Other Ways

Crocheted motifs don't have to be joined to other crocheted motifs! There must be an unlimited number of ways to connect crochet shapes. How many ways can you think of?

A checkerboard arrangement of crocheted motifs and fabric

A crocheted flower motif knit right into a sock — no seams!

MOTIFS AND JOINS

The shapes in this book are worked in the round from the center out. Most are written as if the motif were worked in one color. To work the motif in more than one color, as shown in the sample photos, refer to the color guide at the top of each page and change color accordingly, using either build-up chains or standing stitches (page 14) to begin the new rounds.

Alongside the motifs you'll find examples of ways they can be arranged and connected. These are by no means the only ways they might be combined. Mix and match the motifs, using the finished size of the sample motifs as a guide.

classic grannies

Rnd 1 A ▨   **Rnds 2 and 4** B ■   **Rnd 3** C ▨

This classic granny square uses chain-1 between 3-dc groups and chain-2 corners. See page 48 for a connection.

Begin with sliding loop.

Rnd 1 Ch 3 (counts as dc), 2 dc in ring, *ch 2, 3 dc in ring; rep from * two more times; join with hdc to top of ch-3 — 12 dc and 4 spaces.

Rnd 2 Ch 3 (counts as dc), (2 dc, ch 2, 3 dc) in same space, *ch 1, (3 dc, ch 2, 3 dc) in next space; rep from * two more times, join with sc to top of ch-3.

Rnd 3 Ch 3 (counts as dc), 2 dc in same space, *ch 1, (3 dc, ch 2, 3 dc) in next space**, ch 1, 3 dc in next space; rep from * around, ending last rep at **, join with sc to top of ch-3.

Rnd 4 Ch 3 (counts as dc), 2 dc in same space, *ch 1, 3 dc in next space, ch 1, (3 dc, ch 2, 3 dc) in next space, ch 1**, 3 dc in next space; rep from * around, ending last rep at **, join with slip st to top of ch-3. Fasten off.

SQUARE: 3¼" (8.5 CM)

This granny square is slightly smaller than the previous one, using chain-1 corners instead of chain-2 corners, and omitting the chain-1s between the double crochet groups.

SQUARE: 3" (7.5 CM)

Begin with sliding loop.

Rnd 1 Ch 3 (counts as dc), 2 dc in ring, *ch 1, 3 dc in ring; rep from * two more times; join with sc to top of ch-3 — 12 dc and 4 spaces.

Rnd 2 Ch 3 (counts as dc), (2 dc, ch 1, 3 dc) in same space, *(3 dc, ch 1, 3 dc) in next space; rep from * two more times, join with slip st to top of ch-3.

Rnd 3 Ch 3 (counts as dc), 2 dc in same space between 3-dc groups, *(3 dc, ch 1, 3 dc) in next space**, 3 dc in next space between 3-dc groups; rep from * around, ending last rep at **, join with slip st to top of ch-3.

Rnd 4 Ch 3 (counts as dc), 2 dc in same space between 3-dc groups, *3 dc in next space between 3-dc groups, (3 dc, ch 1, 3 dc) in next space**, 3 dc in next space between 3-dc groups; rep from * around, ending last rep at **, join with slip st to top of ch-3. Fasten off.

[**CLASSIC GRANNIES**]

Oh-so-classic grannies (squares or not) are among the most versatile of shapes when it comes to connections. You can sew them together, crochet them together, or work continuous final rounds.

connect

The 3-dc/ch-space edge of the classic granny square lends itself perfectly to a continuous final join. Making the final round the same color for all the squares is a nice unifying feature for even wildly differently-colored squares. Once you get the hang of the technique, it is fast and fun. You can use any of the three basic connection methods (see pages 36–37) to connect granny squares. This one uses the flat join.

FEATURES:

- JAYGo continuous final round
- Flat join
- Connection in adjoining spaces
- Inconspicuous seam

To work this example, work four individual squares through Round 3, fastening off each one. Round 4 is the continuous final round.

Referring to the stitch diagram for details, start by working Round 4 around three sides of the first motif, ending with 3 dc in the corner space, ch 2 (counts as ch 1 for Motif #1 and ch 1 for Motif #2); 3 dc in any corner space of Motif #2. Now, continue working Round 4 along the top edge of Motif #2, connecting to Motif #1 with flat joins at each space. Follow the green arrows to complete the round. You can do this to a whole blanket's worth of squares, too!

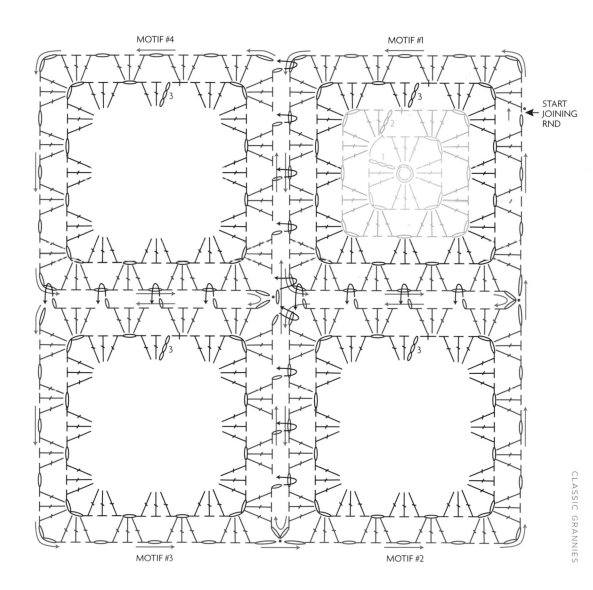

MOTIF #4   MOTIF #1

START JOINING RND

MOTIF #3   MOTIF #2

CLASSIC GRANNIES

Rnds 1 and 4 A ▢ **Rnd 2** B ▨ **Rnd 3** C ▪

A granny-style circle is created with groups of evenly distributed double crochet groups separated by chain-1 spaces.

Begin with sliding loop.

Rnd 1 Ch 3 (counts as dc), dc in ring, *ch 1, 2 dc in ring; rep from * four more times, join with sc to top of ch-3 — 12 dc and 6 spaces.

Rnd 2 Ch 3 (counts as dc), (dc, ch 1, 2 dc) in same space, *ch 1, (2 dc, ch 1, 2 dc) in next space; rep from * around, join with sc to top of ch-3.

Rnd 3 Ch 3 (counts as dc), 2 dc in same space, *ch 1, 3 dc in next space; rep from * around, join with sc to top of ch-3.

Rnd 4 Ch 3 (counts as dc), 3 dc in same space, *ch 1, 4 dc in next space; rep from * around, ch 1, join with slip st to top of ch-3. Fasten off.

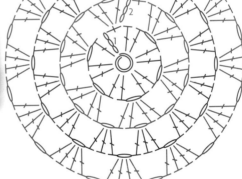

CIRCLE: 4" (10 CM)

This granny starts as a circle, but morphs into a square on Round 4, when the increases are made at four corners, and groups of treble crochet stitches are added to stretch the edges out to the corners. The colorway shown here is subtle; try working the "circle" and the "square" in highly contrasting colors for a more dramatic look.

SQUARE: 4¾" (12 CM)

Begin with sliding loop.

Rnd 1 Ch 3 (counts as dc), dc in ring, *ch 1, 2 dc in ring; rep from * four more times, join with sc to top of ch-3 — 12 dc and 6 spaces.

Rnd 2 Ch 3 (counts as dc), (dc, ch 1, 2 dc) in same space, *ch 1, (2 dc, ch 1, 2 dc) in next space; rep from * around, join with sc to top of ch-3.

Rnd 3 Ch 3 (counts as dc), 2 dc in same space, *ch 1, 3 dc in next space; rep from * around, join with sc to top of ch-3.

Rnd 4 Ch 3 (counts as dc), 2 dc in same space, *ch 1, 3 dc in next space, ch 1, (3 tr, ch 2, 3 tr) in next space**, ch 1, 3 dc in next space; rep from * around, ending last rep at **, join with sc to top of ch-3.

Rnd 5 Ch 3 (counts as dc), 2 dc in same space, ch 1, *(3 dc in next space, ch 1) two times, (3 dc, ch 2, 3 dc) in next space**, ch 1, 3 dc in next space, ch 1; rep from * around, ending last rep at **, join with sc to top of ch-3.

Rnd 6 Ch 1, sc in same space, *(ch 1, skip 1 dc, sc in next dc, ch 1, skip 1 dc, sc in next space) three times, ch 1, skip 1 dc, sc in next dc, ch 1, skip 1 dc, (sc, ch 1) two times in corner space, skip 1 dc, sc in next dc, ch 1, skip 1 dc, sc in next space; rep from * around, omitting last sc, join with slip st to first sc. Fasten off.

CLASSIC GRANNIES

Rnd 1 A ■ **Rnd 2** B ■ **Rnds 3 and 5** C ■ **Rnd 4** D ■

Here's a six-sided classic-style granny.

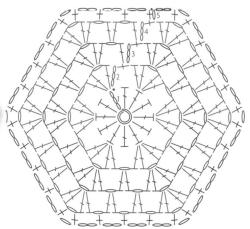

HEXAGON: 4¼" (11 CM)

Begin with sliding loop.

Rnd 1 Ch 3 (counts as dc), 11 dc in ring, join with slip st to top of ch-3 — 12 dc.

Rnd 2 Ch 3 (counts as dc), (dc, ch 1, 2 dc) in same st, *ch 1, skip 1 dc, (2 dc, ch 1, 2 dc) in next dc; rep from * to last st, skip 1 dc, join with sc to top of ch-3.

Rnd 3 Ch 3 (counts as dc), dc in same space, *ch 1, (2 dc, ch 1, 2 dc) in next space**, ch 1, 2 dc in next space; rep from * around, ending last rep at **, join with sc to top of ch-3.

Rnd 4 Ch 3 (counts as dc), dc in same space, *ch 1, 2 dc in next space, ch 1, (2 dc, ch 1, 2 dc) in next space**, ch 1, 2 dc in next space; rep from * around, ending last rep at **, join with sc to top of ch-3.

Rnd 5 Ch 1, *(sc, ch 2) in each space to corner space, (sc, ch 1, sc) in corner space, ch 2; rep from * around, join with slip st to first sc. Fasten off.

Row 1 A ■   **Row 2** B ■   **Row 3** C ■   **Row 4** D ■

Sometimes it's nice to have half a hexagon to fill out a design. Unlike most others in this book, this granny-style motif is worked back and forth in rows. If you are using different colors on each row, you may want to work all rows from the right side as shown in the sample.

Begin with sliding loop.

Row 1 Ch 3 (counts as dc), 6 dc in ring, *do not join*, turn — 7 dc.

Row 2 Ch 3 (counts as dc), dc in same st, ch 1, skip 1 dc, [(2 dc, ch 1, 2 dc) in next dc, ch 1, skip 1 dc] two times, 2 dc in last dc, turn.

Row 3 Ch 3 (counts as dc), dc in same st, *ch 1, 2 dc in next space, ch 1, (2 dc, ch 1, 2 dc) in next space; rep from * once, ch 1, 2 dc in next space, skip 1 dc, 2 dc in last dc, turn.

Row 4 Ch 3 (counts as dc), dc in same st, (ch 1, 2 dc in next space) two times, ch 1, *(2 dc, ch 1, 2 dc) in next space, ch 1, (2 dc, ch 1) in next 2 spaces; rep from * once, skip 1 dc, 2 dc in last dc. Fasten off.

HALF HEXAGON: 2" (5 CM)

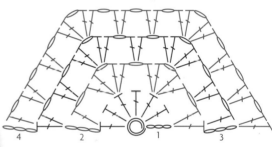

connect

Half hexagons flatten out the side edges in this combination of Motifs 5 and 6. This example also uses flat joins in a continuous final round, but because it's a single crochet/chain-space round, it looks different from the one shown on page 48. The order of joining is slightly different, as well, giving you another way to think about this type of connection.

Make individual hexagons and half-hexagons to the next-to-last round, fastening off each one.

Again, the stitch diagram tells the story. Start out working Round 5 around two sides of the first half-hexagon, and then follow the green arrows.

FEATURES:

- Partial shapes
- JAYGo continuous final round
- Flat join
- Connection in adjoining spaces
- Braided look

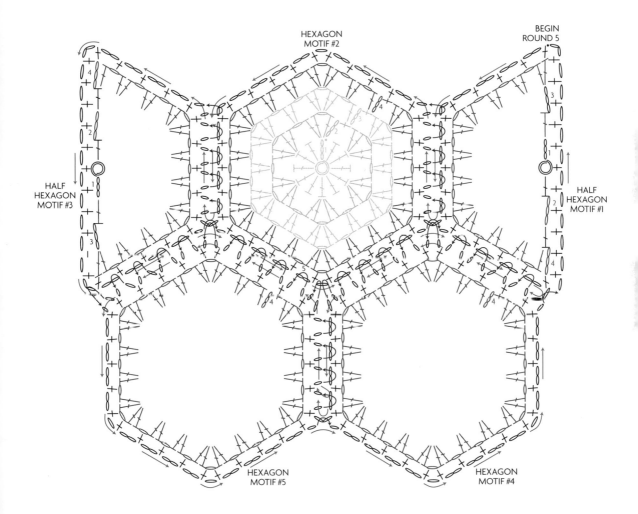

This granny triangle uses groups of 4 double crochet stitches separated by chain-1 spaces.

Begin with sliding loop.

Rnd 1 Ch 3 (counts as dc), 3 dc in ring, (ch 3, 4 dc in ring) two times, ch 1, join with hdc to top of ch-3 — 12 dc and 3 spaces.

Rnd 2 Ch 3 (counts as dc), 3 dc in space formed by joining hdc, [ch 1, (4 dc, ch 3, 4 dc) in next space] two times, ch 1, 4 dc in first space, ch 1, join with hdc to top of ch-3.

Rnd 3 Ch 3 (counts as dc), 3 dc in space formed by joining hdc, *ch 1, 4 dc in next space, ch 1**, (4 dc, ch 3, 4 dc) in next space; rep from * around, ending last rep at **, 4 dc in first space, ch 1, join with hdc to top of ch-3.

Rnd 4 Ch 3 (counts as dc), 3 dc in space formed by joining hdc, *ch 1, (4 dc in next space, ch 1) two times**, (4 dc, ch 3, 4 dc) in next space; rep from * around, ending last rep at **, two times, 4 dc in first space, ch 3, join with slip st to top of ch-3. Fasten off.

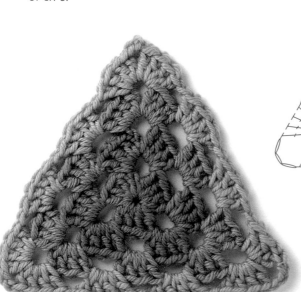

TRIANGLE: 4¾" (12 CM)

This triangle is really a half-square granny worked in rows. It complements Motif 1. To complement Motif 2 instead, make the top corner chain-1 and omit the other chains between the 3-dc groups. Note how wrong-side Rows 2 and 5 on the sample are bumpier than the right-side rows. If you prefer a smooth look to all the right-side rows, work all rows as right-side rows, fastening off and adding new yarn at the beginning of each row.

Begin with sliding loop. Tighten loop only slightly at the end of Row 1 and keep beginning chains fairly loose.

Row 1 Ch 3 (counts as dc), 3 dc in ring, ch 2, 4 dc in ring, turn — 8 dc and 1 space.

Row 2 Ch 3 (counts as dc), 3 dc in same st, ch 1, (3 dc, ch 2, 3 dc) in next space, ch 1, skip 3 dc, 4 dc in last st, turn.

Row 3 Ch 3 (counts as dc), 3 dc in same st, ch 1, 3 dc in next space, ch 1, (3 dc, ch 2, 3 dc) in next space, ch 1, 3 dc in next space, ch 1, skip 3 dc, 4 dc in last st, turn.

Row 4 Ch 3 (counts as dc), 3 dc in same st, ch 1, (3 dc in next space, ch 1) two times, (3 dc, ch 2, 3 dc) in next space, ch 1, (3 dc in next space, ch 1) two times, skip 3 dc, 4 dc in last st, turn.

Row 5 Ch 3 (counts as dc), 3 dc in same st, ch 1, (3 dc in next space, ch 1) three times, (3 dc, ch 2, 3 dc) in next space, ch 1, (3 dc in next space, ch 1) three times, skip 3 dc, 4 dc in last st, turn.

Row 6 Ch 1, sc in each dc and ch-1 space around, placing 2 sc in the corner ch-2 space. Fasten off, or if desired, place 3 sc in each bottom corner st and sc evenly along bottom edge of triangle; join with slip st to first sc. Fasten off.

TRIANGLE: 3½" (9 CM)

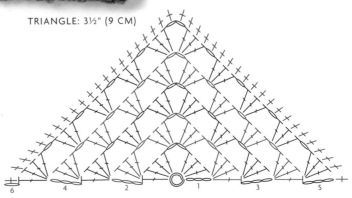

a little double crochet

Even a shape as simple as a mesh square with solid columns of double crochet can become something special. For proof, take a look at the Poet Vest on page 245.

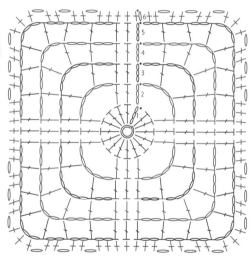

SQUARE: 4¾" (12 CM)

Begin with sliding loop.

Rnd 1 Ch 3 (counts as dc), 15 dc in ring, join with slip st to top of ch-3 — 16 dc.

Rnd 2 Ch 3 (counts as dc), dc in next 2 dc, *ch 5, skip 1 dc**, dc in next 3 dc; rep from * around, ending last rep at **, join with slip st to top of ch-3.

Rnd 3 Ch 3 (counts as dc), dc in next 2 dc, *ch 2, (dc, ch 5, dc) in next space, ch 2**, dc in next 3 dc; rep from * around, ending last rep at **, join with slip st to top of ch-3.

Rnd 4 Ch 3 (counts as dc), dc in next 2 dc, *ch 2, dc in next dc, ch 2, (dc, ch 3, dc) in next space, ch 2, dc in next dc, ch 2**, dc in next 3 dc; rep from * around, ending last rep at **, join with slip st to top of ch-3.

Rnd 5 Ch 3 (counts as dc), dc in next 2 dc, *(ch 2, dc in next dc) two times, ch 2, (dc, ch 3, dc) in next space, (ch 2, dc in next dc) two times, ch 2**, dc in next 3 dc; rep from * around, ending last rep at **, join with slip st to top of ch-3.

Rnd 6 Ch 1, sc in same st and in next 2 dc, *(2 sc in next space, ch 1) three times, 3 sc in corner space, (ch 1, 2 sc in next space) three times**, dc in next 3 dc; rep from * around, ending last rep at **, join with slip st to first sc. Fasten off.

While still working with double crochet and chain-spaces, decreasing the lace portion by adding more solid stitches along the sides creates a completely different look!

Begin with sliding loop.

Rnd 1 Ch 4 (counts as dc and ch 1), *dc in ring, ch 1; rep from * six more times, join with slip st to 3rd ch of ch-4 — 8 dc and 8 spaces.

Rnd 2 Ch 6 (counts as dc and ch 3), *dc in next dc, ch 3; rep from * around, join with slip st to 3rd ch of ch-6.

Rnd 3 Ch 3 (counts as dc), 2 dc in same st, *ch 2, (dc, ch 3, dc) in next dc, ch 2**, 3 dc in next dc; rep from * around, ending last rep at **, join with slip st to top of ch-3.

Rnd 4 Ch 3 (counts as dc), dc in same st, *dc in next dc, 2 dc in next dc, ch 1, dc in next dc, ch 5, dc in next dc, ch 1, 2 dc in next dc; rep from * around, omitting last 2 dc, join with slip st to top of ch-3.

Rnd 5 Ch 3 (counts as dc), dc in same st, *dc in next 3 dc, 2 dc in next dc, ch 1, dc in next dc, ch 2, (dc, ch 3, dc) in next space, ch 2, dc in next dc, ch 1, 2 dc in next dc; rep from * around, omitting last 2 dc, join with slip st to top of ch-3.

Rnd 6 Ch 3 (counts as dc), dc in next 6 dc, *ch 1, dc in next dc, ch 1, dc in next space, ch 1, dc in next dc, ch 1, tr in next space, ch 1, dc in next dc, ch 1, dc in next space, ch 1, dc in next dc, ch 1**, dc in next 7 dc; rep from * around, ending last rep at **, join with slip st to top of ch-3. Fasten off.

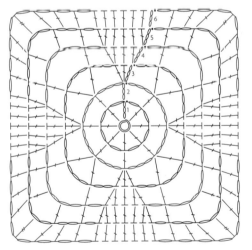

SQUARE: 5" (12.5 CM)

[A LITTLE DOUBLE CROCHET]

In this family of motifs, groups of double crochet stitches alternate with chain-spaces to create positive and negative space. Your connections for this family will depend on what types of edges they have. Straight, even edges might call for a sewn or crocheted seam, while points and chain-spaces beg for a JAYGo method.

These four motifs were held with right sides together while working a whipstitch seam (page 32) through the inside loops. Paying careful attention to the proper tension creates a very flat and unobtrusive seam. Note how the joined motifs create a fabric that subtly shifts the balance of positive and negative space from that of the single motif.

FEATURES

- Join when you're done
- Whipstitch seam
- Sew in one loop only
- Connection in every stitch
- Inconspicuous seam

– – – – = WHIPSTITCHED SEAM

MOTIF #2

MOTIF #1

MOTIF #3

MOTIF #4

Rnd 1 A ■   **Rnds 2 and 3** B ■   **Rnds 4–6** C ▨

While a circle doesn't have corners, you can still see the alternating columns of solid and openwork stitches. The simple cables in the solid portion are a variation you could try on any shape.

FPtr *(front post treble crochet)* (Yarn over) two times, insert hook from front to back to front around post of stitch indicated and pull up a loop (yarn over and pull through 2 loops on hook) three times.

Begin with sliding loop.

Rnd 1 Ch 3 (counts as dc), 17 dc in ring, join with slip st to top of ch-3 — 18 dc.

Rnd 2 Ch 3 (counts as dc), dc in next 2 dc, *ch 3, dc in next 3 dc; rep from * around, ch 1, join with hdc to top of ch-3 — 6 spaces and six 3-dc groups.

Rnd 3 Ch 5 (counts as dc and ch 2), *FPtr in 3rd dc of next 3-dc group, dc in center dc of same group, FPtr in first dc of same group; ch 2**, dc in next space, ch 2; rep from * around, ending last rep at **, join with slip st to 3rd ch of ch-5.

Rnd 4 Ch 5 (counts as dc and ch 2), dc in same st, *ch 2, skip 2 ch, dc in next 3 sts, ch 2**, (dc, ch 2, dc) in next dc; rep from * around, ending last rep at **, join with slip st to 3rd ch of ch-5.

Rnd 5 Ch 6 (counts as dc and ch 3), *dc in next dc, ch 2, FPtr in 3rd dc of next 3-dc group, dc in center dc of same group, FPtr in first dc of same group, ch 2**, dc in next dc, ch 3; rep from * around, ending last rep at **, join with slip st to 3rd ch of ch-6, slip st in next space.

Rnd 6 Ch 1, 3 sc in same space, 3 sc in next space, *sc in next 3 sts, 3 sc in next 3 spaces; rep from * four times, sc in next 3 sts, 3 sc in next space, join with slip st to first sc. Fasten off.

CIRCLE: 5" (12.5 CM)

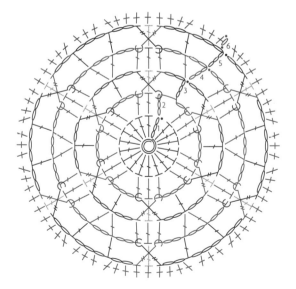

Here's a trianglar version of Motif 10, with the mesh-style corners and solid double crochet sides.

Begin with sliding loop.

Rnd 1 Ch 5 (counts as dc and ch 2), *tr in ring, ch 2, dc in ring, ch 2; rep from * once more, tr in ring, ch 2, join with slip st to top of ch-3 — 3 tr, 3 dc, and 6 spaces.

Rnd 2 Ch 6 (counts as dc and ch 3), *(tr, ch 3, tr) in next tr, ch 3**, dc in next dc, ch 3; rep from * around, ending last rep at **, join with slip st to 3rd ch of ch-6.

Rnd 3 Ch 3 (counts as dc), 2 dc in same st, *ch 3, dc in next tr, ch 5, dc in next tr, ch 3**, 3 dc in next dc; rep from * around, ending last rep at **, join with slip st to top of ch-3.

Rnd 4 Ch 3 (counts as dc), dc in same st, *dc in next dc, 2 dc in next dc, ch 2, dc in next dc, ch 3, (tr, ch 3) two times in next space, dc in next dc, ch 2, 2 dc in next dc; rep from * around, omitting last 2 dc, join with slip st to top of ch-3.

Rnd 5 Ch 3 (counts as dc), dc in same st, *dc in next 3 dc, 2 dc in next dc, ch 1, dc in next dc, ch 3, dc in next dc, ch 2, (tr, ch 3, tr) in next space, ch 2, dc in next tr, ch 3, dc in next dc, ch 1, 2 dc in next dc; rep from * around, omitting last 2 dc, join with slip st to top of ch-3.

Rnd 6 Ch 1, sc in each st around, placing 1 sc in each ch-1 space, 2 sc in each ch-2 space, 3 sc in each ch-3 space, and 5 sc in each corner space around, join with slip st to 3rd ch of ch-3. Fasten off.

TRIANGLE: 6" (15 CM)

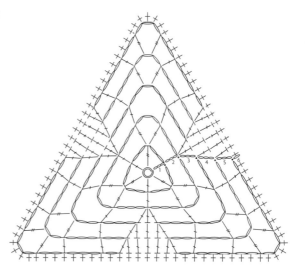

Solid columns of double crochet are topped off with fans to create this simple hexagon.

HEXAGON: 4½" (11.5 CM)

Begin with sliding loop.

Rnd 1 Ch 3 (counts as dc), dc in ring, ch 1, *2 dc in ring, ch 1; rep from * four more times, join with slip st to top of ch 3 — 12 dc and 6 spaces.

Rnd 2 Ch 3 (counts as dc), dc in next dc, ch 3, *dc in next 2 dc, ch 3; rep from * around, join with slip st to top of ch-3.

Rnd 3 Ch 3 (counts as dc), dc in next dc, *ch 3, sc in next space, ch 3, dc in next 2 dc; rep from * around, omitting last 2 dc, join with slip st to top of ch-3.

Rnd 4 Ch 3 (counts as dc), dc in next dc, *ch 4, sc in next sc, ch 4, dc in next 2 dc; rep from * around, omitting last 2 dc, join with slip st to top of ch-3.

Rnd 5 Ch 3 (counts as dc), dc in same st, *ch 2, 2 dc in next dc, sc in next space, ch 3, sc in next space, 2 dc in next dc; rep from * around, omitting last 2 dc, join with slip st to top of ch-3. Fasten off.

Rnds 1–6 A ■

Here's another double crochet–based square. This time, the solid portions are created with 5-dc shells at the corners and openwork along the edges. The shells soften the corners and lines of the motif when compared with the opening motif in this family.

Begin with sliding loop.

Rnd 1 Ch 3 (counts as dc), 15 dc in ring, join with slip st to top of ch-3 — 16 dc.

Rnd 2 Ch 4 (counts as dc and ch 1), skip 1 dc, *3 dc in next dc, ch 1, skip 1 dc**, dc in next dc, ch 1, skip 1 dc; rep from * around, ending last rep at **, join with slip st to 3rd ch of ch-4.

Rnd 3 Ch 5 (counts as dc and ch 2), *skip 1 dc, 5 dc in next dc, ch 2, skip 1 dc**, dc in next dc, ch 2; rep from * around, ending last rep at **, join with slip st to 3rd ch of ch-5.

Rnd 4 Ch 7 (counts as dc and ch 4), *skip 2 dc, 5 dc in next dc, ch 4, skip 2 dc**, dc in next dc, ch 4; rep from * around, ending last rep at **, join with slip st to 3rd ch of ch-7.

Rnd 5 Ch 9 (counts as dc and ch 6), *skip 2 dc, 5 dc in next dc, ch 6, skip 2 dc**, dc in next dc, ch 6; rep from * around, ending last rep at **, join with slip st to 3rd ch of ch-9.

Rnd 6 Ch 9 (counts as dc and ch 6), dc in same dc, *ch 1, (sc, ch 3) two times in next space, skip 2 dc, 5 dc in next dc, (ch 3, sc) two times in next space, ch 1**, (dc, ch 6, dc) in next dc; rep from * around, ending last rep at **, join with slip st to 3rd ch of ch-9. Fasten off.

SQUARE: 5½" (14 cm)

Motifs can be adapted from their original state to form better-fitting and more stable joins. This example uses 3 dc in place of 1 dc at each side of Motif 14's Round 5 to create a more solid fabric to hold the motif in shape as it approaches a connection point. On Round 6, changing the corners from a 5-dc shell to a (2 dc, ch 3, 2 dc) corner elongates the corners and allows them to reach out to the adjacent corners. Because this motif is so lacy, a single crochet join adds a bit of needed heft at the connection points.

Work Rnds 1–4 as for Motif 14 for all motifs, then work Rnds 5 and 6 as described on the next page for Motif #1. For the later motifs, stitch Rnd 6, substituting (ch 1, sc join, ch 1) for the ch-3 at corners, center of sides, and ch-3 space between single crochets.

Rnd 5 Ch 3 (counts as dc), dc in same st, ch 5, *skip 2 dc, 5 dc in next dc, ch 5, skip 2 dc**, 3 dc in next dc, ch 5; rep from * around, ending last rep at **, dc in same st as first dc, join with slip st to top of ch-3.

Rnd 6 Ch 6 (counts as dc and ch 3), dc in same dc, *ch 1, (sc, ch 3) two times in next space, skip 2 dc, (2 dc, ch 3, 2 dc) in next dc, (ch 3, sc) two times in next space, ch 1**,

(dc, ch 3, dc) in next dc; rep from * around, ending last rep at **, join with slip st to 3rd ch of ch-6. Fasten off.

FEATURES:
- Adaptation of original motif
- JAYGo
- Single crochet join
- Connection in adjoining spaces

MOTIF #2 MOTIF #1

MOTIF #4 MOTIF #3

15

Rnds 1–5 A ■

The hexagonal version of the shells and chains is simple yet elegant in a number of different applications. A variation of this motif is used in the Lacy Skirt on page 251.

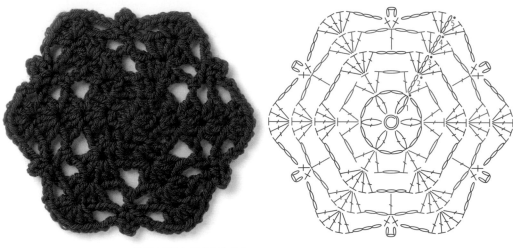

HEXAGON: 5" (12.5 CM)

Dc2tog *(double crochet 2 together)* Yarn over, insert hook into indicated stitch or space and pull up a loop, yarn over, pull through 2 loops, yarn over, insert hook into same stitch and pull up a loop, yarn over and pull through 2 loops, yarn over, and pull through all 3 loops on hook.

Begin with sliding loop.

Rnd 1 Ch 2, dc in ring (counts as dc2tog), ch 2, *dc2tog in ring, ch 2; rep from * four more times, join with slip st to top of first cluster — 6 clusters and 6 spaces.

Rnd 2 Ch 3 (counts as dc), dc in same st, ch 1, *3 dc in next cluster, ch 1; rep from * around, ending dc in first st, join with slip st to top of ch-3 — six 3-dc shells.

Rnd 3 Ch 3 (counts as dc), 2 dc in same st, ch 3, *5 dc in center dc of next 3-dc shell, ch 3; rep from * around, ending 2 dc in first st, join with slip st to top of ch-3 — six 5-dc shells.

Rnd 4 Ch 3 (counts as dc), 2 dc in same st, ch 2, dc in next space, ch 2, *5 dc in center dc of next 5-dc shell, ch 2, dc in next space, ch 2; rep from * around, ending 2 dc in first st, join with slip st to top of ch-3.

Rnd 5 Ch 3 (counts as dc), 2 dc in same st, *ch 3, skip 2 dc, (sc, ch 3, sc) in next dc, ch 3**, 5 dc in center dc of next 5-dc shell; rep from * around, ending last repeat at **, 2 dc in first st, join with slip st to top of ch-3. Fasten off.

Since the full version of this hexagon is so versatile, here's a half-hex version to offer even more options.

HALF HEXAGON: 4½" (11.5 CM)
ACROSS LOWER EDGE

Dc2tog *(double crochet 2 together)* Yarn over, insert hook into indicated stitch or space and pull up a loop, yarn over, pull through 2 loops, yarn over, insert hook into same stitch and pull up a loop, yarn over and pull through 2 loops, yarn over and pull through all 3 loops on hook.

Begin with sliding loop.

Row 1 Ch 4 (counts as hdc and ch-2), (dc2tog in ring, ch 2) two times, ch 2, hdc in ring, turn — 2 clusters, 3 spaces, and 2 hdc.

Row 2 Ch 3 (counts as dc), dc in same st, ch 1, (3 dc in next cluster, ch 1) two times, 2 dc in top of 2nd ch of ch-4, turn.

Row 3 Ch 3 (counts as dc), dc in same st, ch 3, (5 dc in center dc of next 3-dc shell, ch 3) two times, skip 2 dc, 2 dc in last st, turn.

Row 4 Ch 3 (counts as dc), dc in same st, ch 2, dc in next space, ch 2, (5 dc in center dc of next 5-dc shell, ch 2, dc in next space, ch 2) two times, skip 1 dc, 2 dc in last st, turn.

Row 5 Ch 3 (counts as dc), dc in same st, ch 3, skip 1 dc, (sc, ch 3, sc) in next dc, ch 3, [5 dc in center dc of next shell, ch 3, skip 2 dc, (sc, ch 3, sc) in next dc, ch 3] two times, skip 1 dc, 2 dc in last st. Fasten off.

gathered chains

Rnds 1, 3, and 4 A ▨   **Rnd 2** B ▨   **Rnd 5** C ▨

Working a single crochet stitch over existing chains and into a space several rounds down is a simple-as-can-be variation on an ordinary square.

Begin with sliding loop.

Rnd 1 Ch 3 (counts as dc), 2 dc in ring, ch 3, *3 dc in ring, ch 3; rep from * two more times, join with slip st to top of ch-3 — 12 dc and 3 spaces.

Rnd 2 Ch 3 (counts as dc), dc in next 2 dc, ch 7, *dc in next 3 dc, ch 7; rep from * around, join with slip st to top of ch-3.

Rnd 3 Ch 3 (counts as dc), dc in next 2 dc, ch 9, *dc in next 3 dc, ch 9; rep from * around, join with slip st to top of ch-3.

Rnd 4 Ch 3 (counts as dc), dc in next 2 dc, ch 11, *dc in next 3 dc, ch 11; rep from * around, join with slip st to top of ch-3.

Rnd 5 Ch 3 (counts as dc), dc in next 2 dc, *ch 7, working over 3 ch-loops, sc into space from Rnd 2, ch 7**, dc in next 3 dc; rep from * around, ending last rep at **, join with slip st to top of ch-3. Fasten off.

SQUARE: 3¾" (9.5 CM)

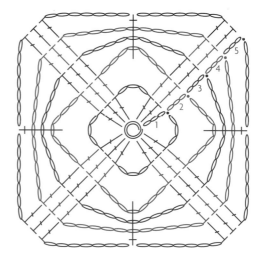

[**GATHERED CHAINS**]

Take the columns of double crochet separated by chains from the last family of motifs, throw in a few spike single crochets to change the shape of the motifs, meta-chain the corners, or use post stitches to create a textured, reversible square. When who's to say which is the right side, what kind of connection offers the most reversibility? JAYGo may be the way to go.

Gathering chains from the top down isn't the only way to do it. Here, long corner chains are looped through each other before working the final round. Want another option? Try it with standard stitches instead of post stitches.

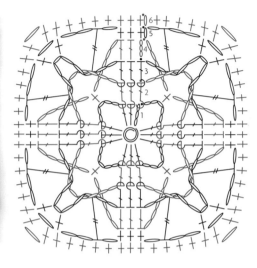

SQUARE: 4" (10 CM)

FPdc *(front post double crochet)* Yarn over, insert hook from front to back to front around post of stitch indicated and pull up a loop, (yarn over and pull through 2 loops on hook) two times.

Standing FPdc *(standing front post double crochet)* Beginning with slip knot on hook, yarn over, insert hook from front to back to front around post of stitch indicated and pull up a loop, (yarn over and pull through 2 loops on hook) two times.

Begin with sliding loop.

Rnd 1 Ch 3 (counts as dc), 2 dc in ring, ch 5, *3 dc in ring, ch 5; rep from * two more times, join with slip st to top of ch-3 — 12 dc and 4 spaces. Fasten off.

Rnd 2 Standing FPdc in first dc of any 3-dc group, FPdc in next 2 dc, ch 9, *FPdc in next 3 dc, ch 9; rep from * two more times, join with slip st to top of first FPdc. Fasten off.

Rnd 3 Standing FPdc in first dc of any 3-dc group, FPdc in next 2 dc, ch 11, *FPdc in next 3 dc, ch 11; rep from * two more times, join with slip st to top of first FPdc. Fasten off.

Rnd 4 Ch 3 (counts as dc), dc in next 2 dc, *ch 5; sc in next Rnd-1 space behind Rnd-2 and Rnd-3 chains, ch 5, dc in next 3 dc; rep from *, omitting last 3 dc, join with slip st to top of ch-3.

Slip one Rnd-2 chain over each corresponding chain in Rnd-3 at all four corners.

Rnd 5 Ch 1, sc in same st and in next 2 dc, *ch 1, tr in Rnd-2 space, ch 2, (sc, ch 1, sc) in Rnd-3 space, ch 2, tr in Rnd-2 space, ch 1, sc in next 3 dc; rep from * around, omitting last 3 sc, join with slip st to first sc.

Rnd 6 Ch 1, sc evenly around, working 1 sc in each st and ch-1 space, 2 sc in each ch-2 space, and placing (sc, ch 1, sc) in each corner space, join with slip st to first sc. Fasten off.

This is the three-sided version of this family. What would this one look like joined to others? Try it and see!

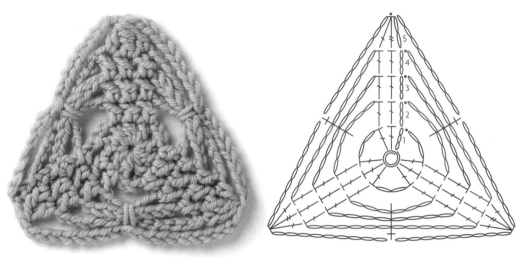

TRIANGLE: 3½" (9 CM)

Partial dc *(partial double crochet)* Yarn over, insert hook into stitch or space indicated and pull up a loop, yarn over and pull through 2 loops on hook.

Partial tr *(partial treble)* (Yarn over) twice, insert hook into stitch or space indicated and pull up a loop, (yarn over and pull through 2 loops on hook) two times.

Begin with sliding loop.

Rnd 1 Ch 3 (counts as dc), 2 dc in ring, ch 2, *3 dc in ring, ch 2; rep from * once more, join with slip st to top of ch-3 — 9 dc and 3 spaces.

Rnd 2 Ch 3 (counts as dc), dc in next 2 dc, ch 6, *dc in next 3 dc, ch 6; rep from * once more, join with slip st to top of ch-3.

Rnd 3 Ch 3 (counts as dc), dc in next 2 dc, ch 8, *dc in next 3 dc, ch 8; rep from * once more, join with slip st to top of ch-3.

Rnd 4 Ch 3 (counts as dc), dc in next 2 dc, ch 12, *dc in next 3 dc, ch 12; rep from * once more, join with slip st to top of ch-3.

Rnd 5 Ch 2 (counts as Partial dc), Partial tr in next dc, Partial dc in next dc, yarn over and pull through all 3 loops on hook, *ch 9, working over 3 ch-loops, sc into space from Rnd 2, ch 9**, Partial dc in next dc, Partial tr in next dc, Partial dc in next dc, yarn over and pull through all 4 loops on hook; rep from * around, ending last rep at **, join with slip st to top of ch-3. Fasten off.

Gathering chains on this six-sided version creates a flowerlike appearance. Play with colorwork and perhaps textured stitches for even more variation.

HEXAGON: 4¼" (11 CM)

Begin with sliding loop.

Note: Do not tighten loop until Rnd 2 is complete; the loop must stay open for motif to lie flat.

Rnd 1 Ch 3 (counts as dc), dc in ring, ch 2, *2 dc in ring, ch 2; rep from * four more times, join with slip st to top of ch-3 — 12 dc and 6 spaces.

Rnd 2 Ch 3 (counts as dc), dc in next dc, ch 4, *dc in next 2 dc, ch 4; rep from * around, join with slip st to top of ch-3.

Rnd 3 Ch 3 (counts as dc), dc in next dc, ch 6, *dc in next 2 dc, ch 6; rep from * around, join with slip st to top of ch-3.

Rnd 4 Ch 3 (counts as dc), dc in next dc, ch 8, *dc in next 2 dc, ch 8; rep from * around, join with slip st to top of ch-3.

Rnd 5 Ch 3 (counts as dc), dc in next dc, *ch 5, working over 3 ch-loops, sc into space from Rnd 2, ch 5**, dc in next 2 dc; rep from * around, ending last rep at **, join with slip st to top of ch-3. Fasten off.

connect

Having an even number of stitches at each point offers a challenge because there is no "center" stitch to use as a connection point. Here, a flat join connects Motif 20, with the join made in both of the double crochets at each point. Where a third motif joins two adjacent motifs, one join is made in the closest double crochet on one motif, and the second flat join is made in the closest double crochet on the next motif. If you prefer, where two motifs are joined, you may place the join in just one of the two double crochets.

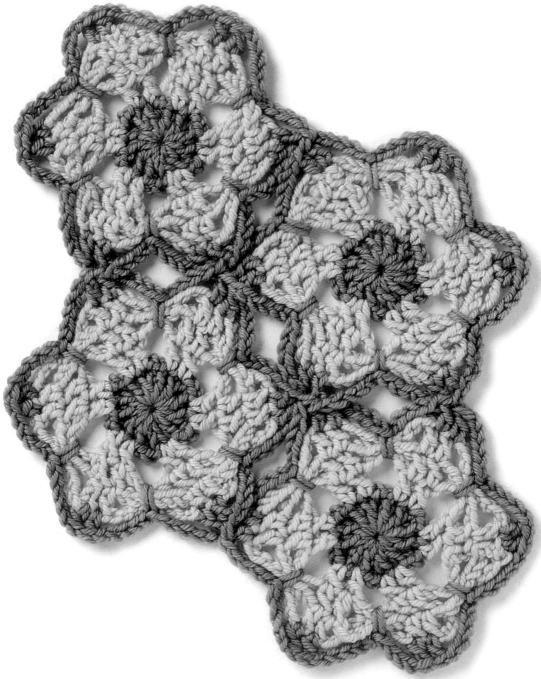

GATHERED CHAINS

74

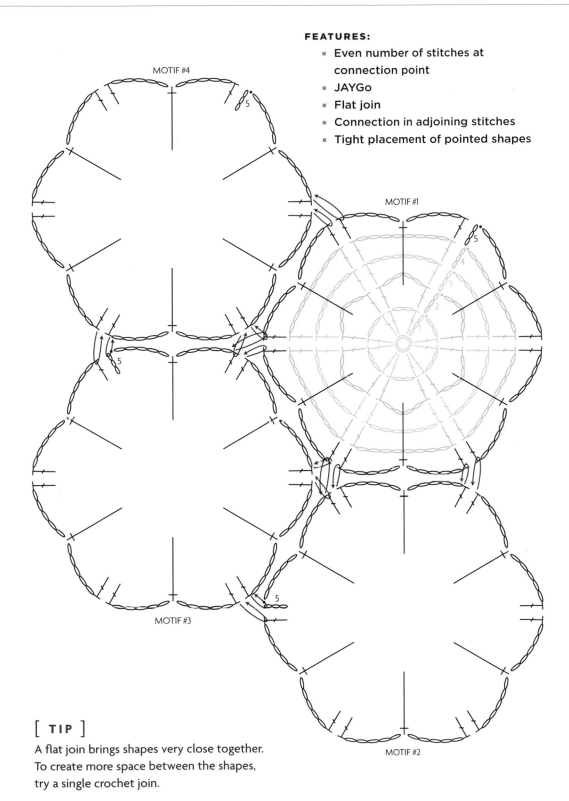

MOTIF #4

MOTIF #1

MOTIF #3

MOTIF #2

- Even number of stitches at connection point
- JAYGo
- Flat join
- Connection in adjoining stitches
- Tight placement of pointed shapes

[**TIP**]

A flat join brings shapes very close together. To create more space between the shapes, try a single crochet join.

Rnds 1–5 A

Until you stitch it, you might find it difficult to understand how this circle relates to others in this family, but it does! The number of points and the depth of the spike stitches (the single crochets that gather the chains by going into previous rounds) determine the final shape of each motif. For another variation, try working the spike stitches only one round down on the final round.

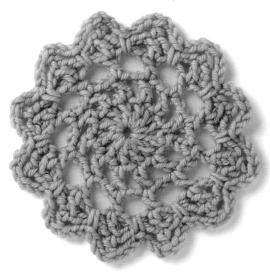

CIRCLE: 4¾" (12 CM)

Begin with sliding loop.

Note: Do not tighten loop until Rnd 2 is complete; the loop must stay open for the motif to lie flat.

Rnd 1 Ch 4 (counts as dc and ch 1), *dc in ring, ch 1; rep from * 10 more times, join with slip st to top of ch-3 — 12 dc and 12 spaces.

Rnd 2 Ch 5 (counts as dc and ch 2), *dc in next dc, ch 2; rep from * around, join with slip st to top of ch-3.

Rnd 3 Ch 6 (counts as dc and ch 3), *dc in next dc, ch 3; rep from * around, join with slip st to top of ch-3.

Rnd 4 Ch 8 (counts as dc and ch 5), *dc in next dc, ch 5; rep from * around, join with slip st to top of ch-3.

Rnd 5 Ch 6 (counts as dc and ch 3), *working over 2 ch-loops, sc into space from Rnd 3, ch 3**, dc in next dc, ch 3; rep from * around, ending last rep at **, join with slip st to top of ch-3. Fasten off.

Add some post stitches for texture and reversibility! This motif is truly reversible, but each side looks quite different — just choose one side or the other as the right side. Even better, put them together for a fabric that looks great on both sides (see Joins on pages 78 and 80).

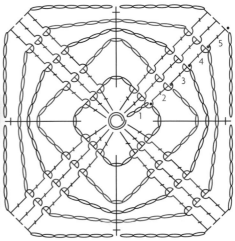

SQUARE (REVERSIBLE): 3¼" (8.5 CM)

FPdc *(front post double crochet)* Yarn over, insert hook from front to back to front around post of stitch indicated and pull up a loop, (yarn over and pull through 2 loops on hook) two times.

Standing FPdc *(standing front post double crochet)* Beginning with slip knot on hook, yarn over, insert hook from front to back to front around post of stitch indicated and pull up a loop, (yarn over and pull through 2 loops on hook) two times.

Begin with sliding loop.

Rnd 1 Ch 3 (counts as dc), 2 dc in ring, ch 3, *3 dc in ring, ch 3; rep from * two more times, join with slip st to top of ch-3 — 12 dc and 4 spaces. Fasten off.

Rnd 2 Standing FPdc in first dc of any 3-dc group, FPdc in next 2 dc, ch 7, *FPdc in next 3 dc, ch 7; rep from * two more times, join with slip st to top of first FPdc. Fasten off.

Rnd 3 Standing FPdc in first dc of any 3-dc group, FPdc in next 2 dc, ch 9, *FPdc in next 3 dc, ch 9; rep from * two more times, join with slip st to top of first FPdc. Fasten off.

Rnd 4 Standing FPdc in first dc of any 3-dc group, FPdc in next 2 dc, ch 11, *FPdc in next 3 dc, ch 11; rep from * two more times, join with slip st to top of first FPdc. Fasten off.

Rnd 5 Standing FPdc in first dc of any 3-dc group, FPdc in next 2 dc, *ch 7, working around 4 ch-loops, sc into space from Rnd 1, ch 7**, FPdc in next 3 dc; rep from * around, ending last rep at **, join with slip st to top of first FPdc. Fasten off.

GATHERED CHAINS

Reversible shapes offer all kinds of fun options for connections. In this example, Motif 22 is connected using alternating sides as the "right" side. Just make all the motifs as for Motif 22, but flip the connected piece over as needed to attach each additional motif. And of course, the other side looks just like this! A tiny filler motif connects to each shape and fills the center space.

Work the first motif through Rnd 5. Make additional motifs the same as the first motif, joining to previous motif(s) in Rnd 5, by working (ch 3, sc in space of previous motif, ch 3, sc over 4 chs into Rnd-1 space, ch 3, sc in space of previous motif, ch 3, 3 FPdc) across each side to be joined.

FILLER MOTIF

Begin with sliding loop.

Ch 1, sc in ring, ch 1, sc in center dc of interior 3-dc group on any joined motif, ch 1, *sc in ring, ch 1, sc in center dc of next interior 3-dc group, ch 1; rep from * two more times; tighten sliding loop, join with slip st to first sc. Fasten off.

FEATURES:

- Reversibility
- JAYGo
- Single crochet join
- Connection in adjoining spaces
- Filler motif

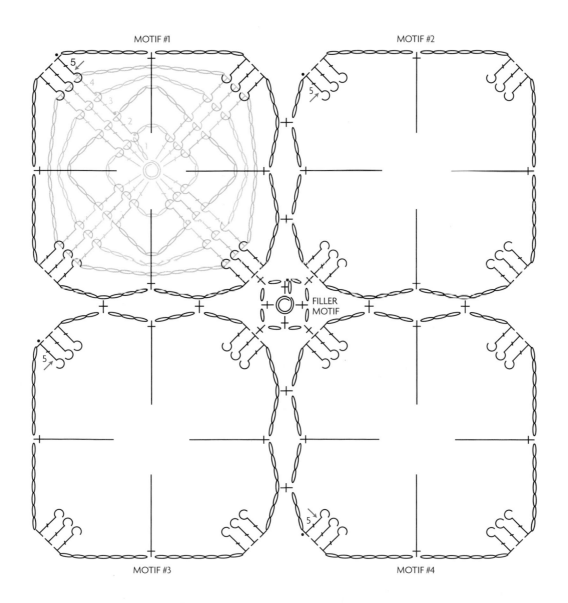

MOTIF #1

MOTIF #2

FILLER MOTIF

MOTIF #3

MOTIF #4

Connecting Motif 22 at the square tips gives an entirely different look from the previous connection example.

After working the first motif through Rnd 5, make and join additional motifs, joining each new motif to previous motif(s) in Rnd 5. Work (FPdc in next dc, flat join to corresponding dc on previous motif) three times at each tip to be connected. Note that the stitch diagram shows the "right" side of the connected fabric, as it is worked, while the photograph shows the reverse side of the same fabric. Although no filler motif is shown, this might be an excellent place to create a space-filling shape.

FEATURES:

- Reversibility
- JAYGo
- Flat join
- Connection in adjoining stitches
- Connections in multiple stitches

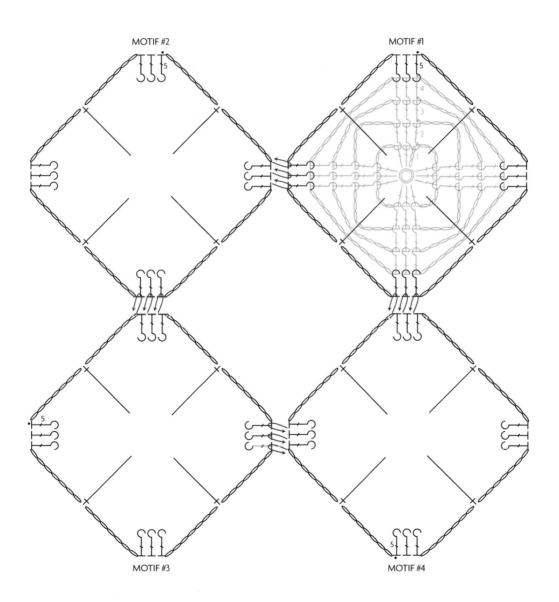

MOTIF #2

MOTIF #1

MOTIF #3

MOTIF #4

lacy links

Rnds 1–3 A ■

This little square is deceptively easy to stitch — and to memorize. A lot of style for not much work!

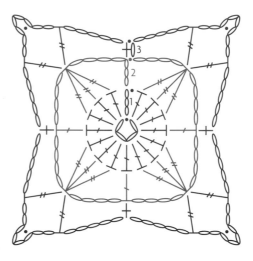

SQUARE: 3" (7.5 CM)

Picot-4 Ch 4, slip st in 4th ch from hook.

Tr3tog *(treble crochet 3 together)* (Yarn over) two times, insert hook into indicated stitch or space and pull up a loop, (yarn over, pull through 2 loops) two times, [(yarn over) two times, insert hook into next stitch or space and pull up a loop, (yarn over, pull through 2 loops) two times] two times, yarn over and pull through all 4 loops on hook.

Ch 4, join with slip st to form ring.

Rnd 1 Ch 3 (counts as dc), 15 dc in ring, join with slip st to top of ch-3 — 16 dc.

Rnd 2 Ch 7 (counts as dc and ch 4), *tr3tog over next 3 dc, ch 4, dc in next dc; rep from * around, omitting last dc, join with slip st to 3rd ch of ch-7.

Rnd 3 Ch 1, sc in same st, *ch 5, (tr, ch 2, Picot-4, ch 2, tr) in next cluster, ch 5, sc in next dc; rep from * around, omitting last sc, join with slip st to first sc. Fasten off.

24

The three-sided version is also pretty and easy to stitch.

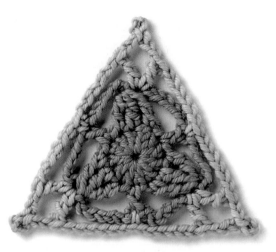

TRIANGLE: 3½" (9 CM)

Picot-4 Ch 4, slip st in 4th ch from hook.

Tr3tog *(treble crochet 3 together)* (Yarn over) two times, insert hook into indicated stitch or space and pull up a loop, (yarn over, pull through 2 loops) two times, [(yarn over) two times, insert hook into next stitch or space and pull up a loop, (yarn over, pull through 2 loops) two times] two times, yarn over and pull through all 4 loops on hook.

Ch 4, join with slip st to form ring.

Rnd 1 Ch 3 (counts as dc), 11 dc in ring, join with slip st to top of ch-3 — 12 dc.

Rnd 2 Ch 9 (counts as dc and ch 6), *tr3tog over next 3 dc, ch 6**, dc in next dc, ch 6; rep from * around, ending last repeat at ᐱᐱ, join with slip st to 3rd ch of ch-11.

Rnd 3 Ch 1, sc in same st, ch 6, (tr, ch 2, Picot-4, ch 2, tr) in next cluster, ch 6, sc in next dc; rep from * around, omitting last sc, join with slip st to first sc. Fasten off.

[**LACY LINKS**]

All of the lacy shapes in this family have nice picot-tipped points that form perfect connection spots. Extend and adapt points and corners as needed to create the ideal join. The continuous-motif technique (see pages 41–42) works well with this family.

connect

Motif 23   **Rnds 1–3** A ■

This join is a series of Motif 23 squares worked in the continuous-motif method (pages 41–42). Additional chain-loops were added to the sides of Motif 23 to offer additional connection points. Beginning with the lower left-hand motif (lower right-hand for lefties), you work a series of joined partial motifs for the first tier. Complete the first-tier motifs as you work back across the top of the tier to the first motif. Work a portion of the last round of the first motif, then move on to begin the second tier, joining each motif to the first tier and to previous motifs as indicated. Refer to the chart as you follow these step-by-step instructions:

CONTINUOUS MOTIF

Ch 11 for foundation chain, slip st in 4th ch from hook to form ring,

Rnd 1 Slip st in next 2 foundation ch, Crossover slip st [see page 42] in next foundation ch (counts as dc), 15 dc in ring, join with slip st to top of first dc.

Rnd 2 Slip st in next 2 foundation ch, Crossover slip st in next foundation ch (counts as dc), ch 4, *tr3tog over next 3 dc, ch 4, dc in next dc; rep from * around, omitting last dc, join with slip st to top of first dc.

Rnd 3 Crossover slip st in next foundation ch (counts as sc), ch 5, (tr, ch 2, Picot-4, ch 2, tr) in next cluster, ch 5, (sc, ch 5, sc) in next dc, ch 5, (tr, ch 2, Picot-4, ch 2, tr) in next cluster, ch 5, sc in next dc**, ch 5 (counts as 2 dc for this motif, connecting ch, and 2 ch for next motif).

Beginning with ch 11 for foundation chain, work motif two more times, ending last motif at ** — *Motifs #1–3 partially complete.*

Continuing on Motif #3, ch 5, sc in same dc, ch 5, (tr, ch 2, Picot-4, ch 2, tr) in next cluster, *ch 5, (sc, ch 5, sc) in next dc, ch 5, (tr, ch 2,

LACY LINKS

Picot-4, ch 2, tr) in next cluster, ch 5, sc in st at base of first foundation ch, ch 2, skip 2 ch, slip st in next ch — *motif complete,* ch 2, sc in same st as last sc on next motif, ch 5, tr in next cluster, ch 2; ch 2, slip st in adjacent picot of previous motif, ch 2, slip st in 4th ch from hook — *picot join made;* ch 2, tr in same cluster; rep from * once more, ch 5, sc in next dc, ch 5 (counts as 2 dc for this motif, connection ch, and ch 2 for next motif).

Continuing on Motif #4, work continuous motif through Rnd 2.

Rnd 3 Crossover slip st in next foundation ch (counts as sc), ch 5, (tr, ch 2, picot join around adjacent slip st join, ch 2, tr) in next cluster, ch 5, sc in next dc**, ch 5 (counts as 2 dc for this motif, connecting ch, and 2 ch for next motif)

Continuing on Motif #5, work continuous motif through Rnd 2.

Rnd 3 Crossover slip st in next foundation ch (counts as sc), ch 5, (tr, ch 2, picot join around

adjacent slip st join, ch 2, tr) in next cluster, ch 5, sc in next dc, ch 2, slip st in adjacent ch-5 space, ch 2, sc in same dc, ch 5, (tr, ch 2, picot join around adjacent slip st join, ch 2, tr) in next cluster, ch 5, sc in next dc **, ch 5 (counts as 2 dc for this motif, connecting ch, and 2 ch for next motif).

Continue working Motif #6, joining to previous motifs as established, and completing Rnd 3 as for Motif #3. When Motif #6 is complete, work remaining portion of Rnd 3 of Motif #5, making a picot join to Motif #6. When Motif #5 is complete, work remaining portion of Rnd 3 on Motif #4, making a picot join to Motif #5, and ending at the foundation chain with sc in st at base of first foundation ch, ch 2, skip 2 ch, slip st in next ch — *motif complete,* ch 2, sc in same st as last sc on Motif #1, ch 5, (tr, ch 2, picot join, ch 2, tr) in next cluster, ch 5, sc in st at base of foundation ch, ch 5, join with slip st to first sc. Fasten off.

MOTIF #4   MOTIF #5   MOTIF #6

MOTIF #1   MOTIF #2   MOTIF #3

Rnd 1 A **Rnds 2 and 3** B

Change the Round 2 clusters to single stitches, and make the whole thing into eight points for this lacy circular shape.

CIRCLE: 5" (12.5 CM)

Picot-4 Ch 4, slip st in 4th ch from hook.

Ch 4, join with slip st to form ring.

Rnd 1 Ch 3 (counts as dc), 15 dc in ring, join with slip st to top of ch-3 — 16 dc.

Rnd 2 Ch 8 (counts as dc and ch 5), skip 1 dc, dc in next dc, *ch 5, skip 1 dc, dc in next dc; rep from * around to last st, skip 1 dc, ch 2, skip 1 dc, join with dc to 3rd ch of ch-8.

Rnd 3 Ch 1, (sc, ch 3, sc) in same space, *ch 4, Picot-4, ch 5**, (sc, ch 3, sc) in next space; rep from * around, ending last rep at **, join with slip st to first sc. Fasten off.

The simple Motif 23 can be expanded to six points as shown here.

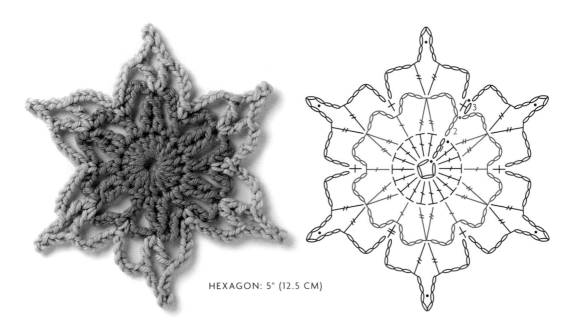

HEXAGON: 5" (12.5 CM)

Picot-4   Ch 4, slip st in 4th ch from hook.

Tr2tog *(treble crochet 2 together)* (Yarn over) two times, insert hook into indicated stitch or space and pull up a loop, (yarn over, pull through 2 loops) two times, (yarn over) two times, insert hook into next stitch or space and pull up a loop, (yarn over, pull through 2 loops) two times, yarn over and pull through all 3 loops on hook.

Ch 4, join with slip st to form ring.

Rnd 1 Ch 3 (counts as dc), 17 dc in ring, join with slip st to top of ch-3 — 18 dc.

Rnd 2 Ch 8 (counts as dc and ch 5), *tr2tog over next 2 dc, ch 5**, dc in next dc, ch 5; rep from * around, ending last rep at **, join with slip st to 3rd ch of ch-8.

Rnd 3 Ch 1, sc in same st, *ch 6, (tr, ch 2, Picot-4, ch 2, tr) in next cluster, ch 6, sc in next dc; rep from * around, omitting last sc, join with slip st to first sc. Fasten off.

Start out as with the previous motif. Then, by working Round 2 into the front loops only, you have the possibility of a double-layered motif! To make it truly reversible, turn after working Round 3, then work Rounds 4 and 5 with the wrong side of Rounds 1–3 facing.

HEXAGON: 5¼" (13.5 CM)

BLsc *(back loop single crochet)* Work 1 single crochet into the back loop only.

BLtr3tog *(back loop treble 3 stitches together)* Work tr3tog into the back loops only.

FLdc *(front loop double crochet)* Work 1 double crochet into the front loop only.

FLsc *(front loop single crochet)* Work 1 single crochet into the front loop only.

FLtr *(front loop treble crochet)* Work 1 treble crochet into the front loop only.

FLtr2tog *(front loop treble 2 stitches together)* Work tr2tog into the front loops only.

Partial tr *(partial treble)* (Yarn over) two times, insert hook into indicated stitch or space and pull up a loop, (yarn over, pull through 2 loops) two times.

Picot-4 Ch 4, slip st in 4th ch from hook.

Standing Partial tr *(standing partial treble)* Beginning with slip knot on hook, (yarn over) two times, insert hook into indicated stitch or space and pull up a loop, (yarn over, pull through 2 loops) two times.

Tr2tog *(treble crochet 2 together)* (Yarn over) two times, insert hook into indicated stitch or space and pull up a loop, (yarn over, pull through 2 loops) two times, (yarn over) two times, insert hook into next stitch or space and pull up a loop, (yarn over, pull through 2 loops) two times, yarn over and pull through all 3 loops on hook.

Tr3tog *(treble crochet 3 together)* (Yarn over) two times, insert hook into indicated stitch or space and pull up a loop, (yarn over, pull through 2 loops) two times, [(yarn over) two times, insert hook into next stitch or space and pull up a loop, (yarn over, pull through 2 loops) two times] two times, yarn over and pull through all 4 loops on hook.

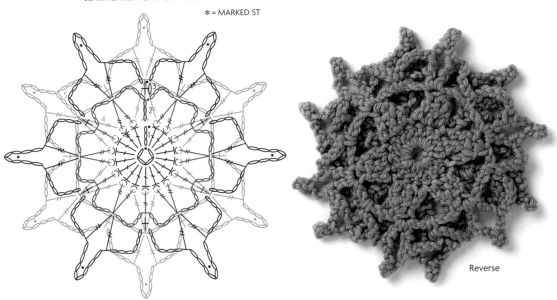

Reverse

Ch 4, join with slip st to form ring.

Rnd 1 Ch 3 (counts as dc), 17 dc in ring, join with slip st to front loop of top of ch-3 18 dc. Place marker in back loop of 3rd st.

Rnd 2 Ch 8 (counts as dc and ch 5), *FLtr2tog over next 2 dc, ch 5, FLdc in next dc, ch 5; rep from * around, omitting last FLdc, join with slip st to 3rd ch of ch-8.

Rnd 3 Ch 1, sc in same st, *ch 6, (tr, ch 2, Picot-4, ch 2, tr) in next cluster, ch 6, sc in next dc; rep from * around, omitting last sc, join with slip st to first sc. Fasten off.

Rnd 4 *Rnd 4 is worked in Rnd-1 sts behind Rnd 2.* Standing Partial tr in back loop of marked dc (behind the second st of the 2-dc cluster), Partial tr in back loop of next 2 dc, yarn over and pull through all 4 loops on hook to BLtr3tog, ch 6, *BLtr3tog over next 3 dcs, ch 6; rep from * around, join with slip st to first cluster.

Rnd 5 Ch 6 (counts as tr and ch 2), Picot-4, ch 2, tr in same st, ch 6, *sc in next Rnd-2 cluster between the two Rnd-3 trs and into next ch-6 space together, ch 6**, (tr, ch 2, Picot-4, ch 2, tr) in next cluster, ch 6; rep from * around, ending last rep at **, join with slip st to 4th ch of ch-6. Fasten off.

Double the layers, double the fun! Four double-layer motifs are joined on both layers, using a flat join to connect the picots. In this arrangement, the points made on Round 5 must be a bit shorter where they will be joined to other Round-5 points. Plan ahead to determine where the tips will join, then work those corners as (tr, ch 1, Picot-4, ch 1, tr) in the appropriate cluster.

The example shown is worked as follows:

MOTIF #1

Work Rounds 1–4 as for Motif 27 (see previous page).

Rnd 5 Ch 5 (counts as tr and ch 1), Picot-4, ch 1, tr in same st, ch 6, [sc in next Rnd-2 cluster between the two Rnd-3 trs and into next ch-6 space together, ch 6, (tr, ch 1, Picot-4, ch 1, tr) in next cluster, ch 6] two times; *sc in next Rnd-2 cluster between the two Rnd-3 trs and into next ch-6 space together, ch 6**, (tr, ch 2, Picot-4, ch 2, tr) in next cluster, ch 6; rep from * around, ending last rep at **, join with slip st to 4th ch of ch-5. Fasten off.

MOTIF #2

Work Rounds 1 and 2 as for Motif 27 (see previous page).

Rnd 3 Ch 1, sc in same st, [ch 6, (tr, ch 2, Picot-4, ch 2, tr) in next cluster, ch 6, sc in next dc] four times, *ch 6, (tr, ch 2; ch 2, flat

join to corresponding Rnd-3 Picot of previous motif [see diagram], ch 2, slip st in 4th ch from hook to complete joined Picot-4; ch 2, tr) in next cluster, ch 6, **sc in next dc; rep from * to ** once more, join with slip st to first sc. Fasten off.

Rnd 4 Work as for Rnd 4 of Motif 27.

Rnd 5 Ch 6 (counts as tr and ch 2), Picot-4, ch 2, tr in same st, ch 6, [*sc in next Rnd-2 cluster between the two Rnd-3 trs and into next ch-6 space together, ch 6, (tr, ch 2, Picot-4, ch 2, tr) in next cluster, ch 6**] twice; sc in next Rnd-2 cluster between the 2 Rnd-3 trs and into next ch-6 space together, ch 6, (tr, ch 1, Picot-4, ch 1, tr) in next cluster, ch 6;

sc in next Rnd-2 cluster and next ch-6 space together, ch 6, (tr, ch 1, joined Picot-4 to corresponding Rnd-5 picot of previous motif, ch 1, tr) in next cluster, ch 6; rep from * to ** once more, sc in next Rnd-2 cluster and next ch-6 space together, ch 6, join with slip st to 4th ch of ch-5. Fasten off.

Continue in this manner to join additional motifs to previous motifs on Rnds 3 and 5; shortening the joined points on Rnd 5.

FEATURES:

- JAYGo
- **Connections on two layers**
- **Flat join**
- **Adaptation of original motif**
- **Connection at picots**
- **3-D appearance**

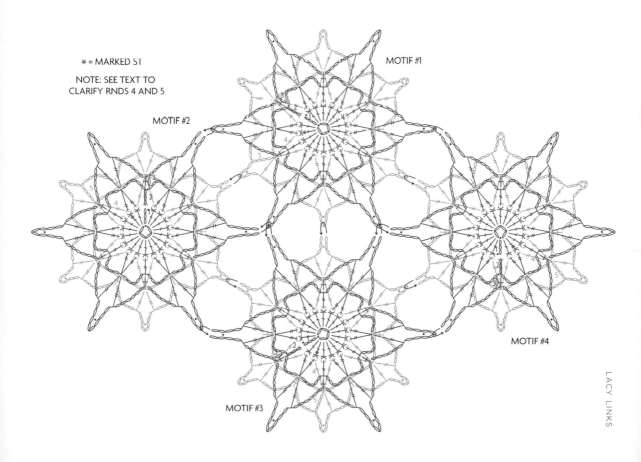

∗ = MARKED ST

NOTE: SEE TEXT TO
CLARIFY RNDS 4 AND 5

MOTIF #1

MOTIF #2

MOTIF #4

MOTIF #3

Rnds 1–3 A ■

This motif is a cousin in this family. The first couple of rounds begin like the others, with double crochets and clusters, but the asymmetrical stitches of the final round soften the sharp points of the previous shapes and add an interesting sense of movement.

CIRCLE: 4" (10 CM)

Dc3tog *(double crochet 3 together)* Yarn over, insert hook into indicated stitch or space and pull up a loop, yarn over, pull through 2 loops on hook, (yarn over, insert hook into same stitch and pull up a loop, yarn over and pull through 2 loops) two times, yarn over and pull through all 4 loops on hook.

Picot-4 Ch 4, slip st in 4th ch from hook.

Ch 5, join with slip st to form ring.

Rnd 1 Ch 4 (counts as dc and ch 1), *dc in ring, ch 1; rep from * nine more times, dc in ring, join with sc to top of ch-3 — 12 dc and 12 spaces.

Rnd 2 Ch 6 (counts as dc and ch 3), *dc3tog in next space**, ch 3, dc in next space, ch 3;

rep from * around, ending last rep at **, ch 1, join with hdc to 3rd ch of ch-6.

Rnd 3 Ch 1, sc in space formed by joining hdc, *ch 1, (tr, ch 3, Picot-4, ch 1, dc) in next st, ch 1, sc in next space; rep from * around, omitting last sc, join with slip st to first sc. Fasten off.

Circular motifs are connected here in a classic 2×2 arrangement. Although you might expect the connection points to be at the picots of this motif, they are actually in the ch-3 spaces. On Round 3, substitute (ch 2, flat join, ch 1) for the ch-3 on the final round. If you prefer a slip stitch or single crochet join, those would work well here, also.

The space in the center of the motifs is filled with a filler motif that blends with the design of the motifs. While the filler motif is not absolutely necessary here, it does add stability.

FILLER MOTIF

Ch 4, join with slip st to form ring.

Rnd 1 Ch 1, sc in ring, *ch 3, flat join to adjacent ch-3 space, ch 2, sc in ring; rep from * twice, ch 3, flat join to adjacent ch-3 space, ch 2, join with slip st to first sc. Fasten off.

FEATURES:

- JAYGo
- Flat join
- Connection in adjoining spaces
- Filler motif

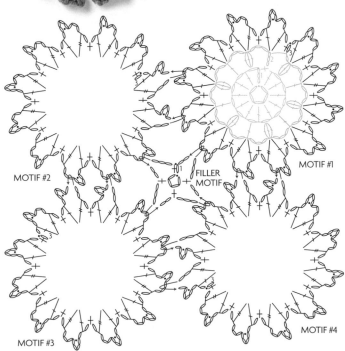

MOTIF #2   FILLER MOTIF   MOTIF #1

MOTIF #3   MOTIF #4

connect

Here's the same motif and the same join technique used on page 93, but this arrangement offsets the circular motifs by a half-drop, closing up the space between the shapes and obviating the need for a filler motif. As in the previous connection example, on Round 3, substitute (ch 2, flat join, ch 1) for the ch-3 on the final round.

FEATURES:

- JAYGo
- Flat join
- Connection in adjoining spaces
- Half-drop arrangement

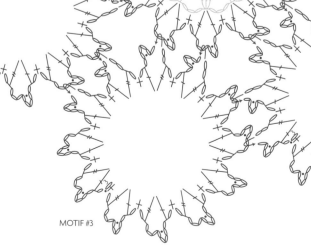

MOTIF #1

MOTIF #2

MOTIF #3

MOTIF #4

layered mesh

Rnds 1–3 A ■   **Rnd 4** B ■   **Rnd 5** C ■

Here's another simple double crochet–based square that can be the basis for many variations.

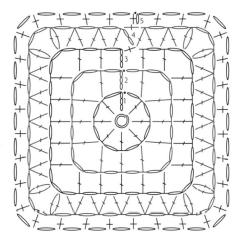

SQUARE: 3¾" (9.5 CM)

Dc2tog *(double crochet 2 together)* Yarn over, insert hook into indicated stitch or space and pull up a loop, yarn over, pull through 2 loops, yarn over, insert hook into next indicated stitch or space and pull up a loop, yarn over and pull through 2 loops, yarn over and pull through all 3 loops on hook.

Begin with sliding loop.

Rnd 1 Ch 4 (counts as dc and ch 1), (dc, ch 1) seven times in ring, join with slip st to top of ch-3 — 8 dc and 8 spaces.

Rnd 2 Ch 4 (counts as dc and ch 1), (dc, ch 3, dc) in next dc, ch 1, *dc in next dc, ch 1, (dc, ch 3, dc) in next dc, ch 1; rep from * around, join with slip st to 3rd ch of ch-4.

Rnd 3 Ch 4 (counts as dc and ch 1), *dc in next dc, ch 1, (dc, ch 3, dc) in next space**, (ch 1, dc in next dc) two times, ch 1; rep from * around, ending last rep at **, ch 1, dc in next dc, join with sc to 3rd ch of ch-4.

Rnd 4 Ch 2, dc in next space, ch 1, (dc2tog over same and next space, ch 1) two times, *(dc2tog, ch 2, dc2tog) in same space, ch 1**, (dc2tog over same and next space, ch 1) five times; rep from * around, ending last rep at **, dc2tog over same and next space, ch 1, dc2tog over same and next space, join with sc to first cluster.

Rnd 5 Ch 1, sc in space formed by joining sc, ch 1, (sc in next space, ch 1) three times, *(sc, ch 1) two times in next space**, (sc in next space, ch 1) six times; rep from * around, ending last rep at **, (sc in next space, ch 1) two times, join with slip st to first sc. Fasten off.

Working into the front and back loops in the first round creates the opportunity for layering. The layers on this hexagon are joined on only two rounds, making it one of the easier ones in this family to stitch. This is the hexagon used in the Layered Motif Afghan on page 234.

Standing tr Beginning with a slip knot on the hook, (yarn over) two times, insert hook into stitch or space indicated, pull up a loop (4 loops on hook), (yarn over and pull through 2 loops on hook) three times.

Begin with sliding loop.

Rnd 1 (RS) Ch 3 (counts as dc), 11 dc in ring, join with slip st in top of ch-3 — 12 dc.

Rnd 2 Ch 5 (counts as dc and ch 2), dc in same dc, ch 1, skip 1 dc, *(dc, ch 2, dc) in next dc, ch 1, skip 1 dc; rep from * around, join with slip st to 3rd ch of ch-5.

Rnd 3 Ch 4 (counts as dc and ch 1), *(dc, ch 2, dc) in next space**, ch 1, (dc in next dc, ch 1) two times; rep from * around, ending last rep at **, ch 1, dc in next dc, ch 1, join with slip st to 3rd ch of ch-4.

Rnd 4 Ch 4 (counts as dc and ch 1), dc in next dc*, ch 1, (dc, ch 3, dc) in next space**, (ch 1, dc in next dc) four times, ch 1; rep from * around, ending last rep at **, (ch 1, dc in next dc) two times, ch 1, join with slip st to 3rd ch of ch-4. Fasten off. Turn.

Rnd 5 (WS) *Rnd 5 is worked into Rnd-1 sts.* Standing tr any skipped st of Rnd 1, ch 2, tr in same st, ch 1, *(tr, ch 2, tr) in next skipped dc, ch 1; rep from * around, join with slip st to first tr.

Rnd 6 Ch 4 (counts as dc and ch 1), *(dc, ch 2, dc) in next ch-2 space, ch 1**, (dc in next tr, ch 1) two times; rep from * around, ending last rep at **, dc in next tr, ch 1, join with slip st to 3rd ch of ch-4.

Rnd 7 Ch 4 (counts as dc and ch 1), dc in next dc, *ch 1, (dc, ch 2, dc) in next space and in corresponding Rnd-4 space together [*See Note*]**, (ch 1, dc in next dc) four times; rep from * around, ending last rep at **, (ch 1, dc in next dc) two times, ch 1, join with slip st to 3rd ch of ch-4. Turn.

Note: The "corresponding Rnd-4 space" is the center ch-1 space along the side of Rnd 4.

Rnd 8 (RS) Ch 4 (counts as dc and ch 1), (dc in next dc, ch 1) three times, *(dc, ch 2, dc) in next space**, (ch 1, dc in next dc) six times, ch 1; rep from * around, ending last rep at **, (ch 1, dc in next dc) two times, ch 1, join with slip st to 3rd ch of ch-4. Fasten off.

[**LAYERED MESH**]

The relatively solid straight edges of these simple mesh motifs make good candidates for join-after-you-stitch options such as crocheted seams. The chain-spaces also make great spots for JAYGo methods. Connection-wise, this is a very adaptable family of motifs.

HEXAGON: 5½" (14 CM)

NOTE: SEE TEXT
TO CLARIFY RND 7

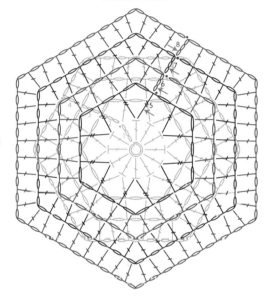

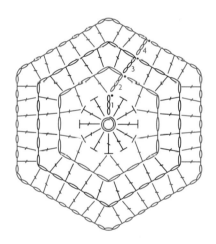

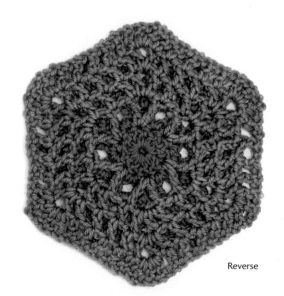

Reverse

31

Rnds 1, 2, 4, and 6 A (top color) ■
Rnds 3, 5, 7, and 8 B (background color) ■

In this reversible square, alternating rounds are working in contrasting colors, creating joins at the corner on every layer. Although the square is reversible, right-side and wrong-side rounds are stated to clarify the instructions. If you prefer, turn and work the final round as a right-side round. Use both the chart and the text instructions as needed.

NOTE: REFER TO THE TEXT FOR PLACEMENT OF STITCHES IN FRONT OF, BEHIND, OR OVER EXISTING STITCHES

SQUARE (REVERSIBLE): 4¾" (12 CM)

Begin with sliding loop.

Rnd 1 (RS) Ch 3 (counts as dc), 15 dc in ring, join with slip st to top of ch-3 — 16 dc.

Rnd 2 (RS) Ch 4 (counts as dc and ch 1), skip 1 dc, (dc, ch 3, dc) in next dc, ch 1, skip 1 dc, *dc in next dc, ch 1, skip 1 dc, (dc, ch 3, dc) in next dc, ch 1, skip 1 dc; rep from * around, join with slip st to 3rd ch of ch-4, drop loop from hook, turn.

Rnd 3 (WS) (Standing sc, ch 3, sc) in any ch-3 space, ch 1, *keeping Rnd-2 sts to the back, (tr in next skipped dc from Rnd 1, ch 1) two times**, (sc, ch 3, sc) in next ch-3 space, ch 1; rep from * around, ending last rep at **, join with slip st to first sc, drop loop from hook, turn.

Rnd 4 (RS) *Rnd 4 is worked into Rnd-2 sts and corner spaces, in front of Rnd 3 sts.* Place dropped loop from Rnd-2 onto hook, ch 4 (counts as dc and ch 1); dc in next dc, ch 1, *(dc, ch 3, dc) in next ch-3 space between Rnd-3 scs**, (ch 1, dc in next dc) three times, ch 1; rep from * around, ending last rep at **, ch 1, dc in next dc, ch 1, join with slip st to 3rd ch of ch-4, drop loop from hook, turn.

Rnd 5 (WS) *Rnd 5 is worked into Rnd-3 sts in front of Rnd 4 sts and into Rnd-3 and Rnd-4 corner spaces.* Place dropped loop from Rnd-3 onto hook, ch 4 (counts as dc and ch 1); *(dc, ch 3, dc) in next ch-3 space over Rnd-4 ch, ch 1; working in Rnd-3 sts holding Rnd-4 sts to the back, dc in next sc, (ch 1, dc in next tr) two times, ch 1**, dc in next sc, ch 1; rep from * around, ending last rep at **, join with slip st to 3rd ch of ch-4, drop loop from hook, turn.

Rnd 6 (RS) *Rnd 6 is worked into Rnd-4 sts and corner spaces, in front of Rnd 5 sts.* Place dropped loop from Rnd-4 onto hook, ch 4 (counts as dc and ch 1), *(dc in next dc, ch 1) two times, (dc, ch 3, dc) in next ch-3 space between Rnd-5 dcs**, (ch 1, dc in next dc) three times; rep from * around, ending last rep at **, (ch 1, dc in next dc) two times, ch 1, join with slip st to 3rd ch of ch-4. Fasten off. Turn.

Rnd 7 (WS) *Rnd 7 is worked into Rnd-5 sts in front of Rnd 6 sts and into Rnd-5 and Rnd-6 corner spaces.* Place dropped loop from Rnd-5 onto hook, ch 4 (counts as dc and ch 1), dc in next dc, ch 1, *(dc, ch 3, dc) in next space through both layers, ch 1**, working in Rnd-5 sts, (dc in next dc, ch 1) six times; rep from * around, ending last rep at **, (dc in next dc, ch 1) four times, join with slip st to 3rd ch of ch-4.

Rnd 8 (WS) Ch 4 (counts as dc and ch 1), *(dc in next dc, ch 1) two times, (dc, ch 3, dc) in corner space, ch 1**, (dc in next dc, ch 1) six times; rep from * around, ending last rep at **, (dc in next dc, ch 1) five times, join with slip st to 3rd ch of ch-4. Fasten off.

32

Rnds 1–4 A ▮   **Rnds 5–7** B ▮

Here's another layered reversible shape. Pay careful attention to the text and the chart in order to get your stitches in the right place. You'll need to use a stitch marker.

SQUARE (REVERSIBLE): 4" (10 CM)

Begin with sliding loop.

Rnd 1 Ch 3 (counts as dc), 15 dc in ring, join with slip st to top of ch-3 — 16 dc. Place marker in second dc.

Rnd 2 Ch 4 (counts as dc and ch 1), skip 1 dc, (dc, ch 3, dc) in next dc, ch 1, skip 1 dc, *dc in next dc, ch 1, skip 1 dc, (dc, ch 3, dc) in next dc, ch 1, skip 1 dc; rep from * around, join with slip st to 3rd ch of ch-4.

Rnd 3 Ch 4 (counts as dc and ch 1); dc in next dc, *ch 1, (dc, ch 3, dc) in next space**, (ch 1, dc in next dc) three times; rep from * around, ending last rep at **, ch 1, dc in next dc, ch 1, join with slip st to 3rd ch of ch-4.

continued on next page

continued

Reverse

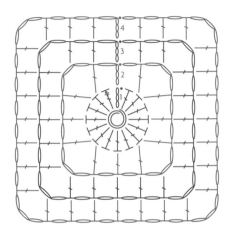

NOTE: REFER TO TEXT
TO CLARIFY RNDS 5–7

Rnd 4 Ch 4 (counts as dc and ch 1), *(dc in next dc, ch 1) two times, (dc, ch 3, dc) in next space**, (ch 1, dc in next dc) three times, ch 1; rep from * around, ending last rep at **, (ch 1, dc in next dc) two times, ch 1, join with slip st to 3rd ch of ch-4. Fasten off. Turn.

Rnd 5 *Rnd 5 is worked into skipped Rnd-1 dcs, keeping Rnds 2–4 to the back, unless otherwise stated.* Standing tr in marked st, *ch 1, tr in next skipped dc, ch 1, sc in next Rnd-2 space before the 2 Rnd-3 dcs, ch 3, sc in same space after the 2 Rnd-3 dcs, ch 1**, tr in next skipped dc; rep from * around, ending last rep at **, join with slip st to first tr.

Rnd 6 Ch 4 (counts as dc and ch 1), dc in next tr, ch 1, *dc in next sc, ch 1, (dc, ch 3, dc) in next corner space, ch 1, dc in next sc, ch 1**, (dc in next tr, ch 1) two times; rep from * around, ending last rep at **, join with slip st to 3rd ch of ch-4.

Rnd 7 *Rnd 7 is worked into Rnd-6 sts and into Rnd-4 spaces together.* Ch 1, sc in same st and in corresponding Rnd-4 space

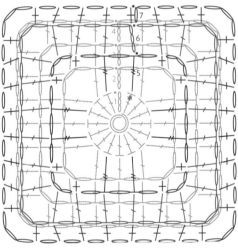

* = MARKED ST

together, ch 1; [(sc, ch 1) in next dc and in corresponding space in Rnd 4] three times, *(sc, ch 3, sc, ch 1) in corresponding corner spaces**, [(sc, ch 1) in next dc and in corresponding space in Rnd 4] six times; rep from * around, ending last rep at **, [(sc, ch 1) in next dc and in corresponding space in Rnd 4] two times, join with slip st to first sc. Fasten off.

The decision to work in front of, in back of, or over chain-spaces of previous rounds makes a huge difference to the design. This pin-striped square comes from working *over* most of the chains. This is the square used in the Reversible Camp Rug (page 228) and the Mary Frances Pincushion (page 233). Rounds 1–3 are the same as in the previous motif. See page 104 for a connection.

REFER TO THE TEXT FOR PLACEMENT OF STITCHES IN FRONT OF, BEHIND, OR OVER EXISTING STITCHES.

SQUARE (REVERSIBLE): 4¼" (11 CM)

Begin with sliding loop.

Rnd 1 (RS) Ch 3 (counts as dc), 15 dc in ring, join with slip st to top of ch-3 — 16 dc.

Rnd 2 (RS) Ch 4 (counts as dc and ch 1), skip 1 dc, (dc, ch 3, dc) in next dc, ch 1, skip 1 dc, *dc in next dc, ch 1, skip 1 dc, (dc, ch 3, dc) in next dc, ch 1, skip 1 dc; rep from * around, join with slip st to 3rd ch of ch-4, drop loop from hook, turn.

Rnd 3 (WS) (Standing sc, ch 3, sc) in any ch-3 corner space, ch 1, *keeping Rnd-2 sts to the back, (tr in next skipped dc from Rnd 1, ch 1) two times**, (sc, ch 3, sc) in next ch-3 space, ch 1; rep from * around, ending last rep at **, join with slip st to first sc, drop loop from hook, turn.

Rnd 4 (RS) *Rnd 4 is worked into Rnd-2 sts over Rnd-3 chs unless otherwise stated.* Place dropped loop from Rnd 2 onto hook, insert hook into Rnd-3 space and ch 1 to slip st over Rnd-3 ch, ch 3 (counts as dc and ch 1); dc in next dc*, ch 1; keeping Rnd-3 space to the back, (dc, ch 3, dc) in next ch-3 space between Rnd-3 scs**; working over Rnd-3 chs, (ch 1, dc in next dc) three times; rep from * around, ending last rep at **, ch 1, dc in next dc, ch 1, join with slip st to 3rd ch of ch-4, drop loop from hook, turn.

Rnd 5 (WS) *Rnd 5 is worked into Rnd-3 sts over Rnd-4 chs unless otherwise stated.* Place dropped loop from Rnd 3 onto hook, insert hook into Rnd-4 space and ch 1 to slip st around Rnd-4 ch, ch 3 (counts as dc and

continued on next page

LAYERED MESH

ch 1); *(dc, ch 3, dc) in next spaces (through both layers), ch 1, dc in next sc, (ch 1, dc in next tr) two times, ch 1**, dc in next sc, ch 1; rep from * around, ending last rep at **, join with slip st to 3rd ch of ch-4, drop loop from hook, turn.

Rnd 6 (RS) *Rnd 6 is worked into Rnd-4 sts over Rnd-5 chs unless otherwise stated.* Place dropped loop from Rnd-4 onto hook, and ch 1 to slip st over Rnd-5 chain, ch 3 (counts as dc and ch 1), *(dc in next dc, ch 1) two times; keeping Rnd-5 ch to the back, (dc, ch 3, dc) in next ch-3 space between Rnd-5 dcs**; (ch 1, dc in next dc) three times, ch 1; rep from * around, ending last rep at **, (ch 1, dc in next dc) two times, ch 1, join with slip st to 3rd ch of ch-4. Fasten off. Turn.

Rnd 7 (WS) *Rnd 7 is worked into Rnd-5 sts over Rnd-6 chs unless otherwise stated.* Place dropped loop from Rnd 5 onto hook, insert hook into Rnd-6 space and ch 1 to slip st around Rnd-6 ch, ch 3 (counts as dc and ch 1), dc in next dc, ch 1, *(dc, ch 3, dc) in next space through both layers, ch 1**, working over Rnd-6 chs, (dc in next dc, ch 1) six times; rep from * around, ending last rep at **, (dc in next dc, ch 1) four times, join with slip st to 3rd ch of ch-4. Fasten off.

Reverse

Staying with the pin-striped theme, here's a nice circle. Make two and sew them together to make a pincushion or sachet (page 231).

V-st (Dc, ch 1, dc) in 1 stitch.

___

Begin with sliding loop.

Rnd 1 (RS) Ch 3 (counts as dc), 11 dc in ring, join with slip st to top of ch-3 — 12 dc.

Rnd 2 (RS) Ch 6 (counts as dc and ch 3), skip 1 dc, *dc in next dc, ch 3, skip 1 dc; rep from * around, join with slip st to 3rd ch of ch-4, drop loop from hook, turn.

Rnd 3 (WS) Standing sc in any ch-3 space, ch 1*, keeping Rnd-2 sts to the back, tr in next skipped dc from Rnd 1, ch 1, sc in same space, ch 1, **sc in next space, ch 1; rep from * around ending last rep at **, join with slip st to first sc, drop loop from hook, turn.

Rnd 4 (RS) *Rnd 4 is worked into Rnd-2 sts over Rnd-3 chs unless otherwise stated.* Place dropped loop from Rnd 2 onto hook, insert hook into Rnd-3 space and ch 1 to slip st over Rnd-3 ch, ch 3 (counts as dc and ch 1); dc in same st, ch 1, *keeping Rnd-3 space to the back, dc in next ch-3 space in Rnd 2 after next sc in Rnd-3, ch 1, dc in same ch-3 space in Rnd 2 after next tr in Rnd 3, ch 1**; working over Rnd-3 ch, V-st in next dc, ch 1; rep from * around, ending last rep at **, join with slip st to 3rd ch of ch-4, drop loop from hook, turn.

Rnd 5 (WS) *Rnd 5 is worked into Rnd-3 sts over Rnd-4 chs unless otherwise stated.* Place dropped loop from Rnd 3 onto hook, ch 1, insert hook into Rnd-4 space and ch 1 to slip st over Rnd-4 ch, ch 2 (counts as dc and ch 1), *sc in next tr in Rnd-3, ch 1, dc in next sc, ch 1, sc in next ch-1 space, ch 1**, dc in

NOTE: REFER TO THE TEXT FOR
PLACEMENT OF STITCHES IN FRONT OF, BEHIND,
OR OVER EXISTING STITCHES

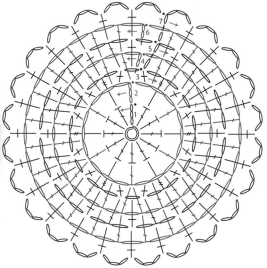

CIRCLE (REVERSIBLE): 4¼" (11 CM)

next sc, ch 1; rep from * around, ending last rep at **, join with slip st to 3rd ch of ch-4, drop loop from hook, turn.

Rnd 6 (RS) *Rnd 6 is worked into Rnd-4 sts over Rnd-5 chs unless otherwise stated.* Place dropped loop from Rnd 4 onto hook, ch 1 to slip st over Rnd-5 ch, ch 3 (counts as dc and ch 1), *dc in next dc, ch 1; rep from * around, join with slip st to 3rd ch of ch-4. Fasten off. Turn.

Rnd 7 (WS) *Rnd 7 is worked into Rnd-5 sts over Rnd-6 chs unless otherwise stated.* Place dropped loop from Rnd 5 onto hook, ch 1, slip st over Rnd-6 ch, ch 1, *ch 3, sc in next sc, ch 3**, sc in next dc; rep from * around, ending last rep at **, join with slip st to first slip st. Fasten off.

Because these motifs are reversible, it's good to join them using a method that also looks good on both sides. Here the squares are arranged in a half-drop pattern. To join, hold pieces with wrong sides (or right sides) together and working into both layers, (sc into dc, ch 1) across. This is a fairly dense motif because of its double layer, so a sturdy seam is in order. Besides the sc-with-chain seam shown here, another good option would be a double-crochet-together seam, or a whipstitch seam. It all depends on the look you desire, and the function you want it to fill.

LAYERED MESH

Rnds 1, 2, 4, and 6 A ▢ ▢ ■ ▢ ▢ **Rnds 3, 5, and 7** B ■

FEATURES:

- Join when you're done
- Sc-with-chain seam
- Connection in adjoining stitches
- Half-drop arrangement

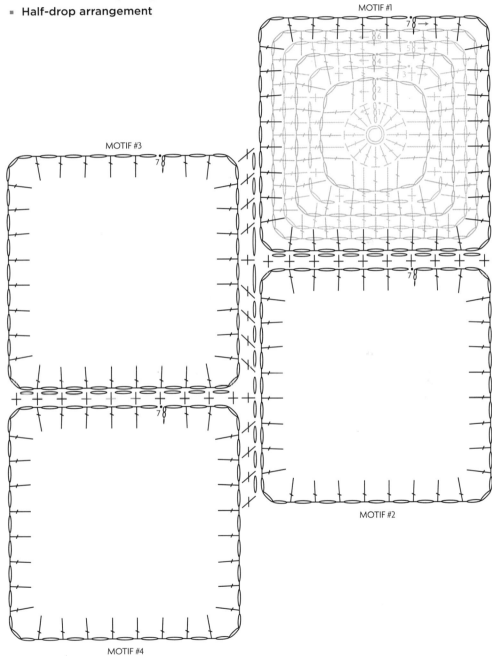

MOTIF #1

MOTIF #3

MOTIF #2

MOTIF #4

When you start playing with the idea of working all around a chain-space, you realize the vast number of permutations possible! The final round of this circle takes the simple layered shape to a new level. It looks different on each side, yet it's fully reversible. Although both sides are really the right side, the text designates right side and wrong side to clarify the instructions.

V-st (Dc, ch 1, dc) in 1 stitch.

Begin with sliding loop.

Rnd 1 (RS) Ch 3 (counts as dc), 11 dc in ring, join with slip st to top of ch-3 — 12 dc.

Rnd 2 (RS) Ch 4, dc in same st (counts as V-st), ch 1, skip 1 dc, *V-st in next dc, ch 1, skip 1 dc; rep from * around, join with slip st to 3rd ch of ch-4.

Rnd 3 (RS) Ch 4 (counts as dc and ch 1), *(dc, ch 1) two times in center of next V-st**, (dc in next dc, ch 1) two times; rep from * around, ending last rep at **, dc in next dc, ch 1, join with slip st to 3rd ch of ch-4.

Rnd 4 (RS) Ch 5 (counts as dc and ch 2), *dc in next dc, ch 2; rep from * around, join with slip st to 3rd ch of ch-5; drop loop from hook, turn.

Rnd 5 (WS) *Rnd 5 is worked into Rnd-1 sts.* Standing tr in any skipped st of Rnd 1, ch 2, tr in same st, ch 1, *(tr, ch 2, tr) in next skipped dc, ch 1; rep from * around, join with slip st to top of first tr.

Rnd 6 (WS) Ch 4 (counts as dc and ch 1), *(dc, ch 1) two times in next space**, (dc in next tr, ch 1) two times; rep from * around, ending last rep at **, dc in next tr, ch 1, join with slip st to 3rd ch of ch-4.

Rnd 7 (WS) *Rnd 7 is worked into Rnd-6 sts over Rnd-4 chs.* Ch 1, insert hook into corresponding Rnd-4 ch and ch 1 to slip st over Rnd-4 ch, ch 3 (counts as dc and ch 2), *dc in next dc, ch 2; rep from * around, join with slip st to 3rd ch of ch-4. Fasten off. Turn.

Rnd 8 (RS) *Rnd 8 is worked into Rnd-4 sts.* Place Rnd-4 st onto hook; ch 1, sc in same st in front of Rnd 7, ch 4, *sc in next dc behind Rnd 7, ch 4**, sc in next dc in front of Rnd 7, ch 4, rep from * around, ending last rep at **, join with slip st in front of Rnd 7 to first sc. Fasten off.

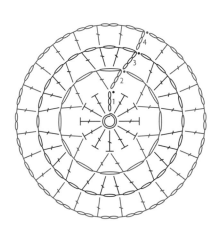

CIRCLE (REVERSIBLE): 4½" (11.5 CM)

Reverse

Take advantage of the reversibility of this motif when connecting them. Just flip one over every now and then to add a bit of flair. These four motifs are joined with a flat join in the center of each of two chain loops. Refer to the chart for joining points. The filler is not precisely a motif, but rather 8 partial double treble stitches worked together.

FILLER

Begin with a slip knot on the hook. *(Yarn over) three times, insert hook into joining point and pull up a loop, (yarn over and pull through 2 loops) three times; rep from * seven more times, yarn over and pull through all 9 loops on hook. Fasten off. Thread a tapestry needle with the yarn tail and weave it in a circular pattern around the tops of stitches to create a tight circle where stitches meet. Untie knot at beginning of round and weave in ends.

FEATURES:

- Reversibility
- JAYGo
- Flat join
- Connection in adjoining spaces
- Filler motif

MOTIF #1

FILLER
MOTIF

sc/dc

Rnds 1 and 4 A ■   **Rnds 2 and 5** B ■   **Rnds 3 and 6** C ■

This square is perfect for beginning crocheters. It can serve as the basis for many variations in color, textured stitches, and shape.

SQUARE: 4" (10 CM)

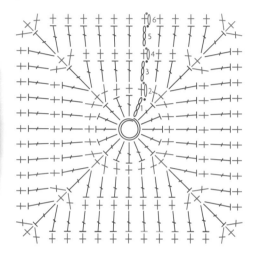

Begin with sliding loop.

Rnd 1 Ch 3 (counts as dc), 15 dc in ring, join with slip st to top of ch-3 — 16 dc.

Rnd 2 Ch 1, sc in same st, *sc in next 2 dc, 3 sc in next dc, sc in next dc; rep from * around, omitting last sc, join with slip st to first sc.

Rnd 3 Ch 3 (counts as dc), *dc in next 3 sc, 3 dc in next sc, dc in next 2 sc; rep from * around, omitting last dc, join with slip st to top of ch-3.

Rnd 4 Ch 1, sc in same st, *sc in next 4 dc, 3 sc in next dc, sc in next 3 dc; rep from * around, omitting last sc, join with slip st to first sc.

Rnd 5 Ch 3 (counts as dc), *dc in next 5 sc, 3 dc in next sc, dc in next 4 sc; rep from * around, omitting last dc, join with slip st to top of ch-3.

Rnd 6 Ch 1, sc in same st, *sc in next 6 dc, 3 sc in next dc, sc in next 5 dc; rep from * around, omitting last sc, join with slip st to first sc. Fasten off.

[SC/DC]

The concept behind this family is basic: alternating rounds of double crochet and single crochet. But look what can happen with this simple concept! From nicely striped squares to three-dimensional ruffles, the mind boggles at the possibilities, especially when you add in all the connection options available. Smooth straight edges are great for seaming, of course, but don't stick with the expected; try a zigzag seam or other fancy connection. Try JAYGo before you reach the final round, or a complex filler motif.

Longer post stitches and spike stitches add an overlay of color on this variation.

SQUARE: 3½" (9 CM)

FPdc *(front post double crochet)* Yarn over, insert hook from front to back to front around post of stitch indicated and pull up a loop, (yarn over and pull through 2 loops on hook) two times.

FPtr *(front post treble crochet)* (Yarn over) two times, insert hook from front to back to front around post of stitch indicated and pull up a loop (yarn over and pull through 2 loops on hook) three times.

Spike sc Insert hook into stitch or space one or more rounds below next stitch and pull up a loop to level of current round, yarn over and pull through both loops on hook.

Begin with sliding loop.

Rnd 1 Ch 3 (counts as dc), 15 dc in ring, join with slip st to top of ch-3 — 16 dc.

Rnd 2 Ch 1, sc in same st, *3 sc in next dc, sc in next dc, FPdc in next dc, sc in next dc; rep from * around, omitting last sc, join with slip st to first sc.

Rnd 3 Ch 3 (counts as dc), dc in next sc, *3 dc in next sc, dc in next 5 sts; rep from * around, omitting last 2 dc, join with slip st to top of ch-3.

Rnd 4 Ch 1, sc in same st, *Spike sc in next corner st of Rnd 2, skip 1 dc, sc in next 2 dc, Spike sc in same corner st of Rnd 2, sc in same dc and in next dc, Spike sc in same corner st of Rnd 2, skip 1 dc, sc in next dc, FPtr around post of FPdc from Rnd 2, skip dc behind last st, sc in next dc; rep from *, omitting last sc, join with slip st to first sc.

Rnd 5 Ch 1, sc in same sc, *ch 1, skip 1 sc, sc in next sc, ch 1, skip 1 sc, (sc, ch 1, sc) in next sc, (ch 1, skip 1 sc, sc in next sc) three times; rep from * around, omitting last sc, join with slip st to first sc, slip st in next space.

Rnd 6 Ch 1, *(working over ch-1 space, Spike sc in free sc from Rnd 4, ch 1, skip 1 sc) two times, sc in next space, Spike sc in corner st from Rnd 4, sc in same space, (ch 1, skip 1 sc, Spike sc in next free st from Rnd 4) two times, ch 1, skip 1 sc, FPtr around post of FPtr from Rnd 4, ch 1, skip 1 sc; rep from * around, join with slip st to first sc. Fasten off.

connect

Motif 36

You might think a plain square like this means a plain join. You could, of course, just stitch the squares together or use a single crochet seam. Instead, why not try a JAYGo join that happens on the next-to-last round? This allows the edges of the motif to curl inward (intentionally!) to create a three-dimensional connection. You may find yourself experimenting with this technique on other I-thought-they-were-plain shapes.

Rnds 1–4 Work as for Motif 36 (page 110).

Rnd 5 (Joining Rnd) Work as for Motif 36, placing all sts into the front loops only.

Beginning with the second motif, join the current motif to previous motif(s) in every stitch along the side edges, leaving the 3 dcs in the corner of each motif unjoined, as follows on the next page.

SC/DC

With WS together and RS of current motif facing, yarn over, insert hook through both front and back loops of current motif and through the free Rnd-4 loop of previous motif, yarn over and pull up a loop, (yarn over and pull through 2 loops) two times to complete dc; continue in this manner across the edge.

When all adjacent stitches are joined, continue working Rnd-5 dcs into the front loops only.

Note: If you prefer not to have the outside (nonjoined) edges pop up toward the front, work those edges into both loops on Round 5.

Rnd 6 Work as for Motif 36. Fasten off.

FEATURES:

- JAYGo
- **Connection on next-to-last round**
- **Connection in adjoining stitches**
- **Stitching through two motif layers**
- **3-D appearance**

REFER TO TEXT FOR
JOINING INSTRUCTIONS

MOTIF #1   MOTIF #2

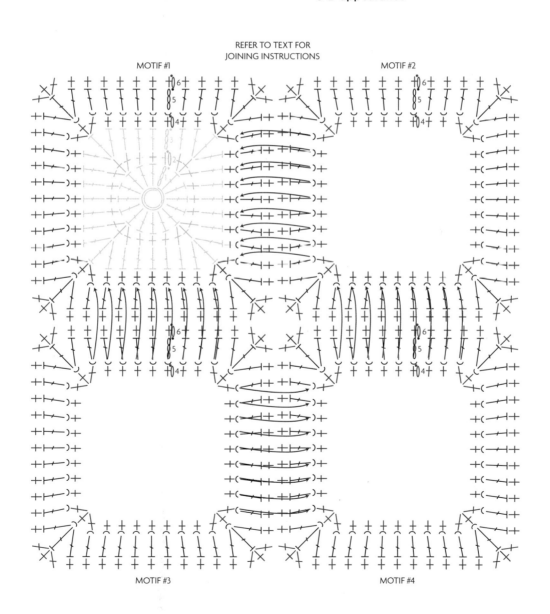

MOTIF #3   MOTIF #4

Here's another way post stitches can be used to create a color pattern that lies on top of a background. Following the tips for keeping motifs flat (Creating Shapes, page 23, and Waves and Curls, page 24), try making this one even larger by adding rounds of flat background stitches and dimensional post stitches.

FPdc *(front post double crochet)* Yarn over, insert hook from front to back to front around post of stitch indicated and pull up a loop, (yarn over and pull through 2 loops on hook) two times.

FPdtr *(front post double treble crochet)* (Yarn over) three times, insert hook from front to back to front around post of designated stitch and pull up a loop, (yarn over and pull through 2 loops on hook) four times.

Partial FPdtr *(partial front post double treble crochet)* (Yarn over) three times, insert hook from front to back to front around post of designated st and pull up a loop, (yarn over and pull through 2 loops on hook) three times.

Begin with sliding loop.

Rnd 1 Ch 3 (counts as dc), 15 dc in ring, join with slip st to top of ch-3 — 16 dc.

Rnd 2 Ch 1, sc in same st, *3 sc in next dc, sc in next dc, FPdc in next dc**, sc in next dc; rep from * around, omitting last sc, join with slip st to first sc.

Rnd 3 Ch 3 (counts as dc), dc in each st around, placing 3 dc in each corner st, join with slip st to top of ch-3.

Rnd 4 Ch 1, sc in same st, *FPdtr around post of FPdc 2 sts back and 2 rnds below, skip dc behind st just made, sc in next dc, (sc, FPdc, sc) in corner dc, sc in next dc, FPdtr around post of FPdc 2 sts ahead and 2 rnds below,

skip dc behind st just made, sc in next 3 dc; rep from * around, omitting last sc, join with slip st to first sc.

Rnd 5 Rep Rnd 3.

Rnd 6 Ch 1, sc in same st, sc in next 3 dc, *FPdtr in corner FPdc 2 rnds below, skip dc behind st just made, 3 sc in next dc, FPdtr in same corner FPdc 2 rnds below, skip dc behind st just made, sc in next 4 dc, Partial FPdtr in FPdtr 2 sts back and 2 rnds below, Partial FPdtr in FPdtr 2 sts ahead and 2 rnds below, insert hook into next st and pull up a loop, yarn over and pull through 3 loops on hook to dtr2tog, ** sc in next 4 dc; rep from * around, ending last rep at **, join with slip st to first sc. Fasten off.

SQUARE: 4" (10 CM)

Unless you examine this one closely, you'd never know this is another variation of Motif 36! This one has evenly spaced increases, three-dimensional texture on Round 4, and petal-like clusters on the final round.

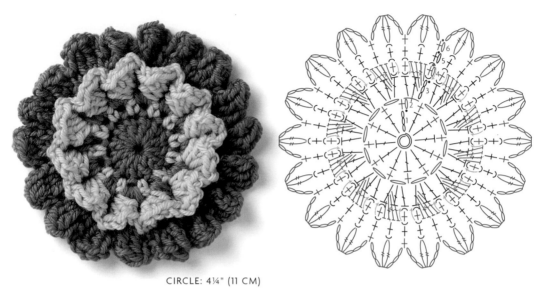

CIRCLE: 4¼" (11 CM)

BLsc *(back loop single crochet)* Work 1 single crochet into the back loop only.

FLsc *(front loop single crochet)* Work 1 single crochet into the front loop only.

FLtr2tog *(front loop treble 2 stitches together)* Work tr2tog into the front loops only.

Tr2tog *(treble crochet 2 together)* (Yarn over) two times, insert hook into indicated stitch or space and pull up a loop, (yarn over, pull through 2 loops) two times, (yarn over) two times, insert hook into same stitch or space and pull up a loop, (yarn over, pull through 2 loops) two times, yarn over and pull through all 3 loops on hook.

Begin with sliding loop.

Rnd 1 Ch 3 (counts as dc), 11 dc in ring, join with slip st to top of ch-3 — 12 dc.

Rnd 2 Ch 1, sc in same st, *ch 1, sc in next dc; rep from * around, join with sc to first sc.

Rnd 3 Ch 3 (counts as dc), 2 dc in space formed by joining sc, 3 dc in each space around, join with slip st to top of ch-3.

Rnd 4 Ch 1, FLsc in same st, *(hdc, 3 dc) around post of same dc, skip 1 dc, FLsc in next 2 dc; rep from * around, omitting last FLsc, join with slip st to first sc.

Rnd 5 Working into sts from Rnd 3, ch 1, BLsc in same st, *sc in next dc, BLsc in next 2 dc; rep from * around, omitting last BLsc, join with slip st to first sc.

Rnd 6 Ch 1, sc in same st, *ch 3, FLtr2tog in next st, ch 3, sc in next st; rep from * around, omitting last sc, join with slip st to first sc. Fasten off.

SC/DC

As we've seen before, connecting circular shapes in a grid pattern creates large spaces that need to be filled. Using just a portion of the main motif as a filler can be a wonderful way to create a coordinated fabric.

Referring to chart for joining locations, work four complete motifs, joining motifs on Round 6 with a flat join to tops of clusters.

FEATURES:

- JAYGo
- Flat join
- Filler motif
- Connection in adjoining stitches
- 3-D appearance

FILLER MOTIF

Work Rnds 1 and 2 of Motif 39, then join the filler to the completed motifs on Rnd 3, using a single crochet join between the double crochet stitches, as follows:

Rnd 3 Ch 3 (counts as dc), 2 dc in space formed by joining sc, dc in next space, sc join to adjacent motif, 2 dc in same space, sc join to next point of adjacent motif, (3 dc in each of next 2 spaces, dc in next space, sc join to next motif, 2 dc in same space, sc join to next point of motif) three times, 3 dc in next space, join with slip st to top of ch-3. Fasten off.

Rnd 4 Work as Rnd 4 of Motif 39.

MOTIF #3

MOTIF #4

FILLER
MOTIF

MOTIF #1

MOTIF #2

SC/DC

The fretwork look of this motif comes from using chain-spaces to open up the double crochet rounds. Single crochet rounds worked into these chain-spaces add color without overwhelming the lacy look.

Dc2tog *(double crochet 2 together)* Yarn over, insert hook into indicated stitch or space and pull up a loop, yarn over, pull through 2 loops, yarn over, insert hook into same stitch and pull up a loop, yarn over and pull through 2 loops, yarn over and pull through all 3 loops on hook.

HEXAGON: 4¼" (11 CM)

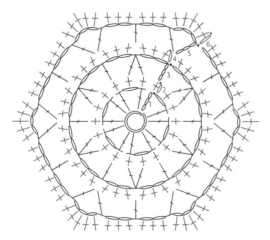

Begin with sliding loop.

Rnd 1 Ch 3 (counts as dc), dc in ring, ch 1, *2 dc in ring, ch 1; rep from * four more times, join with slip st to top of ch-3 — 12 dc and 6 spaces.

Rnd 2 Ch 1, sc in each st and space around, join with slip st to first sc.

Rnd 3 Ch 5 (counts as dc and ch 2), *dc2tog over next 2 dc, ch 2**, dc in next dc, ch 2; rep from * around, ending last rep at **, join with slip st to top of first dc, slip st in next space.

Rnd 4 Ch 1, 3 sc in each space around, join with slip st to first sc — *12 sc-groups made.*

Rnd 5: Placing dcs in between each group of 3-sc, ch 6 (counts as dc and ch 3), dc in same space between last sc and first sc, *ch 2, skip next 3 sc, dc in next space between 2 sc groups, ch 2, skip next 3 sc**, (dc, ch 3, dc) in next space between 2 sc groups; rep from * around, ending last rep at **, join with slip st to 3rd ch of ch-6.

Rnd 6: Ch 1, 5 sc in next space, 3 sc in next 2 spaces, *5 sc in next ch-3 space, 3 sc in next 2 spaces; rep from * around, join with slip st to first sc. Fasten off.

Take the combination of double crochet groups alternating with chain-spaces in a different direction with this snowflake-like motif.

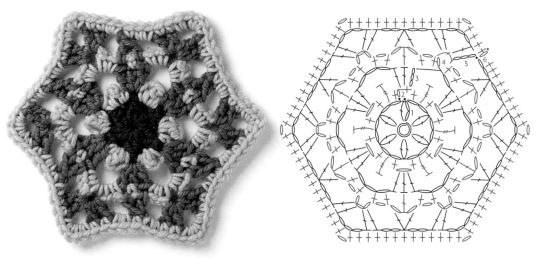

HEXAGON: 5" (12.5 CM)

Dc2tog *(double crochet 2 together)* Yarn over, insert hook into indicated stitch or space and pull up a loop, yarn over, pull through 2 loops, yarn over, insert hook into same stitch and pull up a loop, yarn over and pull through 2 loops, yarn over and pull through all 3 loops on hook.

Partial dc *(partial double crochet)* Yarn over, insert hook into stitch or space indicated and pull up a loop, yarn over and pull through 2 loops on hook.

Begin with sliding loop.

Rnd 1 Ch 2 (counts as Partial dc), Partial dc in ring, yarn over and pull through all 3 loops on hook to dc2tog, ch 2, *dc2tog in ring, ch 2; rep from * four more times, join with slip st to top of first cluster, slip st in next space — 6 clusters and 6 spaces.

Rnd 2 Ch 1, (sc, tr, sc) in same space, *ch 1, (sc, tr, sc) in next space; rep from * around, join with sc to first sc.

Rnd 3 Ch 3 (counts as dc), 2 dc in space formed by joining sc, ch 3, 3 dc in next space; rep from * around, ch 1, join with hdc to top of ch-3.

Rnd 4 Ch 1, (sc, ch 1, sc) in space formed by joining hdc, *ch 1, skip 1 dc, dc in next dc, ch 1, skip 1 dc**, (sc, ch 1, sc, ch 3, sc, ch 1, sc) in next space; rep from * around, ending last rep at **, (sc, ch 1, sc) in next space, join with dc to first sc.

Rnd 5 Ch 3 (counts as dc), (dc, ch 3, 2 dc) in space formed by joining dc, *ch 2, dc2tog over next 2 spaces, ch 2**, (2 dc, ch 3, 2 dc) in next space; rep from * around, ending last rep at **, join with slip st to top of ch-3.

Rnd 6 Ch 1, sc in each st around, placing 2 sc in each ch-2 space and (2 sc, ch 1, 2 sc) in each corner space, join with slip st to first sc. Fasten off.

SC/DC

all clustered

Rnds 1 and 2 A ■	Rnds 3 and 4 B ■	Rnds 5–7 C ▦

This is a lovely and versatile square with pronounced corners for a true square shape. The Linen Place Mat (page 222) uses a variation of this motif as its main theme.

Dc2tog *(double crochet 2 together)* Yarn over, insert hook into indicated stitch or space and pull up a loop, yarn over, pull through 2 loops, yarn over, insert hook into same stitch and pull up a loop, yarn over and pull through 2 loops, yarn over and pull through all 3 loops on hook.

Dc3tog *(double crochet 3 together)* Yarn over, insert hook into indicated stitch or space and pull up a loop, yarn over, pull through 2 loops on hook, (yarn over, insert hook into same stitch and pull up a loop, yarn over and pull through 2 loops) two times, yarn over and pull through all 4 loops on hook.

Dtr3tog *(double treble crochet 3 together)* (Yarn over) three times, insert hook into indicated stitch or space and pull up a loop, (yarn over, pull through 2 loops) three times, [(yarn over) three times, insert hook into same stitch or space and pull up a loop, (yarn over, pull through 2 loops) three times] two times, yarn over and pull through all 4 loops on hook.

Tr2tog *(treble crochet 2 together)* (Yarn over) two times, insert hook into indicated stitch or space and pull up a loop, (yarn over, pull through 2 loops) two times, (yarn over) two times, insert hook into same stitch or space and pull up a loop, (yarn over, pull through 2 loops) two times, yarn over and pull through all 3 loops on hook.

Tr3tog *(treble crochet 3 together)* (Yarn over) two times, insert hook into indicated stitch or space and pull up a loop, (yarn over, pull through 2 loops) two times, [[(yarn over) two times, insert hook into same stitch or space and pull up a loop, (yarn over, pull through 2 loops) two times] two times, yarn over and pull through all 4 loops on hook.

[ALL CLUSTERED]

The initial clusters in this motif family help establish the shape of the motif. But see how the shape of the motif can be tweaked by what happens on the outer rounds, and how a simple picot stitch or the use of popcorns instead of clusters creates a whole new look! Each of the motifs has handy points and/or spaces to serve as connection points. Most are easily adaptable on their final round(s), allowing you to adjust the shapes to fit a multiplicity of arrangements. These features also make them good candidates for free-form work.

SQUARE: 5" (12.5 CM)

Begin with sliding loop.

Rnd 1 Ch 1, 8 sc in ring, join with slip st to first sc — 8 sc.

Rnd 2 Ch 3, tr2tog in same st — *beginning cluster made*, *ch 4, sc in next sc, ch 4**, tr3tog in next sc; rep from * around, ending last rep at **, join with slip st to beginning cluster.

Rnd 3 Ch 1, sc in same st, *ch 5, sc in next sc, ch 5, sc in next cluster; rep from * around, omitting last sc, join with slip st to first sc.

Rnd 4 Ch 1, sc in first sc, *ch 6, dtr3tog in next sc, ch 6, sc in next sc; rep from * around, omitting last sc, join with slip st to first sc.

Rnd 5 Ch 1, sc in same st, *ch 6, (sc, ch 1, sc) in next cluster, ch 6, sc in next sc; rep from * around, omitting last sc, join with slip st to first sc.

Rnd 6 Ch 2, dc2tog in same st, *ch 4, sc in Rnd 4 space over 2 chains, ch 5, tr3tog in next ch-1 space, ch 5, sc in Rnd-4 space over 2 chains, ch 4**, dc3tog in next sc; rep from * around, ending last rep at **, join with slip st to top of first cluster.

Rnd 7 Ch 1, sc in same st, *ch 4, sc in next sc, ch 5, (sc, ch 3, sc) in next cluster; ch 5, sc in next sc, ch 4, sc in next cluster; rep from * around, omitting last sc, join with slip st to first sc. Fasten off.

Four clusters grow into eight points on the final rounds to create a shape rounded enough to be considered either an octagon or a circle.

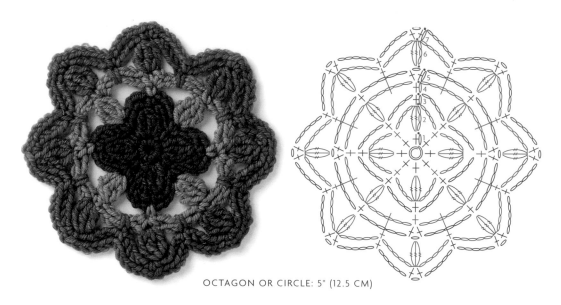

OCTAGON OR CIRCLE: 5" (12.5 CM)

Tr2tog *(treble crochet 2 together)* (Yarn over) two times, insert hook into indicated stitch or space and pull up a loop, (yarn over, pull through 2 loops) two times, (yarn over) two times, insert hook into same stitch or space and pull up a loop, (yarn over, pull through 2 loops) two times, yarn over and pull through all 3 loops on hook.

Tr3tog *(treble crochet 3 together)* (Yarn over) two times, insert hook into indicated stitch or space and pull up a loop, (yarn over, pull through 2 loops) two times, [(yarn over) two times, insert hook into same stitch or space and pull up a loop, (yarn over, pull through 2 loops) two times] two times, yarn over and pull through all 4 loops on hook.

Begin with sliding loop.

Rnd 1 Ch 1, 8 sc in ring, join with slip st to 1st sc — 8 sc.

Rnd 2 Ch 3, tr2tog in same st — *beginning cluster made,* *ch 4, sc in next sc, ch 4**, tr3tog in next sc; rep from * around, ending last rep at **, join with slip st to beginning cluster.

Rnd 3 Ch 1, sc in same st, *ch 4, sc in next sc, ch 4, sc in next cluster; rep from * around, omitting last sc, join with slip st to first sc.

Rnd 4 Ch 1, sc in same st, *ch 5, tr3tog in next sc, ch 5, sc in next sc; rep from * around, omitting last sc, join with slip st to first sc.

Rnd 5 Ch 1, (sc, ch 1, sc) in same st, *ch 5, sc in next cluster, ch 5**, (sc, ch 1, sc) in next sc; rep from * around, ending last rep at **, join with slip st to first sc, slip st in next space.

Rnd 6 Beginning cluster in same space, *ch 5, sc in Rnd-4 space over 2 chains, ch 5, tr3tog in next sc, ch 5, sc in Rnd-4 space over 2 chains, ch 5**, tr3tog in next space; rep from * around, ending last rep at **, join with slip st to top of first cluster.

Rnd 7 Ch 1, (sc, ch 1, sc) in same st, *ch 5, sc in next sc, ch 5**, (sc, ch 1, sc) in next cluster; rep from * around, ending last rep at **, join with slip st to first sc. Fasten off.

The simple substitution of (sc, ch 3, sc) for (sc, ch 1, sc) in the final round of the previous motif creates a more defined shape.

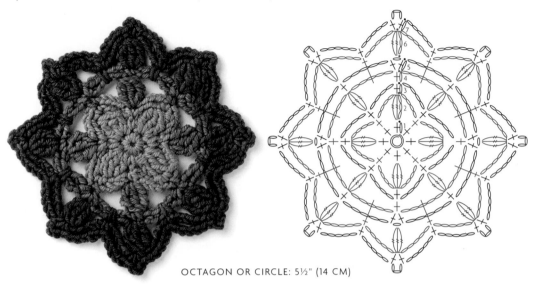

OCTAGON OR CIRCLE: 5½" (14 CM)

Tr2tog *(treble crochet 2 together)* (Yarn over) two times, insert hook into indicated stitch or space and pull up a loop, (yarn over, pull through 2 loops) two times, (yarn over) two times, insert hook into same stitch or space and pull up a loop, (yarn over, pull through 2 loops) two times, yarn over and pull through all 3 loops on hook.

Tr3tog *(treble crochet 3 together)* (Yarn over) two times, insert hook into indicated stitch or space and pull up a loop, (yarn over, pull through 2 loops) two times, [(yarn over) two times, insert hook into same stitch or space and pull up a loop, (yarn over, pull through 2 loops) two times] two times, yarn over and pull through all 4 loops on hook.

Begin with sliding loop.

Rnd 1 Ch 1, 8 sc in ring, join with slip st to first sc — 8 sc.

Rnd 2 Ch 3, tr2tog in same st — *beginning cluster made*, *ch 4, sc in next sc, ch 4**, tr3tog in next sc; rep from * around, ending last rep at **, join with slip st to beginning cluster.

Rnd 3 Ch 1, sc in same st, *ch 4, sc in next sc, ch 4, sc in next cluster; rep from * around, omitting last sc, join with slip st to first sc.

Rnd 4 Ch 1, sc in same st, *ch 5, tr3tog in next sc, ch 5, sc in next sc; rep from * around, omitting last sc, join with slip st to first sc.

Rnd 5 Ch 1, (sc, ch 1, sc) in same st, *ch 5, sc in next cluster, ch 5, (sc, ch 1, sc) in next sc; rep from * around, omitting last sc, join with slip st to first sc, slip st in next space.

Rnd 6 Beginning cluster in same space, *ch 5, sc in Rnd-4 space over 2 chains, ch 5, tr3tog in next sc, ch 5, sc in Rnd-4 space over 2 chains, ch 5**, tr3tog in next space; rep from * around, ending last rep at **, join with slip st to top of first cluster.

Rnd 7 Ch 1, (sc, ch 3, sc) in same st, *ch 5, sc in next sc, ch 5**, (sc, ch 3, sc) in next cluster; rep from * around, ending last rep at **, join with slip st to first sc. Fasten off.

This group of joined motifs uses all eight points of the shape to join to other motifs. The first tier of shapes joins to previous ones at two corners, while the second tier is offset from the first. This example shows (sc, ch 1, sc join, ch 1, sc) in place of (sc, ch 3, sc) on the joined corners. Note that the judicious use of a complementary color adds pop.

FEATURES:

- JAYGo
- Single crochet join
- Offset arrangement
- Connection in adjoining points

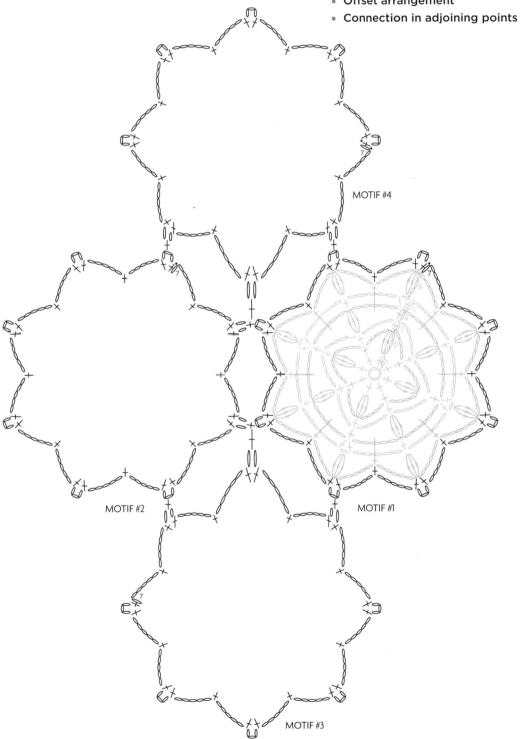

MOTIF #4

MOTIF #2

MOTIF #1

MOTIF #3

ALL CLUSTERED

Here's another variation of the basic motif, using Popcorn stitches instead of clusters.

Popcorn Make 5 dc in 1 stitch or space, drop loop from hook and insert hook from front to back through top of first stitch in the Popcorn then into dropped loop, yarn over and pull through 2 loops on hook.

Begin with sliding loop.

Rnd 1 Ch 1, 8 sc in ring, join with slip st to first sc — 8 sc.

Rnd 2 Ch 3, Popcorn in same st, *ch 4, sc in next sc, ch 4**, Popcorn in next sc; rep from * around, ending last rep at **, join with slip st to beginning Popcorn.

Rnd 3 Ch 1, sc in same st, *ch 4, sc in next sc, ch 4, sc in next Popcorn; rep from * around, omitting last sc, join with slip st to first sc.

Rnd 4 Ch 1, sc in first st, *ch 5, Popcorn in next sc, ch 5, sc in next sc; rep from * around, omitting last sc, join with slip st to first sc.

Rnd 5 Ch 1, (sc, ch 1, sc) in same st, *ch 5, sc in next Popcorn, ch 5**, (sc, ch 1, sc) in next sc; rep from * around, ending last rep at **, join with slip st to first sc, slip st in next space.

Rnd 6 Ch 3, Popcorn in same space, *ch 5, sc in Rnd-4 space over 2 chains, ch 5, Popcorn in next sc, ch 5, sc in Rnd-4 space over 2 chains, ch 5**, Popcorn in next space; rep from * around, ending last rep at **, join with slip st to top of first cluster.

Rnd 7 Ch 1, (sc, ch 1, sc) in same st, *ch 5, sc in next sc, ch 5**, (sc, ch 1, sc) in next cluster; rep from * around, ending last rep at **, join with slip st to first sc. Fasten off.

OCTAGON OR CIRCLE: 4½" (11.5 CM)

This variation on circle-becomes-a-square is the coaster feature in the Linen Place Mat (page 222). Encourage the clusters to pop to the front if necessary to allow Round 3 to lie flat.

SQUARE: 4" (10 CM)

Tr2tog *(treble crochet 2 together)* (Yarn over) two times, insert hook into indicated stitch or space and pull up a loop, (yarn over, pull through 2 loops) two times, (yarn over) two times, insert hook into same stitch or space and pull up a loop, (yarn over, pull through 2 loops) two times, yarn over and pull through all 3 loops on hook.

Tr3tog *(treble crochet 3 together)* (Yarn over) two times, insert hook into indicated stitch or space and pull up a loop, (yarn over, pull through 2 loops) two times, [(yarn over) two times, insert hook into same stitch or space and pull up a loop, (yarn over, pull through 2 loops) two times] two times, yarn over and pull through all 4 loops on hook.

Begin with sliding loop.

Rnd 1 Ch 1, 8 sc in ring, join with slip st to first sc — 8 sc.

Rnd 2 Ch 1, 2 sc in each sc around, join with slip st to first sc.

Rnd 3 Ch 3, tr2tog in same st — *beginning cluster made*, *ch 4, sc in next sc, ch 4**, tr3tog in next sc; rep from * around, ending last rep at **, join with slip st to beginning cluster.

Rnd 4 Ch 1, sc in top of same cluster, *ch 3, tr in next sc, ch 3, sc in top of next cluster; rep from * around, omitting last sc, join with slip st to first sc.

Rnd 5 Ch 1, sc in same st, *ch 3, sc in next tr, ch 3, (tr2tog, ch 5, tr2tog) in next sc, ch 3, sc in next tr, ch 3, sc in next sc; rep from * around, omitting last sc, join with slip st to first sc.

Rnd 6 Ch 1, sc in same st, *ch 3, sc in next sc, ch 3, sc in next cluster, ch 3, sc in corner space, ch 3, sc in next cluster, (ch 3, sc in next sc) two times; rep from * around, omitting last sc, join with slip st to first sc. Fasten off.

ALL CLUSTERED

Here's a three-sided version of the basic motif. This is a rounded triangle; for a more pronounced one, lengthen the clusters at the points and shorten the stitches along the sides.

Dc3tog *(double crochet 3 together)* Yarn over, insert hook into indicated stitch or space and pull up a loop, yarn over, pull through 2 loops on hook, (yarn over, insert hook into same stitch and pull up a loop, yarn over and pull through 2 loops) two times, yarn over and pull through all 4 loops on hook.

Partial dc *(partial double crochet)* Yarn over, insert hook into stitch or space indicated and pull up a loop, yarn over and pull through 2 loops on hook.

Tr2tog *(treble crochet 2 together)* (Yarn over) two times, insert hook into indicated stitch or space and pull up a loop, (yarn over, pull through 2 loops) two times, (yarn over) two times, insert hook into same stitch or space and pull up a loop, (yarn over, pull through 2 loops) two times, yarn over and pull through all 3 loops on hook.

Tr3tog *(treble crochet 3 together)* (Yarn over) two times, insert hook into indicated stitch or space and pull up a loop, (yarn over, pull through 2 loops) two times, [(yarn over) two times, insert hook into same stitch or space and pull up a loop, (yarn over, pull through 2 loops) two times] two times, yarn over, and pull through all 4 loops on hook.

Begin with sliding loop.

Rnd 1 Ch 1, 6 sc in ring, join with slip st to first sc — 6 sc.

Rnd 2 Ch 1, sc in same st, *ch 4, tr3tog in next sc, ch 4, sc in next sc; rep from * around, omitting last sc, join with slip st to first sc.

Rnd 3 Ch 1, sc in same st, *ch 4, (sc, ch 1, sc) in top of next cluster, ch 4, sc in next sc; rep from * around, omitting last sc, join with slip st to first sc.

Rnd 4 Ch 2 (counts as Partial dc), 2 Partial dc in same st, yarn over and pull through all

3 loops on hook to dc3tog, *ch 5, skip 1 space, (tr3tog, ch 3, tr3tog) in next ch-1 space, ch 5**, dc3tog in next sc; rep from * around, ending last rep at **, join with slip st to first cluster.

Rnd 5 Ch 1, sc in same st, *ch 5, sc in next cluster, ch 1, (sc, ch 3, sc, ch 1) in next space, sc in next cluster, ch 5, sc in next cluster; rep from * around, omitting last sc, join with slip st to first sc.

Rnd 6 Ch 2 (counts as Partial dc), 2 Partial dc in same st, yarn over and pull through all 3 loops on hook to dc3tog, *ch 3, sc in next Rnd-4 space over 2 chains, ch 3, dc3tog in next

TRIANGLE:
5" (12.5 CM)

sc, ch 3, skip 1 space, (sc, ch 3, dc3tog, ch 3, sc) in next space, ch 3, skip 1 sc, dc3tog in next sc, ch 3, sc in next Rnd-4 space over 2 chains, ch 3**, dc3tog in next sc; rep from * around, ending last rep at **, join with slip st to first cluster.

Rnd 7 Ch 1, sc in same st, *ch 3, sc in next sc, ch 3**, sc in next cluster; rep from * around, ending last rep at **, join with slip st to first sc. Fasten off.

48

Rnds 1, 2, and 6 A ■   **Rnd 3** B ☐   **Rnds 4 and 5** C ■

Here's another cluster-based shape that can be considered either a hexagon or a circle. The bright white of Round 3 offers nice contrast.

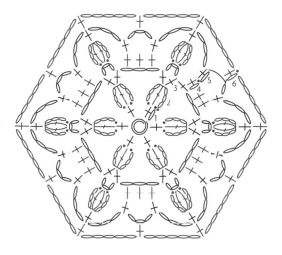

HEXAGON OR CIRCLE: 4" (10 CM)

Dc2tog *(double crochet 2 together)* Yarn over, insert hook into indicated stitch or space and pull up a loop, yarn over, pull through 2 loops, yarn over, insert hook into same stitch and pull up a loop, yarn over and pull through 2 loops, yarn over and pull through all 3 loops on the hook.

Begin with sliding loop.

Rnd 1 Ch 1, 6 sc in ring, join with slip st to first sc — 6 sc.

Rnd 2 *(Ch 3, dc, ch 3, slip st) in same st, slip st in next sc; rep from * around, placing last slip st in first slip st. Fasten off.

Rnd 3 (Standing sc, ch 3, sc) in any dc, *ch 3, (sc, ch 3, sc) in next dc; rep from * around, ending ch 2, join with sc to first sc.

Rnd 4 Ch 1, sc in space formed by joining sc, *(slip st, ch 3, dc2tog, ch 3, slip st) in next space, 3 sc in next space; rep from * around, omitting last sc, join with slip st to first st.

Rnd 5 Ch 1, sc in first sc, *ch 3, sc in next cluster, ch 3, sc in next sc**, ch 3, skip 1 sc, sc in next sc; rep from * around, ending last rep at **, ch 1, join with hdc in first sc.

Rnd 6 Ch 1, sc in space formed by joining hdc, *ch 5, skip 1 sc, sc in next sc, ch 5, skip 1 space, sc in next space; rep from * around, omitting last sc, join with slip st to first sc. Fasten off.

Motifs with final rounds like this one offer oh-so-many possibilities for connection! You can join at the corners, where there is a tiny ch-1 space, or you could join more tightly, connecting at both the corners and along each side edge. The motifs in the sample were joined with a flat join (sc, ch 1, flat join, sc) at the center of the adjacent points. The filler motif is the first two rounds of the motif, joined with a flat join after completing the double crochet at each point (ch 3, dc, flat join, ch 3, slip st).

FILLER MOTIF

Begin with sliding loop.

Rnd 1 Ch 1, 6 sc in ring, join with slip st to first sc — 6 sc.

Rnd 2 *(Ch 3, dc, flat join to ch-1 space of adjacent motif, ch 3, slip st) in same st, slip st in next sc, [(ch 3, dc, flat join to sc of adjacent motif, ch 3, slip st) in same st, slip st in next sc] two times; rep from * once more, placing last slip st in first slip st. Fasten off.

FEATURES:

- JAYGo
- Single crochet join
- Flat join
- Filler motif
- Connection in adjoining points
- Connection in adjoining stitches

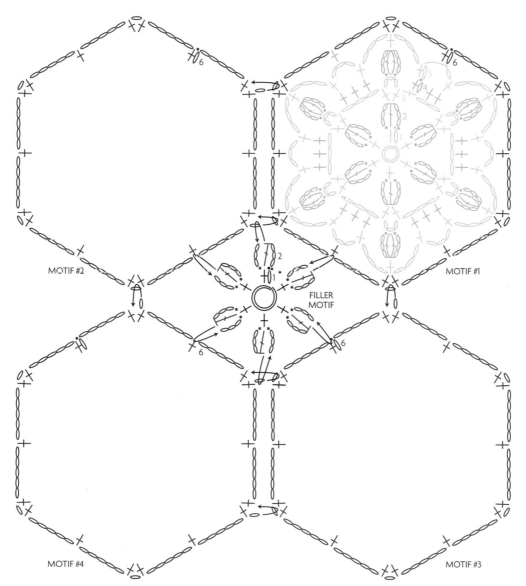

ALL CLUSTERED

triple petals

49

Rnd 1 A ■   **Rnd 2** B ■   **Rnds 3 and 4** C ■

This square gets its charm from the groups of three petals arranged just so. Can't you see this stitched in many different colors and joined to create a riotous flowering fabric? For joining locations, look to the top of each petal and the ch-3 space along each side.

Begin with sliding loop.

Rnd 1 Ch 3 (counts as dc), 11 dc in ring, join with slip st to top of ch-3 — 12 dc.

Rnd 2 Ch 1, sc in same st, *ch 6, [dc, ch 3, slip st, (ch 3, dc, ch 3, slip st) two times] in 4th ch from hook — *tri-petal cluster made*, ch 2, skip 2 dc**, sc in next dc; rep from * around, ending last rep at **, join with slip st to first sc. Fasten off.

Rnd 3 (Standing sc, ch 3, sc) in top of any corner petal, *(ch 3, sc in top of next petal) two times, ch 3**, (sc, ch 3, sc) in next petal; rep from * around, ending last rep at **, join with slip st to first sc.

Rnd 4 *[Slip st, (ch 3, dc, ch 3, slip st) 3 times] in next ch-3 space — *tri-petal cluster made*, 3 sc in next space, (sc, dc, ch 3, dc, sc) in next space, 3 sc in next space; rep from * around, join with slip st to first space. Fasten off.

[**TIP**] When working into the 4th chain from the hook in Round 2, work into the bump on the wrong side of the chain for a larger hole, or into the front of the chain for a smaller, less symmetrical gap.

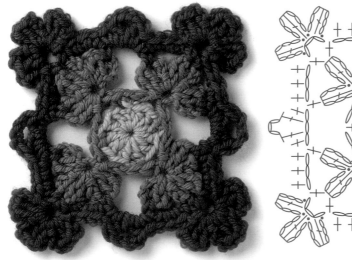

SQUARE: 3¾" (9.5 CM)

The three-pointed version is particularly cute. The addition of petals along the sides helps flatten out the triangle.

TRIANGLE:
4" (10 CM)

Begin with sliding loop.

Rnd 1 Ch 1, 12 sc in ring, join with slip st to first sc — 12 sc.

Rnd 2 Ch 1, sc in same st, *ch 8, [dc, ch 3, slip st, (ch 3, dc, ch 3, slip st) 2 times] in 4th ch from hook — *tri-petal cluster made*, ch 4, skip 3 sc**, sc in next sc; rep from * around, ending last rep at **, join with slip st to first sc. Fasten off.

Rnd 3 (Standing sc, ch 3, sc) in center dc of any tri-petal cluster, *ch 3, sc in top of next petal, ch 2, dc in next sc, ch 2, sc in top of next petal, ch 3**, (sc, ch 3, sc) in next petal; rep from * around, ending last rep at **, join with slip st to first sc.

Rnd 4 *[Slip st, (ch 3, dc, ch 3, slip st) three times] in next ch-3 space — *tri-petal cluster made*, 3 sc in next space, ch 1, skip 1 sc, 2 sc in next space, (slip st, ch 3, dc, ch 3, slip st) in next dc, 2 sc in next space, ch 1, skip 1 sc, 3 sc in next space; rep from * around, join with slip st in first space. Fasten off.

[**TRIPLE PETALS**]

Petal-like stitches form the basis for whimsical shapes in this family of motifs. Possible connection locations for most of this family include the top of any of the petals of the tri-petal clusters, as well as the chain-spaces between the petal clusters. These are also perfect for using just the first several rounds of the shape to add variety — another great option for free-form work.

Sometimes using just a portion of a larger motif works well. Here Rounds 1 and 2 of Motif 50 are joined at the tips of petals with flat joins. Can't you just see this little cascade of flowers as a summer scarf? Or try connecting other portions of petal-like shapes for a flowery free-form sweater.

FEATURES:

- JAYGo
- Flat join
- Connection in adjoining stitches
- Offset arrangement

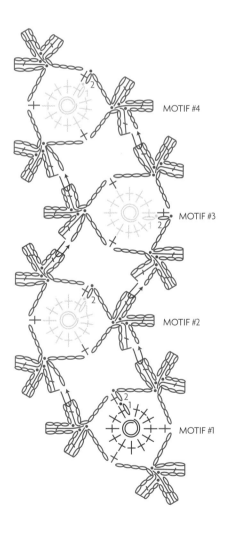

MOTIF #4

MOTIF #3

MOTIF #2

MOTIF #1

Here's a flowery hexagon that would be perfect as a coaster or as the basis for a shawl or afghan.

Begin with sliding loop.

Rnd 1 Ch 4 (counts as dc and ch 1), (dc, ch 1) 11 times into ring, join with slip st to 3rd ch of ch-4 — 12 dc and 12 spaces.

Rnd 2 Ch 1, sc in same st, *ch 6, [dc, ch 3, slip st, (ch 3, dc, ch 3, slip st) two times] in 4th ch from hook — *tri-petal cluster made*, ch 2, skip (ch 1, dc, ch 1)**, sc in next dc; rep from * around, ending last rep at **, join with slip st to first sc. Fasten off.

Rnd 3 (Standing sc, ch 3, sc) in center dc of any tri-petal cluster, *ch 3, (insert hook into top of next petal and pull up a loop) two times, yarn over and pull through all 3 loops on hook to sc2tog, ch 3**, (sc, ch 3, sc) in next petal; rep from * around, ending last rep at **, join with slip st to first sc.

Rnd 4 *[Slip st, (ch 3, dc, ch 3, slip st) three times] in next ch-3 space — *tri-petal cluster made*, 3 sc in next 2 ch-3 spaces; rep from * around, join with slip st to first space. Fasten off.

HEXAGON: 5¼" (13.5 CM)

In order to encompass six points instead of the four in the original square, the triple petals on Round 2 must be farther from the center to fit within the available circumference. These loose petals are joined in Round 3.

CIRCLE: 5" (12.5 CM)

Begin with sliding loop.

Rnd 1 Ch 1, 12 sc in ring, join with slip st to first sc — 12 sc.

Rnd 2 Ch 1, sc in same st, *ch 8, [dc, ch 3, slip st, (ch 3, dc, ch 3, slip st) two times] in 4th ch from hook — *tri-petal cluster made*, ch 4, skip 1 sc, sc in next sc; rep from * around, omitting last sc, join with slip st to first sc. Fasten off.

Rnd 3 Standing sc in center petal of any tri-petal cluster, *ch 4, (insert hook into top of next petal and pull up a loop) two times, yarn over and pull through all 3 loops on hook to sc2tog, ch 4**, sc in top of next petal; rep from * around, ending last rep at **, join with slip st to first sc.

Rnd 4 Ch 1, (sc, ch 3, sc) in same st, *5 sc in next space, sc2tog over same and next space, 5 sc in same space**, (sc, ch 3, sc) in next space; rep from * around, ending last rep at **, join with slip st to first sc. Fasten off.

Because the petals are squeezed into a tighter space on this shape, they begin to ruffle a bit, adding to the flowerlike quality of the motif.

Begin with sliding loop.

Rnd 1 Ch 1, 12 sc in ring, join with slip st to 1st sc — 12 sc.

Rnd 2 Ch 1, sc in same st, ch 8, [dc, ch 3, slip st, (ch 3, dc, ch 3, slip st) two times] in 4th ch from hook — *tri-petal cluster made*, ch 4, skip 1 sc, sc in next sc; *ch 8, dc in 4th ch from hook, flat join to third petal of previous cluster, [ch 3, slip st, (ch 3, dc, ch 3, slip st) two times] in same chain, ch 4, skip 1 sc, sc in next sc; rep from * three more times, ch 8, dc in 4th ch from hook, flat join to third petal of previous cluster, (ch 3, slip st, ch 3, dc, ch 3, slip st, ch 3, dc) in same chain, flat

join to first petal of first cluster, ch 3, slip st in same chain, ch 4, join with slip st to first sc. Fasten off.

Rnd 3 Standing sc over join between any two petals, ch 3, sc in same space, *ch 4, sc in top of center petal of next tri-petal cluster, ch 4**, (sc, ch 3, sc) over next join between clusters; rep from * around, ending last rep at **, join with slip st to first sc.

Rnd 4 *[Slip st, (ch 3, dc, ch 3, slip st) three times] in next ch-3 space — *tri-petal cluster made*, 3 sc in next space, (sc, ch 3, sc) in next sc, 3 sc in next space; rep from * around, join with slip st to first space. Fasten off.

HEXAGON: 5" (12.5 CM)

You couldn't ask for more joining points than this frilly shape offers! Not only could you use just the center section as a motif on its own, petals and ch-3 spaces are also available for connecting. In this example, the pieces were joined with a flat join at the (sc, ch 3, sc) corners, leaving the tri-petal corners free. The filler motif is connected by working flat joins around the existing joins.

FILLER MOTIF
Begin with sliding loop.

Rnd 1 Ch 1, 12 sc in ring, join with slip st to first sc.

Rnd 2 Ch 1, sc in same st, ch 7, flat join at intersection of two motifs on side where motifs are joined at one point, *ch 7, skip 2 sc, sc in next sc, ch 5, flat join at next intersection of two motifs, ch 5, skip 2 sc**, sc in next sc, ch 7, flat join at next intersection of two motifs; rep from * to ** once more, join with slip st to first sc. Fasten off.

FEATURES:
- JAYGo
- Flat join
- Connection in adjoining spaces
- Connection around existing join
- Filler motif

MOTIF #2

MOTIF #1

FILLER MOTIF

MOTIF #4

MOTIF #3

TRIPLE PETALS

This versatile little square has four petal-like clusters in its center with tri-petal corners and side arches, offering many opportunities for joining to other motifs.

SQUARE: 3½" (9 CM)

Dc3tog *(double crochet 3 together)* Yarn over, insert hook into indicated stitch or space and pull up a loop, yarn over, pull through 2 loops on hook, (yarn over, insert hook into same stitch and pull up a loop, yarn over and pull through 2 loops) two times, yarn over and pull through all 4 loops on hook.

Begin with sliding loop.

Rnd 1 Ch 1, *sc in ring, ch 3; rep from * six more times, sc in ring, ch 2, join with sc to first sc — 8 sc and 8 spaces.

Rnd 2 Ch 1, sc in space formed by joining sc, ch 5, dc3tog in next space, *ch 5, sc in next space, ch 5, dc3tog in next space; rep from * two more times, ch 2, join with dc to first sc.

Rnd 3 Ch 1, sc in space formed by joining dc, *ch 3, sc in next space, ch 2, (sc, ch 3, sc) in top of cluster, ch 2, sc in next space; rep from * around, omitting last sc, join with slip st to first sc.

Rnd 4 Ch 1, *(sc, dc, ch 3, dc, sc) in next space, 3 sc in next space, [slip st, (ch 3, dc, ch 3, slip st) three times] in next space, 3 sc in next space; rep from * around, join with slip st to first sc. Fasten off.

55

Rnd 1 A ■   **Rnd 2** B ■   **Rnds 3–5** C ■

This square will lend itself to so many variations, you may have trouble deciding where to stop!

SQUARE: 3¾" (9.5 CM)

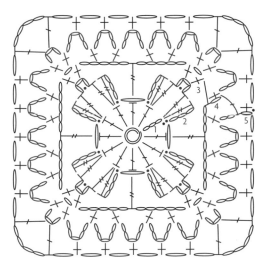

Picot-3 Ch 3, slip st in 3rd ch from hook.

Begin with sliding loop.

Rnd 1 Ch 3 (counts as dc), 11 dc in ring, join with slip st to top of ch-3 — 12 dc.

Rnd 2 *Ch 3, 2 tr in same st, Picot-3, (2 tr, ch 3, slip st) in next st, ch 1, skip 1 st, slip st in next st; rep from * around — 4 petals. Fasten off.

Rnd 3 (Standing sc, ch 1, sc) in any Picot-3, *ch 5, tr in next ch-1 space between two petals**, ch 5, (sc, ch 1, sc) in next picot; rep from * around, ending last rep at **, ch 3, join with hdc to first sc.

Rnd 4 Ch 1, sc in space formed by joining hdc, *ch 5, (sc, ch 3, sc) in next space**, (ch 5, sc in next space, ch 5, sc in same space) two times; rep from * around, ending last rep at **, ch 5, sc in next space, ch 5, sc in same space, ch 5, sc in next space, ch 2, join with dc to first sc.

Rnd 5 Ch 1, sc in space formed by joining dc, ch 1, sc in next space, *ch 1, (dc, ch 4, dc) in next space**, (ch 1, sc in next space) five times; rep from * around, ending last rep at **, (ch 1, sc in next space) three times, ch 1, join with slip st to first sc. Fasten off.

Rounds 1–3 are exactly the same as Motif 55, but the final two rounds change it up.

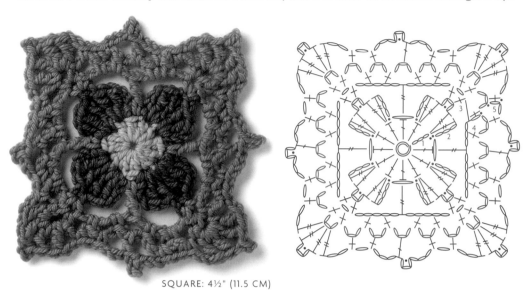

SQUARE: 4½" (11.5 CM)

Picot-3 Ch 3, slip st in 3rd ch from hook.

Begin with sliding loop.

Rnd 1 Ch 3 (counts as dc), 11 dc in ring, join with slip st to top of ch-3 — 12 dc.

Rnd 2 *Ch 3, 2 tr in same st, Picot-3, (2 tr, ch 3, slip st) in next st, ch 1, skip 1 st, slip st in next st; rep from * around — 4 petals. Fasten off.

Rnd 3 (Standing sc, ch 1, sc) in any Picot-3, *ch 5, tr in next ch-1 space between two petals**, ch 5, (sc, ch 1, sc) in next picot; rep from * around, ending last rep at **, ch 3, join with hdc to first sc.

Rnd 4 Ch 1, sc in space formed by joining hdc, *ch 3, (sc, ch 3, sc) in next space, (ch 3, sc in next space, ch 3, sc in same space) two times; rep from * around, omitting last sc, join with slip st to first sc, slip st in next space.

Rnd 5 Ch 1, sc in same space, *ch 2, (2 tr, Picot-3, 2 tr) in next space, ch 2, sc in next space, ch 1, sc in next space, ch 3, dc in next space, Picot-3, ch 3, sc in next space, ch 1, sc in next space; rep from * around, omitting last sc, join with slip st to first sc. Fasten off.

[START WITH A FLOWER]

A single flowerlike center is the basis for this group of shapes. Add three dimensions by layering the petals, or experiment with the outside rounds to create your own unique motif. Those final rounds are easily changed to smaller or larger chain-spaces to create different appearances for the connections. It's also easy to figure out how to add additional rounds to each. All those options mean you can use just about any connection method you choose.

This is the triangular version of Motif 56, with extended corners for a close fit when you are joining to other triangles.

TRIANGLE: 5" (12.5 CM)

Picot-3 Ch 3, slip st in 3rd ch from hook.

Ch 4, join with slip st to form ring.

Rnd 1 Ch 1, 9 sc in ring, join with slip st to first sc — 9 sc.

Rnd 2 *Ch 3, 2 tr in same st, Picot-3, (2 tr, ch 3, slip st) in next st, ch 1, skip 1 sc**, slip st in next st; rep from * around, ending at **, join with slip st in first slip st — 4 petals. Fasten off.

Rnd 3 Standing sc in picot of any Rnd-2 petal, *ch 6, dc in next ch-1 space between two petals, ch 6, sc in picot at tip of next petal; rep from * around, omitting last sc, join with slip st to first sc.

Rnd 4 Ch 1, (sc, ch 3, sc) in same st, (ch 3, sc in next space, ch 3, sc in same space) two times, *ch 3, (sc, ch 3, sc) in next sc, (ch 3, sc in next space, ch 3, sc in same space) two times; rep from * around, ch 1, join with hdc in first sc.

Rnd 5 Ch 1, sc in space formed by joining hdc, *ch 3, [dc, ch 2, tr, ch 3, tr, ch 2, dc] in next space**, (ch 3, sc in next space) 5 times, rep from * around, omitting last sc, join with slip st to first sc. Fasten off.

This triangle has softer tips. Note the gentle scallops along the edges.

Rnds 1–4 Work as for Motif 57 (page 143).

Rnd 5 Ch 1, sc in same space, *ch 1, [dc, (ch 1, dc) three times] in next space, ch 1, sc in next space, (ch 3, sc in next space) four times; rep from * around, omitting last sc, join with slip st to first sc. Fasten off.

TRIANGLE: 4" (10 CM)

[**TIP**] It's easy to enlarge any of the motifs that have a net-like structure on their final rounds. Just add additional rounds of chain loops, increasing as necessary to allow the piece to lie flat.

connect

This join shows Motif 58 with an additional round in color A. In this example, the motifs were joined with only two continuous rounds, rather than with a final round worked separately on each motif.

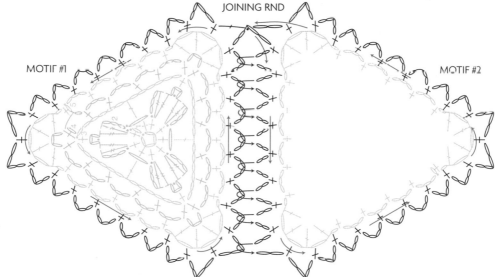

JOINING RND

MOTIF #1

MOTIF #2

On the first motif, join yarn with sc any corner space, (ch 4, sc in next space) around, ending ch 2, join with dc to first sc; on second motif, ch 2, sc in first space to the left of any corner space, (ch 2, flat join to corresponding space of first motif, ch 2, sc in next space) along edge adjoining first motif, then continue working (ch 4, sc in next space) around second motif, ending sc in last space, ch 2, join with slip st to top of dc in first motif. Fasten off.

FEATURES:

- JAYGo
- Continuous final round
- Flat join
- Additional round on original motif
- Connection in adjoining spaces
- Braided look

This six-sided flower surrounded by a simple single crochet/chain stitch would be a good basis for any number of projects. It's easy to add more rounds to make it larger. Or just crochet the flower by itself (see page 242)!

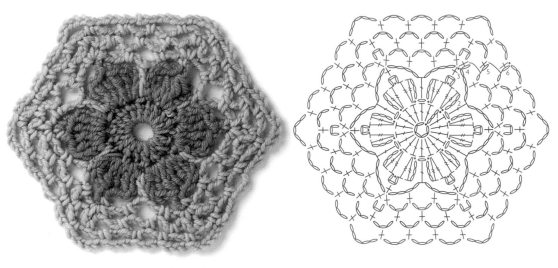

HEXAGON: 5½" (14 CM)

Picot-3 Ch 3, slip st in 3rd ch from hook.

Ch 5, join with slip st to form ring.

Rnd 1 Ch 3 (counts as dc), 17 dc in ring, join with slip st to top of ch-3 — 18 dc.

Rnd 2 *(Ch 3, 2 tr) in same st, Picot-3, (2 tr, ch 3, slip st) in next st, ch 1, skip 1 st**; slip st in next st; rep from * around, ending at **, join with slip st in first slip st — 6 petals. Fasten off.

Rnd 3 Standing sc in picot of any Rnd-2 petal, *ch 4, dc in next ch-1 space between two petals, ch 4, sc in picot at tip of next petal; rep from * around, omitting last sc, join with slip st to first sc.

Rnd 4 Ch 1, (sc, ch 3, sc) in same st, (ch 3, sc in next space) two times, *ch 3, (sc, ch 3, sc) in next sc, (ch 3, sc in next space) two times; rep from * around, ch 1, join with hdc in first sc.

Rnd 5 Ch 1, sc in space formed by joining hdc, *ch 3, sc in next space; rep from * around, ending with ch 1, join with hdc in first sc.

Rnd 6 Ch 1, sc in space formed by joining hdc, ch 3, sc in next space, *ch 5, sc in next space**, (ch 3, sc in next space) three times; rep from * around, ending last rep at **, ch 3, sc in next space, ch 3, join with slip st to first sc. Fasten off.

Here's a nicely circular version of the basic motif. Note how the (dc, tr, dc) cluster stitch on Round 3 fills in the spaces between petals and the (sc, ch 3, sc) on the final round adds definition — and joining points.

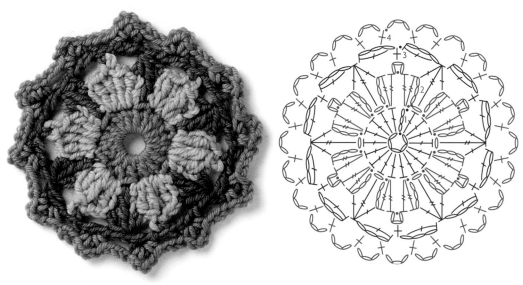

CIRCLE: 4½" (11.5 CM)

Partial dc *(partial double crochet)* Yarn over, insert hook into stitch or space indicated and pull up a loop, yarn over and pull through 2 loops on hook.

Partial tr *(partial treble)* (Yarn over) twice, insert hook into stitch or space indicated and pull up a loop, (yarn over and pull through 2 loops on hook) two times.

Picot-3 Ch 3, slip st in 3rd ch from hook.

Ch 5, join with slip st to form ring.

Rnd 1 Ch 3 (counts as dc), 17 dc in ring, join with slip st to top of ch-3 — 18 dc.

Rnd 2 *(Ch 3, 2 tr) in same st, Picot-3, (2 tr, ch 3, slip st) in next st, ch 1, skip 1 st**, slip st in next st; rep from * around, ending at **, join with slip st in first slip st — 6 petals. Fasten off.

Rnd 3 Standing sc in picot of any Rnd-2 petal, *ch 3, dc in 3rd ch from hook, skip 2 tr, Partial dc in next ch, skip 2 ch, Partial tr in next ch-1 space, skip 2 ch, Partial dc in next ch, yarn over and pull through all 4 loops on hook, ch 3, dc in 3rd ch from hook, skip 2 tr, sc in next picot; rep from * around, omitting last sc, join with slip st to first sc. Fasten off.

Rnd 4 (Standing sc, ch 3, sc, ch 3) in any ch-3 space, (sc, ch 3) two times in each ch-3 space around, join with slip st to first sc. Fasten off.

Rnd 1 A ■ **Rnd 2** B ■ **Rnds 3 and 7** C ■
Rnds 4–6 D ■

Here's another hexagon, this time with 3-D petals. The petals are left loose and allowed to pop to the front, while the background stitches create the shape of the motif.

NOTE: RND 3 IS WORKED
BEHIND RND-2 STITCHES

HEXAGON: 5" (12.5 CM)

BLtr *(back loop treble crochet)* Work 1 treble crochet into the back loop only.

Ch 5, join with slip st to form ring.

Rnd 1 Ch 3 (counts as dc), 17 dc in ring, join with slip st to top of ch-3 — 18 dc. Fasten off.

Rnd 2 *Work Rnd 2 in front loops of Rnd-1 sts.* Join yarn with slip st in front loop of any st, *ch 3, 2 FLtr in same st, Picot-3, (2 FLtr, ch 3, slip st) in next st, ch 1, skip 1 st**, slip st in front loop of next st; rep from * around, ending last rep at **, join with slip st in front loop of first st. Fasten off.

Rnd 3 *Work Rnd 3 in back loops of Rnd-1 sts.* Join yarn with slip st in back loop of first st (behind first ch-3 of Rnd 2), *ch 3, 2 BLtr in same st, (2 BLtr, ch 3, slip st) in next st, ch 1, skip 1 st, slip st in back loop of next st; rep from * around, ending slip st in first st. Fasten off.

Rnd 4 *Work Rnd 4 in both loops of free sts in Rnd 1.* (Standing dc, ch 3, dc) in any free dc from Rnd 1, ch 3, *(dc, ch 3, dc) in next free dc, ch 3; rep from * around, join with slip st to top of first dc.

Rnd 5 Ch 3 (counts as dc), *(2 dc, ch 3, 2 dc) in next space, dc in next 2 dcs; rep from * around, omitting last dc, join with slip st to top of ch-3.

Rnd 6 Ch 3 (counts as dc), dc in each dc around, placing (dc, ch 2, dc) in each ch-3 space, join with slip st to first sc.

Rnd 7 Ch 1, sc in each dc around, placing (2 sc, ch 1, 2 sc) in each ch-3 space, join with slip st to first sc. Fasten off.

Rnd 1 A ■   **Rnds 2 and 6** B ▨   **Rnds 3 and 4** C ■
Rnd 5 D ■

On this flower, both the front and back petals are more rounded. The colorful background fabric lends itself to many joining options.

SQUARE: 4½" (11.5 CM)

Tr3tog *(treble crochet 3 together)* (Yarn over) two times, insert hook into indicated stitch or space and pull up a loop, (yarn over, pull through 2 loops) two times, [(yarn over) two times, insert hook into same stitch or space and pull up a loop, (yarn over, pull through 2 loops) two times] two times, yarn over and pull through all 4 loops on hook.

Ch 5, join with slip st to form ring.

Rnd 1 Ch 3 (counts as dc), 15 dc in ring — 16 dc.

Rnd 2 *(Ch 3, 3 tr, ch 3, slip st) in same st, ch 1, skip 1 dc, slip st in next dc; rep from * around — 8 petals. Fasten off.

Rnd 3 Working behind Rnd-2 sts and into Rnd-1 sts, standing dc in any skipped dc, ch 3, *dc in next skipped dc, ch 3; rep from * around, join with slip st to first dc.

Rnd 4 Ch 1, sc in same st, ch 3, tr3tog in next space, ch 3, sc in next dc; rep from * around, omitting last sc.

Rnd 5 Ch 5 (counts as dc and ch 2), *sc in next cluster, ch 2, (tr, ch 3, tr) in next sc, ch 2, sc in next cluster, ch 2**, dc in next sc, ch 2; rep from * around, ending last rep at **, join with slip st to 3rd ch of ch-5, slip st in next space.

Rnd 6 Ch 1, sc in same space, *ch 5, sc in next space, ch 5, (sc, ch 5, sc) in next space**, (ch 5, sc in next space) three times; rep from * around, ending last rep at **, (ch 5, sc in next space) two times, ch 5, join with slip st in first sc. Fasten off.

In this connection, the corner chains have been extended on the last round to better meet each other. The chain loops along each side of the squares are longer than the ones in the example on page 145, creating a mesh look to the connection instead of that example's more braided look. The sample uses a JAYGo final round with slip-stitch joins, but you could also work a continuous final round with single-crochet join, or any combination.

Work first motif as for Motif 62, making each corner (sc, ch 7, sc) instead of (sc, ch 5, sc).

Make additional motifs with elongated corners and join to previous motifs along adjacent edges, as follows:

Sc in corner space, ch 3, slip st in corner space of adjacent motif, ch 3, sc in same corner space of current motif, (ch 2, slip st in next space of adjacent motif, ch 2, sc in next space of current motif) four times, ch 2, slip st in next space of adjacent motif, ch 2, ch 3, slip st in corner space of adjacent motif, ch 3, sc in same space of current motif, continue working around.

FEATURES:

- JAYGo
- Slip-stitch join
- Extended corners
- Mesh-like appearance

MOTIF #2   MOTIF #1

MOTIF #4   MOTIF #3

3-D fun

QUICK & EASY

63

Rnds 1–3 and 5 A ▨   **Rnds 4 and 6** B ▪

Here's a not-so-basic square with a three-dimensional feature that allows the color underneath to peek out. For the Quick & Easy version, omit Round 6.

Crocodile Stitch Instructions are written for right-handed crochet with left-handed directions in brackets. Holding piece with first st to be worked to the right [left] at 3 o'clock [9 o'clock] position and working from right to left [left to right], starting with standing dc, work 5 dc around post of dc, ch 2; rotate piece 180° to 9 o'clock [3 o'clock] position, 5 dc around post of next dc.

Picot-3 Ch 3, slip st in 3rd ch from hook.

Begin with sliding loop.

Rnd 1 Ch 3 (counts as dc), dc in ring, ch 3, *2 dc in ring, ch 3; rep from * two more times, join with slip st to top of ch-3 — 8 dc and 4 spaces.

Rnd 2 Ch 3 (counts as dc), dc in next dc, *ch 3, dc in next space, ch 3**, dc in next 2 dc; rep from * around, ending last rep at **, join with slip st to top of ch-3.

Rnd 3 Ch 2 (counts as hdc), hdc in next dc, *ch 3, (dc, ch 3, dc) in next dc, ch 3**, hdc in next 2 dc; rep from * around, ending last rep at **, join with slip st to top of ch-2.

Rnd 4 Ch 3 (counts as dc), dc in each hdc and dc, and 3 dc in each side ch-3 space around, placing (2 dc, ch 3, 2 dc) in each corner ch-3 space, join with slip st to top of ch-3.

Rnd 5 Ch 1, sc in same st, *Picot-3, sc in next dc, (Picot-3, ch 1, skip 1 dc, sc in next dc) three times, Picot-3, ch 1, sc in corner space**, Picot-3, ch 1, sc in next dc, (Picot-3, ch 1, skip 1 dc, sc in next dc) three times; rep from * around, omitting last sc, join with slip st to first sc. Fasten off.

[3-D FUN]

The Crocodile Stitch, worked around the posts of pairs of double crochets, creates a fun peek-a-boo effect. Once you get the hang of it, you'll be putting 3-D stitches on everything. The edges of these motifs offer a bit of everything: picots, straight edges, chain loops, and points — and they are a snap to change. Experiment with different edges, arrangements, and color changes to find the connection that suits you.

Rnd 6 *Work Rnd 6 over Rnd-2 sts.* Crocodile Stitch around the first pair of dcs, ch 2, slip st around post of next dc, ch 2; *Crocodile Stitch around next pair of dcs, slip st around post of next dc, ch 2; rep from * around, join with slip st to first dc.

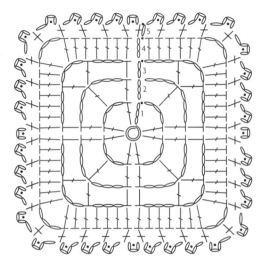

SQUARE: 4½" (11.5 CM)

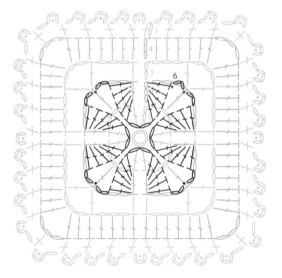

For this JAYGo arrangement, substitute a slip-stitch join in place of the center chain of each picot. Connecting picot-to-picot is an option for many styles of motifs and offers a more tailored look than similar ch-3 loops would. Working all the final rounds in the same color would change the appearance even further.

Rnds 4 and 5 C ▇ D ▨ **Rnd 6** A ▇

FEATURES:

- JAYGo
- Slip-stitch join
- Connection in adjoining picots

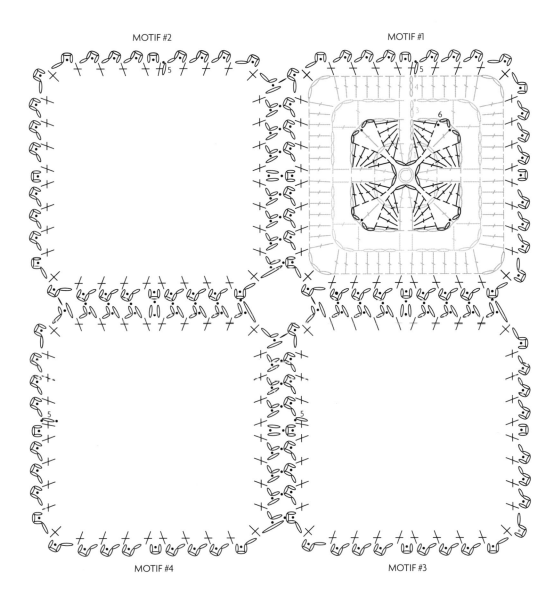

MOTIF #2

MOTIF #1

MOTIF #4

MOTIF #3

Rnds 1 and 2 A ■   **Rnds 3 and 4** B ▫   **Rnd 5** C ■

Here's a simple hexagonal version of the Crocodile Stitch motif. Omit Round 5 for the Quick & Easy version. See page 158 for a connection.

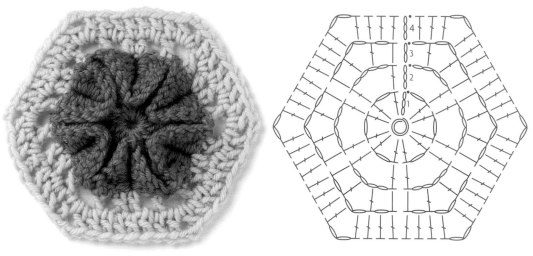

HEXAGON: 4" (10 CM)

Crocodile Stitch Instructions are written for right-handed crochet with left-handed directions in brackets. Holding piece with first st to be worked to the right [left] at 3 o'clock [9 o'clock] position and working from right to left [left to right], starting with standing dc, work 5 dc around post of dc, ch 2; rotate piece 180° to 9 o'clock [3 o'clock] position, 5 dc around post of next dc.

Begin with sliding loop.

Rnd 1 Ch 3 (counts as dc), dc in ring, ch 1, *2 dc in ring, ch 1; rep from * four more times, join with slip st to top of ch-3 — 12 dc and 6 spaces.

Rnd 2 Ch 3 (counts as dc), dc in next dc, ch 4, *dc in next 2 dc, ch 4; rep from * around, join with slip st to top of ch-3.

Rnd 3 Ch 2 (counts as hdc), hdc in next dc, *ch 1, (dc, ch 2, dc) in next space, ch 1**, hdc in next 2 dc; rep from * around, ending last rep at **, join with slip st to top of ch-2.

Rnd 4 Ch 3 (counts as dc), dc in each hdc, dc and ch-1 space around, placing (dc, ch 2, dc) in each corner ch-2 space, join with slip st to top of ch-3. Fasten off.

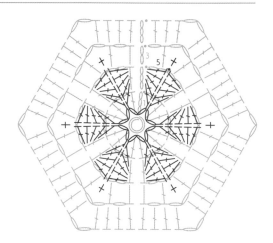

Rnd 5 *Work Rnd 5 over Rnd-2 sts.* Crocodile Stitch around first pair of dcs, sc in next space between 2 Rnd-3 dcs; *Crocodile Stitch around next pair of dcs, sc in next space between two Rnd-3 dcs; rep from * around, join with slip st to first dc. Fasten off.

In the triangular motif, the fancy stitches are closer together and thus tighter than in the previous versions. The Crocodile Stitch here uses a ch-1 instead of a ch-2 at its point to better accommodate the acute angles in the triangle. The picot edging adds charm to the piece; it's a great final round to many shapes.

Crocodile Stitch Instructions are written for right-handed crochet with left-handed directions in brackets. Holding piece with first st to be worked to the right [left] at 3 o'clock [9 o'clock] position and working from right to left [left to right], starting with standing dc, work 5 dc around post of dc, ch 1; rotate piece 180° to 9 o'clock [3 o'clock] position, 5 dc around post of next dc.

Begin with sliding loop.

Rnd 1 Ch 3 (counts as dc), 2 dc in ring, ch 5, *3 dc in ring, ch 5; rep from * once more, join with slip st to top of ch-3 — 9 dc and 3 spaces.

Rnd 2 Ch 3 (counts as dc), dc in next 2 dc, *ch 2, (dc, ch 2, dc) in next space, ch 2**, dc in next 3 dc; rep from * around, ending last rep at **, join with slip st to top of ch-3.

Rnd 3 Ch 2 (counts as hdc), hdc in next 2 dc, *ch 3, tr in next dc, ch 1, (tr, ch 1, tr) in next space, ch 1, tr in next dc, ch 3**, hdc in next 3 dc; rep from * around, ending last rep at **, join with slip st to top of ch-2.

Rnd 4 Ch 1, (sc, ch 3, sc) in same st, *skip 1 hdc, (sc, ch 3, sc) in next hdc, (sc, ch 3, sc) in next space, (sc, ch 3, sc) in next 2 tr, (sc, ch 4, sc) in next space, (sc, ch 3, sc) in next 2 tr, (sc, ch 3, sc) in next space**, (sc, ch 3, sc) in next hdc; rep from * around, ending last rep at **, join with slip st to first sc. Fasten off.

Rnd 5 *Work Rnd 5 over Rnd-2 sts.* Crocodile Stitch around first and third dc of any 3-dc group, ch 3, *Crocodile Stitch around first and third dc of next 3-dc group, ch 3; rep from * once more, slip st to top of first dc. Fasten off.

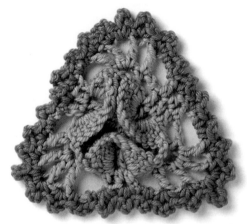

TRIANGLE: 4" (10 CM)

3-D FUN

Simple hexagon shapes are sewn together with a whipstitch (page 32) through one loop of each motif. Holding pieces with right sides together, whipstitch through the outer loops (the loop closest to the wrong side on each motif). The two-color motifs omitted Round 5 of the pattern.

These motifs could just as easily have been joined with a simple JAYGo final round or a continuous final round, which would have eliminated the "outline" effect that sewing through a single loop creates.

Rnds 1 and 2 A ■   **Rnd 3 and 4** B ■   **Rnd 5** C ▨

FEATURES:

- Join when you're done
- Whipstitch seam
- Sew in one loop only
- Connection in every stitch
- Outlined appearance

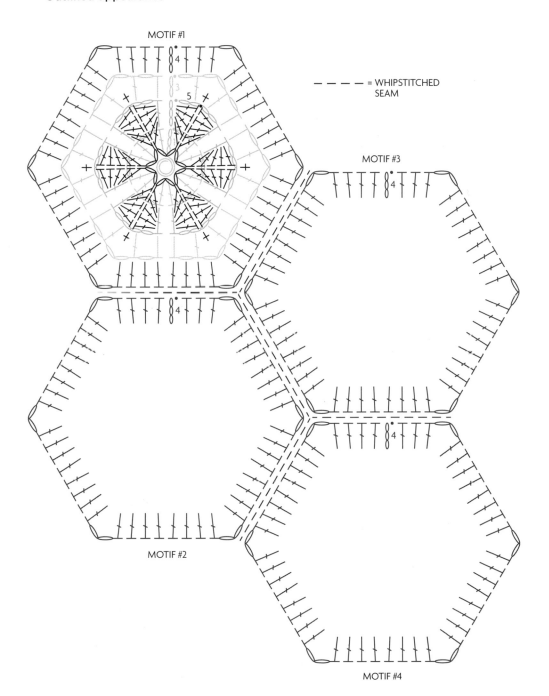

MOTIF #1

MOTIF #3

— — — — — = WHIPSTITCHED
SEAM

MOTIF #2

MOTIF #4

66

This tidy circle starts out the same as Motif 64, through Round 2. It's complete with an (sc, ch 3, sc) edging, which is great for any shape and creates plenty of joining points. The Quick & Easy version omits Round 6.

CIRCLE: 5" (12.5 CM)

Crocodile Stitch Instructions are written for right-handed crochet with left-handed directions in brackets. Holding piece with first st to be worked to the right [left] at 3 o'clock [9 o'clock] position and working from right to left [left to right], starting with standing dc, work 5 dc around post of dc, ch 2; rotate piece 180° to 9 o'clock [3 o'clock] position, 5 dc around post of next dc.

Begin with sliding loop.

Rnd 1 Ch 3 (counts as dc), dc in ring, ch 1, *2 dc in ring, ch 1; rep from * four more times, join with slip st to top of ch-3 — 12 dc and 6 spaces.

Rnd 2 Ch 3 (counts as dc), dc in next dc, ch 4, *dc in next 2 dc, ch 4; rep from * around, join with slip st to top of ch-3.

Rnd 3 Ch 5 (counts as dc and ch 2), dc in next dc, *ch 1, (dc, ch 2, dc) in next space, ch 1**, dc in next dc, ch 2, dc in next dc; rep from * around, ending last rep at **, join with slip st to 3rd ch of ch-5.

Rnd 4 Ch 3 (counts as dc), dc in each dc and space around, join with slip st to top of ch-3.

Rnd 5 Ch 1, (sc, ch 3, sc) in same st, skip 1 dc, *(sc, ch 3, sc) in next dc, skip 1 dc; rep from * around, join with slip st to first sc. Fasten off.

Rnd 6 *Work Rnd 6 over Rnd-2 sts.* Crocodile Stitch around first pair of dcs, sc in center of next ch-4 space between 2 Rnd-3 dcs; *Crocodile Stitch around next pair of dcs, sc in center of next ch-4 space between 2 Rnd-3 dcs; rep from * around, join with slip st to first dc. Fasten off.

This hexagon moves the embossed stitches out in order to open up the center.

Crocodile Stitch Instructions are written for right-handed crochet with left-handed directions in brackets. Holding piece with first st to be worked to the right [left] at 3 o'clock [9 o'clock] position and working from right to left [left to right], starting with standing dc, work 5 dc around post of dc, ch 2; rotate piece 180° to 9 o'clock [3 o'clock] position, 5 dc around post of next dc.

Begin with sliding loop.

Rnd 1 Ch 3 (counts as dc), dc in ring, ch 1, *2 dc in ring, ch 1; rep from * four more times, join with slip st to top of ch-3 — 12 dc and 6 spaces.

Rnd 2 Ch 3 (counts as dc), dc in next dc, ch 3, *sc in next space, ch 3**, dc in next 2 dc, ch 3; rep from * around, ending last rep at **, join with slip st to top of ch-3.

Rnd 3 Ch 3 (counts as dc), dc in next dc, *ch 3, sc in next sc, ch 3**, dc in next 2 dc; rep from * around, ending last rep at **, join with slip st to top of first st.

Rnd 4 Ch 3 (counts as dc), dc in same dc, *ch 2, 2 dc in next dc, ch 2, sc in next space, ch 3, sc in next space**, ch 2, 2 dc in next dc; rep from * around, ending last rep at **, ch 1, join with sc to top of ch-3.

Rnd 5 Ch 1, sc in same space formed by joining sc, *ch 3, (sc, ch 3, sc) in next space, ch 3, sc in next space, ch 3, skip 1 space, sc in next space; rep from * around, omitting last sc, join with slip st to first sc. Fasten off.

Rnd 6 *Work Rnd 6 over Rnd-3 sts.* Crocodile Stitch around first pair of dcs, *ch 2, sc in next sc, ch 2, ** Crocodile Stitch around next pair of dcs; rep from * around, ending last rep at **, join with slip st to first dc. Fasten off.

HEXAGON: 5" (12.5 CM)

3-D FUN

68

Rnds 1, 3, and 8 A ■   **Rnds 2, 4, 6, and 7** B ■   **Rnd 5** C ■

If one round of fancy stitches is good, then two is better! This showstopper would make a beautiful centerpiece for your special project, but be careful not to use too many of them together or your fabric will become heavy. Instead, vary the motif by omitting Round 7, Round 8, or — for the Quick & Easy version — both.

SQUARE: 5" (12.5 CM)

Crocodile Stitch Instructions are written for right-handed crochet with left-handed directions in brackets. Holding piece with first st to be worked to the right [left] at 3 o'clock [9 o'clock] position and working from right to left [left to right], starting with standing dc, work 5 dc around post of dc, ch 2; rotate piece 180° to 9 o'clock [3 o'clock] position, 5 dc around post of next dc.

Begin with sliding loop.

Rnd 1 Ch 3 (counts as dc), dc in ring, ch 3, *2 dc in ring, ch 3; rep from * two more times, join with slip st to top of ch-3 — 8 dc and 4 spaces.

Rnd 2 Ch 3 (counts as dc), dc in next dc, *ch 3, dc in next space, ch 3**, dc in next 2 dc; rep from * around, ending last rep at **, join with slip st to top of ch-3.

Rnd 3 Ch 3 (counts as dc), dc in next dc, *ch 3, (dc, ch 3, dc) in next dc, ch 3**, dc in next 2 dc; rep from * around, ending last rep at **, join with slip st to top of ch-3.

Rnd 4 Ch 3 (counts as dc), dc in next dc, *ch 1, dc in next space, ch 1, dc in next dc, ch 1, (dc, ch 3, dc) in next space, ch 1, dc in next dc, ch 1, dc in next space, ch 1**, dc in next 2 dc; rep from * around, ending last rep at **, join with slip st to top of ch-3.

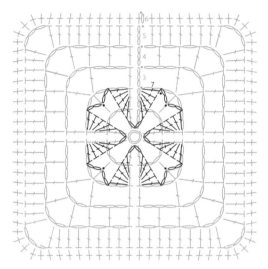

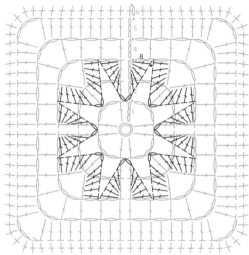

Rnd 5 Ch 3 (counts as dc), dc in each st and ch-1 space around, placing (2 dc, ch 3, 2 dc) in each corner ch-3 space, join with slip st to top of ch-3.

Rnd 6 Ch 1, sc in each dc around, placing 5 sc in each corner space. Fasten off.

Rnd 7 *Work Rnd 7 over Rnd-2 sts.* Crocodile Stitch around first pair of dcs, ch 2, slip st around post of next dc, ch 2; *Crocodile

Stitch around next pair of dcs, slip st around post of next dc, ch 2; rep from * around, join with slip st to first dc. Fasten off.

Rnd 8 *Work Rnd 8 over Rnd-3 sts.* Crocodile Stitch around first pair of dcs, *Crocodile Stitch around pair of dcs that form corner**, Crocodile Stitch around next pair of dcs; rep from * around, ending last rep at **, join with slip st to first dc. Fasten off.

69

Rnds 1 and 4 A ☐   **Rnds 2, 5, and 6** B ▧   **Rnd 3** C ▨

The six-pointed version of this motif evokes a colorful pinwheel. Omit the last two rounds for a more unusual shape.

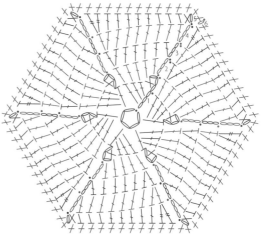

HEXAGON: 6½" (16.5 CM)

Ch 5, join with slip st to form ring.

Rnd 1 Ch 6 (counts as dc and ch-3), sc in 3rd ch from hook, 3 dc around the post of beginning ch-3, *dc in ring, ch 3, sc in 3rd ch from hook, 3 dc around the post of dc; rep from * four times, join with slip st to 3rd ch of ch-6. Fasten off.

Rnd 2 Join yarn with slip st in any ch-3 corner space, *ch 3, dc in same space, dc in next sc, dc in next 3 dc, slip st in 3rd ch of next ch-3; rep from * around. Fasten off.

Rnd 3 Join yarn with slip st in 3rd ch of any ch-3 corner, *ch 3, dc in same space, dc in next 4 dc, 2 dc in next dc, slip st in 3rd ch of next ch-3; rep from * around. Fasten off.

Rnd 4 Join yarn with slip st in 3rd ch of any ch-3 corner, *ch 3, dc in same space, dc in next 6 dc, 2 dc in next dc, slip st in 3rd ch of next ch-3; rep from * around. Fasten off.

Rnd 5 Join yarn with slip st in 3rd ch of any ch-3 corner, *ch 1, sc in same st, hdc in next 3 dc, dc in next 5 dc, 2 tr in next dc, slip st in 3rd ch of next ch-3; rep from * around.

Rnd 6 Ch 1, *2 sc in ch-1, sc in next 11 sts; rep from * around; join with slip st in first sc. Fasten off.

An eight-pointed motif becomes a circle on the last two rounds. Try leaving off those rounds for a pinwheel, or if you want the pinwheel to be prominent without losing the circular shape, work the last two rounds in a color that will fade into the background.

CIRCLE: 5¾" (14.5 CM)

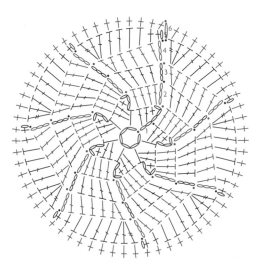

Ch 6, join with slip st to form ring.

Rnd 1: Ch 5 (counts as hdc and ch-3), sc in 3rd ch from hook, 2 dc around the post of ch-2, *hdc in ring, ch 3, sc in 3rd ch from hook, 2 dc around post of hdc; rep from * five more times, join with slip st to 3rd ch of ch-6. Fasten off.

Rnd 2: Join with slip st in any ch-3 corner space, *ch 3, dc in same space, dc in next sc, dc in next 2 dc, slip st in 3rd ch of next ch-3 space; rep from * around. Fasten off.

Rnd 3: Join with slip st in 3rd ch of any ch-3 corner, *ch 3, dc in next 4 dc, slip st in 3rd ch of next ch-3; rep from * around. Fasten off.

Rnd 4: Join with slip st in 3rd ch of any ch-3 corner, *ch 3, dc in same space, dc in next 3 dc, 2 dc in next dc, slip st in 3rd ch of next ch-3; rep from * around. Fasten off.

Rnd 5: Join with slip st in 3rd ch of any ch-3 corner, *ch 1, sc in same st and in next dc, hdc in next 2 dc, dc in next 2 dc, (2 dc, tr) in next dc, slip st in 3rd ch of next ch-3; rep from * around.

Rnd 6: Ch 1, sc in first sc and in each st around; join with slip st in first sc. Fasten off.

[SWIRLS]

The motifs in this group begin with an unusual first round that sets up a quirky swirl. Solid straight edges predominate in this family of motifs, so any of the seaming methods would be a good choice for connecting them. The final couple of rounds of Motifs 69–72 and 74 straighten the edges; try leaving them off for a totally different look. For the motifs with points, of course, JAYGo makes connecting motifs a breeze!

Rnd 1 A ■	Rnds 2, 4, 6, and 7 B ▓	Rnd 3 C ☐
Rnd 5 D ▓		

This doesn't really become a square until the last two rounds. Up to that point, it's just a four-pointed swirl. It is rich with possibilities for experimenting with color and perhaps the addition of textured stitches.

Begin with sliding loop.

Rnd 1 Ch 6 (counts as dc and ch-3), sc in 3rd ch from hook, 3 dc around the post of beginning ch-3, tr in ring, *dc in ring, ch 3, sc in 3rd ch from hook, 3 dc around the post of dc, tr in ring; rep from * two times, join with slip st to 3rd ch of ch-6. Fasten off.

Rnd 2 Join yarn with slip st in ch-3 corner space, *ch 3, 2 dc in same space, dc in next sc, dc in next 4 sts, slip st in next ch-3 corner space; rep from * around. Fasten off.

Rnd 3 Join yarn with slip st in 3rd ch of any ch-3 corner, *ch 3, 2 dc in same st, dc in next 6 dc, 2 dc in next dc, slip st in 3rd ch of next ch-3; rep from * around. Fasten off.

Rnd 4 Join yarn with slip st in 3rd ch of any ch-3 corner, *ch 3, 2 dc in same st, dc in next 9 dc, 2 dc in next dc, slip st in 3rd ch of next ch-3; rep from * around. Fasten off.

Rnd 5 Join yarn with slip st in 3rd ch of any ch-3 corner, *ch 3, 2 dc in same st, dc in next 12 dc, 2 dc in next dc, slip st in 3rd ch of next ch-3; rep from * around. Fasten off.

Rnd 6 Join yarn with slip st in 3rd ch of any ch-3 corner, *ch 3, dc in next 2 dc, hdc in next 2 dc, sc in next 7 sc, hdc in next 2 dc, dc in next 2 dc, 2 tr in next dc, slip st in 3rd ch of next ch-3; rep from * around.

Rnd 7 Ch 1, *sc in next 2 ch, (sc, ch 1, sc) in next ch, sc in next 17 sts, sc in next slip st; rep from * around, join with slip st in first sc. Fasten off.

SQUARE: 5¾" (14.5 CM)

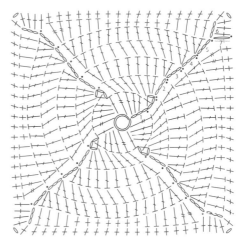

[**TIP**] The next-to-last round of the motifs in this group is used to straighten the edges of each motif. To make this motif larger, add optional additional rounds in the manner of Round 5, then make the next-to-last round an adjusting round in the manner of Round 6. To make the square smaller, end at Round 3 or 4, then make the next-to-last round an adjusting round in the manner of Round 6.

The triangular swirl is quite rounded and may therefore be best suited to joining other triangles at the corners only. But take a look at the Pie Wedge Pillow on page 240 for what happens when you join these triangles along the edges.

TRIANGLE: 6" (15 CM)

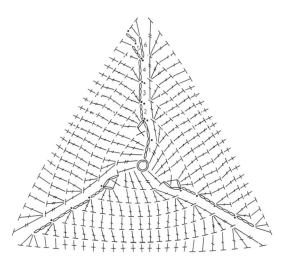

Begin with sliding loop.

Rnd 1 Ch 6 (counts as dc and ch-3), sc in 3rd ch from hook, 3 dc around the post of ch-3, tr in ring, *dc in ring, ch 3, sc in 3rd ch from hook, 3 dc around the post of dc, tr in ring; rep from * once more, join with slip st to 3rd ch of ch-6. Fasten off.

Rnd 2 Join yarn with slip st in any ch-3 corner space, *ch 3, 3 dc in same space, skip 1 sc, dc in next 3 dc, 3 dc in next tr, slip st in next ch-3 corner space; rep from * around. Fasten off.

Rnd 3 Join yarn with slip st in 3rd ch of any ch-3 corner, *ch 3, 2 dc in same st, dc in next 8 dc, 3 dc in next dc, slip st in 3rd ch of next ch-3; rep from * around. Fasten off.

Rnd 4 Join yarn with slip st in 3rd ch of any ch-3 corner, *ch 3, 2 dc in same st, dc in next 12 dc, 3 dc in next dc, slip st in 3rd ch of next ch-3; rep from * around. Fasten off.

Rnd 5 Join yarn with slip st in 3rd ch of any ch-3 corner, ch 3, dc in same st, *dc in next 16 dc, 3 tr in next dc, slip st in 3rd ch of next ch-3**, ch 3, 2 dc in same st; rep from * around, ending last rep at **.

Rnd 6 Ch 3, slip st in 3rd ch of next ch-3, ch 2, hdc in same st, *hdc in next dc, sc in next 14 dc, hdc in next 2 dc, dc in next 2 dc, (2 dc, tr) in next dc**, 3 hdc in 3rd ch of next ch-3, hdc in next dc, rep from * around, ending last rep at **, 2 hdc in base of beg ch-2, join with slip st to top of ch-2. Fasten off.

[**TIP**]
The instructions for Motifs 69–72 change the color on almost every round. To work the motif in a single color, work a round as written, then slip stitch in each chain at the beginning of the same round to reach the bottom of the next round.

SWIRLS

Leaving off the final two rounds of Motif 72 creates a triangular pinwheel. Connect the tips of the pinwheels by working (ch 3, flat join in adjacent ch-3 space of previous motif, 2 dc in same st of current motif). The three-pointed filler motifs connect to the sides of the shapes and serve an important purpose in this arrangement.

FILLER MOTIF

Begin with sliding loop.

Rnd 1 Ch 3 (counts as dc), dc in ring, *ch 1, flat join in dc at center edge of motif, ch 1, 2 dc in ring, rep from * two more times, omitting last 2 dc and joining or working plain ch-2 corners as needed, join with slip st to top of ch-3. Fasten off.

FEATURES:

- Partial motif
- JAYGo
- Flat join
- Connection in adjoining points
- Connection in adjoining sides
- Filler motif

MOTIF #1

MOTIF #2

FILLER MOTIF

MOTIF #3

MOTIF #4

Rnds 1, 2, 4, and 5 A ■   **Rnd 3** B ■

This square incorporates a different technique — Block Stitches — to establish the sawtooth look of the rounds. The rounded corners make it appear more circular than square when all five rounds are complete. For a more defined square, stop after working Round 4.

Block Stitch Sc in st or space indicated, ch 3, 3 dc inside of sc just made.

───────────────────────────────

Begin with sliding loop.

Rnd 1 Ch 1, 8 sc in ring, join with slip st to first sc.

Rnd 2 Ch 1, Block Stitch in same st, skip 1 sc, *Block Stitch in next sc, skip 1 st; rep from * around, join with slip st to first sc.

Rnd 3 Ch 1, Block Stitch in same st, *Block Stitch in top of next ch-3**, Block Stitch in next sc; rep from * around, ending last rep at **, join with slip st to first sc. Fasten off.

Rnd 4 Standing sc in top of first ch-3, *ch 1, (dc, ch 1, dc) in next sc, ch 1, (sc, ch 1, sc) in top of next ch-3, ch 1, dc in next sc, ch 1, sc in top of next ch-3; rep from *, omitting last sc, join with slip st to first sc, slip st in next space.

Rnd 5 Ch 1, Block Stitch in same space, *skip (dc, ch), Block Stitch in next dc, skip (ch, sc), Block Stitch in next space, skip (sc, ch), Block Stitch in next dc, skip (ch, sc)**, Block Stitch in next space; rep from * around, ending last rep at **, join with slip st to first sc. Fasten off.

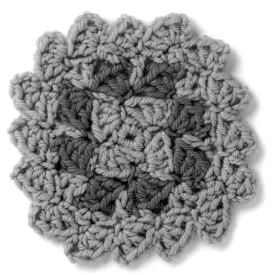

SQUARE: 4" (10 CM)

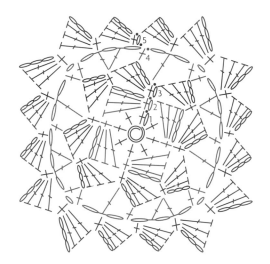

Rnds 1 and 2 A ☐   **Rnd 3** B ▨   **Rnds 4 and 5** C ■

This six-sided shape has nice flat sides, but leave off the last two rounds and you'll have a swirly, sawtooth motif.

HEXAGON: 4¾" (12 CM)

Block Stitch Sc in stitch or space indicated, ch 3, 3 dc in side of sc just made.

Ch 5, join with slip st to form ring.

Rnd 1 Ch 1, 12 sc in ring, join with slip st to first sc.

Rnd 2 Ch 1, Block Stitch in same st, skip 1 sc, *Block Stitch in next sc, skip 1 st; rep from * around, join with slip st to first sc.

Rnd 3 Ch 1, Block Stitch in same st, *Block Stitch in top of next ch-3**, Block Stitch in next sc; rep from * around, ending last rep at **, join with slip st to first sc. Fasten off.

Rnd 4 Standing sc in top of first ch-3, *ch 1, dc in next sc, ch 1, (sc, ch 1, sc) in top of next ch-3, ch 1, dc in next sc, ch 1**, sc in top of next ch-3; rep from * around, ending last rep at **, join with slip st to first sc.

Rnd 5 Ch 1, sc in first sc, *sc in next space, sc in next dc, sc in next space), skip 1 sc, (sc, ch 1, sc) in ch-1 corner space, skip 1 sc, sc in next space, sc in next dc, sc in next space, sc in next sc; rep from * around, omitting last sc, join with slip st to first sc. Fasten off.

It's no problem to decide where to make the connections on Motif 73! Join each of the four points along the sides of this unusual square, using a single crochet join, as follows:

Sc in st or space on current motif, ch 3, sc in ch-3 space of adjoining block st, 3 dc in side of sc at base of block on current motif.

The filler motif complements and completes the look.

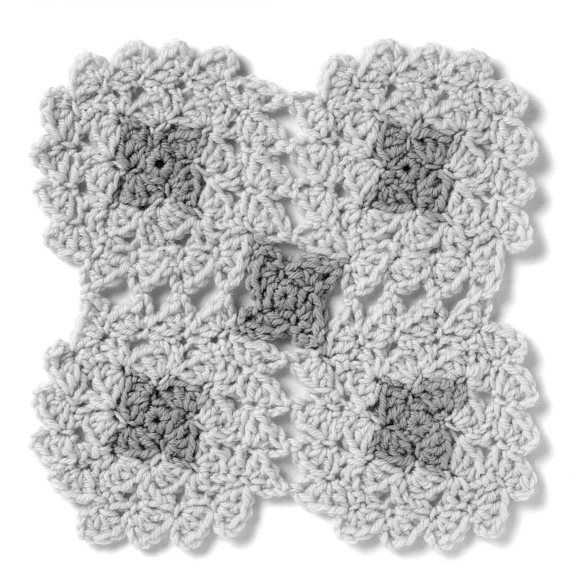

FILLER MOTIF

Work Rnds 1 and 2 of Motif 73, joining Block Stitches on Rnd 2 to the adjoining squares at the free sc at each corner.

FEATURES:

- Partial motif
- JAYGo
- Single crochet join
- Connection in adjoining points
- Filler motif

MOTIF #1

MOTIF #2

FILLER MOTIF

MOTIF #4

MOTIF #3

radiants

75

Rnds 1 and 2 A ■   **Rnd 3** B ■

These circles demonstrate the idea at its most elemental level: chain spokes radiating out from a center point and corralled with another chain that connects the spokes. See page 176 for a connection.

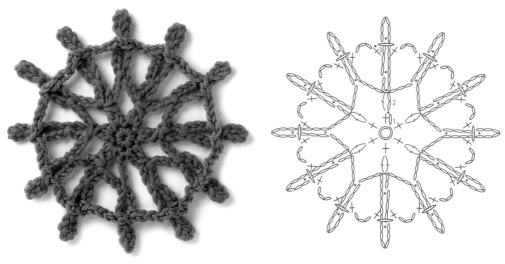

CIRCLE: 5" (12.5 CM)

Long Corner Chain Ch 13, slip st in 6th ch from hook, ch 3, skip 3 ch, slip st in next ch, ch 3 — *3 open loops made.*

Short Corner Chain Ch 12, slip st in 6th ch from hook, ch 3, skip 3 ch, slip st in next ch, ch 2 — *3 open loops made.*

Begin with sliding loop.

Rnd 1 Ch 1, 6 sc in ring, join with slip st to first sc — 6 sc.

Rnd 2 Ch 2, dc in same st (ch-2 and dc count as dc2tog), *make Short Corner Chain, slip st in top of same cluster, make Long Corner Chain, dc2tog in next sc; rep from * around, omitting last dc2tog, join with slip st to first cluster. Fasten off.

Rnd 3 Standing sc in left side of middle open loop of any corner chain, *ch 3, sc in right side of middle open loop of next corner chain, ch 1, holding corner chain to the back, sc in left side of same corner chain; rep from * around, omitting last sc, join with slip st to first sc. Fasten off.

Of this family of motifs, this one looks the most like the classic motifs you may be familiar with. Here double crochet rounds are joined to the corner chains to create a solid fabric. See page 178 for connections.

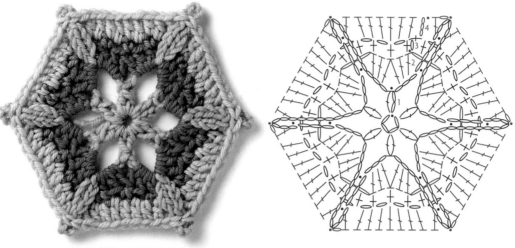

HEXAGON: 5" (12.5 CM)

Corner Chain Ch 13, slip st in 6th ch from hook, ch 3, skip 3 ch, slip st in next ch, ch 3 — *3 open loops made.*

Ch 4, join with slip st to form ring.

Rnd 1 Ch 2, working into ring, dc (ch-2 and dc count as dc2tog), make Corner Chain, *dc2tog, make Corner Chain; rep from * four more times, join with slip st to first cluster. Fasten off.

Rnd 2 Standing dc in left side of lower open loop of any Corner Chain, dc in same space, *dc2tog over same space and next lower open loop on next corner ch, 2 dc in same space, ch 2**; keeping Corner Chain to the front, 2 dc in next lower open loop; rep from * around, ending last rep at **, join with slip st to first dc.

Rnd 3 *Keep Corner Chains to the front while working Rnd 3.* Ch 1, sc in same st, *(ch 1, skip 1 dc, sc in next st) two times, ch 1, (sc, ch 1, sc) in next space**, ch 1, sc in next dc; rep from * around, ending last rep at **, join with sc to first sc.

Rnd 4 Ch 3 (counts as dc), *(dc in next sc, dc in next space) three times, skip 1 sc, dc in next space, slip st in top open loop of Corner Chain, ch 1, dc in same Rnd-3 space, skip 1 sc, dc in next space; rep from * around, omitting last dc, join with slip st to top of ch-3. Fasten off. Pull tips of Corner Chains to allow corner slip sts to move toward center and tips of Corner Chains to extend beyond Rnd 4.

[RADIANTS]

The first rounds of this motif family go all the way out to the corners, then subsequent rounds are worked around those spokes. Use strongly contrasting colors for the inner and outer rounds for best effect. You may want to think ahead to plan connections for this group, for in some cases the points are formed on the first round of the motif, rather than on the final round. This presents more options for creativity, as you may be able to join at the points, along the edges, or both.

Motif 75   **Rnds 1 and 2** A ■   **Rnds 3 and 4** B ■

This join features a variation of Rounds 1–3 of Motif 75. Round 3 is worked holding the corner chains to the front. Each motif is worked separately through Round 3, then joined with a final continuous round worked into the top loop of each corner chain. Several types of joins are used in this example.

[TIP]

The method used to join these circular motifs can be adapted to work continuous joins for a number of different shapes.

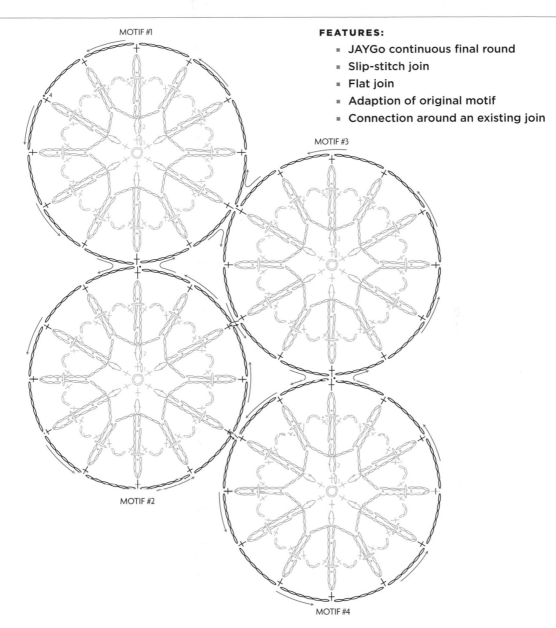

MOTIF #1

MOTIF #3

MOTIF #2

MOTIF #4

FEATURES:

- JAYGo continuous final round
- Slip-stitch join
- Flat join
- Adaption of original motif
- Connection around an existing join

Rnd 4 Join with sc in top loop of any Short Corner Chain, (ch 6, sc in top loop of next corner chain) four times, sc in any Short Corner Chain of Motif #2; continuing working around Motif #2, ch 6, (sc in next corner chain, ch 6) 11 times, slip st over join; continuing around Motif #1, (ch 6, sc in next corner chain) two times; sc in any Short Corner Chain of Motif #3; continuing around Motif #3, (ch 6, sc in next corner chain) two times, flat join to top of adjacent Motif-#2 sc, (ch 6, sc in next corner chain) two times, sc in any Short Corner Chain of Motif #4; continuing around Motif #4, (ch 6, sc in next corner chain) two times, flat join to top of adjacent Motif-#2 sc, ch 6, (sc in next corner chain, ch 6) nine times, slip st over join; continuing around Motif #3, ch 6, (sc in next corner chain, ch 6) seven times, slip st over join; continuing around Motif #1, ch 6, (sc in next corner chain, ch 6) five times, join with slip st to first sc. Fasten off.

Here's an instance where thinking ahead pays off: the corner chains formed in the first round are joined at their tips with a flat join. You could, of course, leave off Rounds 2–4 or connect the Round-4 stitches as well. Or you could change the finished shape to something entirely different, like circles, or triangles. What other shapes could you make using this technique?

FEATURES:

- JAYGo
- Flat join
- Connection in adjoining spaces
- Connection on first round

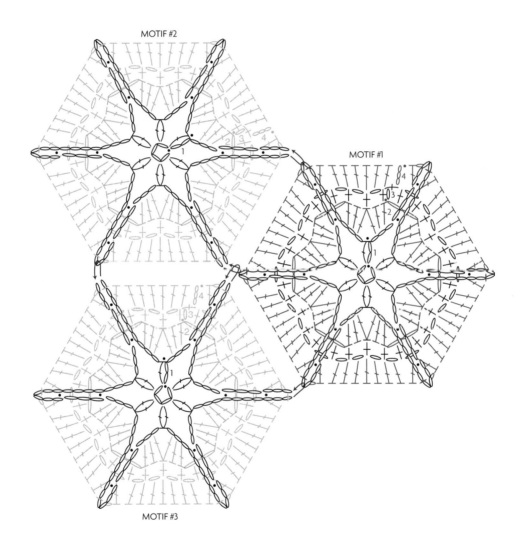

MOTIF #2

MOTIF #1

MOTIF #3

Don't forget the layering option! After forming a circle of connected corner chains, layer on a connected background of double crochet.

Long Corner Chain Ch 13, slip st in 6th ch from hook, ch 3, skip 3 ch, slip st in next ch, ch 3 — *3 open loops made.*

Dc2tog *(double crochet 2 together)* Yarn over, insert hook into indicated stitch or space and pull up a loop, yarn over, pull through 2 loops, yarn over, insert hook into same stitch and pull up a loop, yarn over and pull through 2 loops, yarn over and pull through all 3 loops on hook.

FPdc *(front post double crochet)* Yarn over, insert hook from front to back to front around post of stitch indicated and pull up a loop, (yarn over and pull through 2 loops on hook) two times.

Short Corner Chain Ch 12, slip st in 6th ch from hook, ch 3, skip 3 ch, slip st in next ch, ch 2 — *3 open loops made.*

Standing FPdc Beginning with slip knot on hook, yarn over, insert hook from front to back to front around post of stitch indicated and pull up a loop, (yarn over and pull through 2 loops on hook) two times.

Begin with sliding loop.

Rnd 1 Ch 1, 6 sc in ring, join with slip st to first sc — 6 sc.

Rnd 2 Ch 2, dc in same st (ch-2 and dc count as dc2tog), *make Short Corner Chain, slip st in top of same cluster, make Long Corner Chain, dc2tog in next sc; rep from * around, omitting last dc2tog, join with slip st to first cluster. Fasten off.

Rnd 3 Standing sc in left side of middle open loop of any corner chain, *ch 3, sc in right side of middle open loop of next corner chain, ch 1, holding corner chain to the front, sc in left side of same corner chain; rep from * around, omitting last sc. Fasten off.

Rnd 4 Working around posts of Rnd-1 scs, work Standing FPdc in any sc from Rnd 1, ch 2, *FPdc in next sc, ch 2; rep from * around, join with slip st to top of first dc, slip st in next space.

Rnd 5 Ch 3 (counts as dc), 3 dc in same space, 4 dc in each space around, join with slip st to top of ch-3 — 24 dc.

Rnd 6 Ch 3 (counts as dc), *2 dc in next dc, dc in next 2 dc; rep from * around, omitting last dc, join with slip st to top of ch-3.

CIRCLE: 5" (12.5 CM)

Rnd 7 Ch 3 (counts as dc), *dc in next 2 dc, 2 dc in next dc, dc in next dc; rep from * around, omitting last dc, join with slip st to top of ch-3.

Rnd 8 Ch 3 (counts as dc), *dc in next 3 dc, 2 dc in next dc, dc in next dc; rep from * around, omitting last dc, join with slip st to top of ch-3.

Rnd 9 Ch 1, sc in same st, *2 sc in next dc, sc in next dc, insert hook into upper open loop of next corner chain and into next dc of current rnd, yarn over and pull up a loop, yarn over and pull through 2 loops to join corner chain to current round, sc in next dc; rep from * around, omitting last sc, join with slip st to first sc. Fasten off.

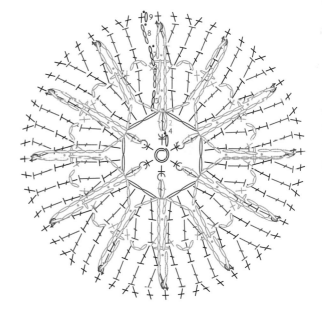

Rnds 1–3 A ▨   **Rnds 4–6** B ▨

The Corner Chains on this motif are enhanced with a lacy square framework.

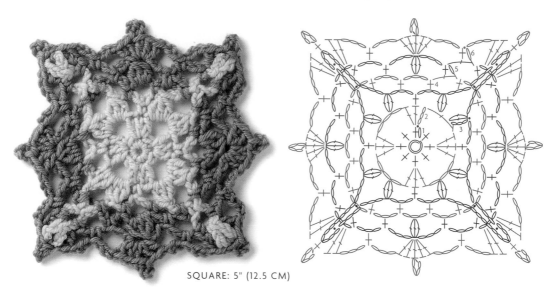

SQUARE: 5" (12.5 CM)

Corner Chain Ch 13, slip st in 6th ch from hook, ch 3, skip 3 ch, slip st in next ch, ch 3 — *3 open loops made.*

Dc2tog *(double crochet 2 together)* Yarn over, insert hook into indicated stitch or space and pull up a loop, yarn over, pull through 2 loops, yarn over, insert hook into same stitch and pull up a loop, yarn over and pull through 2 loops, yarn over and pull through all 3 loops on hook.

Dc3tog *(double crochet 3 together)* Yarn over, insert hook into indicated stitch or space and pull up a loop, yarn over, pull through 2 loops on hook, (yarn over, insert hook into same stitch and pull up a loop, yarn over and pull through 2 loops) two times, yarn over and pull through all 4 loops on hook.

Tight Picot-4 Ch 4, insert hook from top to bottom through top and side edge of st just made and pull a loop through to slip st.

Begin with sliding loop.

Rnd 1 Ch 1, 8 sc in ring, join with slip st to first sc — 8 sc.

Rnd 2 Ch 3 (counts as dc), 2 dc in same st, *ch 3, skip 1 sc, 3 dc in next sc; rep from * two more times, skip 1 sc, join with dc in top of ch-3.

Rnd 3 Ch 2, dc2tog in space formed by joining dc, make Corner Chain, dc3tog in same space, *ch 3, skip 1 dc, sc in next dc, ch 3, skip 1 dc**, (dc3tog, Corner Chain, dc3tog) in next space; rep from * around, ending last rep

at **, join with slip st to top of first cluster. Fasten off.

Rnd 4 Standing sc in ch-3 space after any Corner Chain, *ch 3, sc in next ch-3 space, ch 3, sc in lower open loop of Corner Chain, holding Corner Chain to the front, ch 3, sc on other side of same lower open loop**, ch 3, sc in next ch-3 space; rep from * around, ending last rep at **, join with dc in to first sc.

Rnd 5 Ch 1, sc in same space, *ch 3, dc3tog in next space, ch 3, sc in next space, ch 3, sc in middle open loop of Corner Chain, holding Corner Chain to the front, ch 3, sc on other side of same middle open loop**, ch 3, skip space behind Corner Chain, sc in next space; rep from * around, ending last rep at **, join with dc in first sc.

Rnd 6 Ch 1, sc in same space, *ch 3, (3 dc, Tight Picot-4, 2 dc) in next cluster, ch 3, skip 1 space, sc in next space, ch 3, 2 dc in next space, sc in top open loop of corner chain, Tight Picot-4, 2 dc in same space from Rnd 5, ch 3**, sc in next space; rep from * around, ending last rep at **, join with slip st to first sc. Fasten off.

79

Rnd 1 A ■   **Rnds 2–4** B ■

This is the hexagonal version of Motif 78.

HEXAGON: 5¼" (13.5 CM)

Ch 4, join with slip st to form ring.

Rnd 1 Ch 2, working into ring, dc, make Corner Chain, *dc2tog, make Corner Chain; rep from * four more times, join with slip st to first cluster. Fasten off.

Rnd 2 Standing sc on right side of lower open loop of any Corner Chain, *holding Corner Chain to front, ch 3, sc on other side of lower open loop**, ch 3; sc in next lower open loop; rep from * around, ending last rep at **, join with dc to first sc.

Rnd 3 Ch 2, dc2tog in same space, *ch 3, sc in middle open loop of next Corner Chain, ch 3, holding Corner Chain to front, sc in other side of middle open loop, ch 3, skip space behind Corner Chain**, dc3tog in next space; rep from * around, ending last rep at **, join with slip st to first cluster.

Rnd 4 Ch 4, slip st in same st, *ch 3, skip 1 space, 3 dc in next space, sc in top open loop of Corner Chain, Tight Picot-4, 3 dc in same space from Rnd 3, ch 3**, (slip st, ch 4, slip st) in next cluster; rep from * around, ending last rep at **, join with slip st to first cluster. Fasten off.

Here's a nice three-legged version. Remember, for a close edge-to-edge fit with other triangles, lengthen the corners and shorten the stitches along the sides.

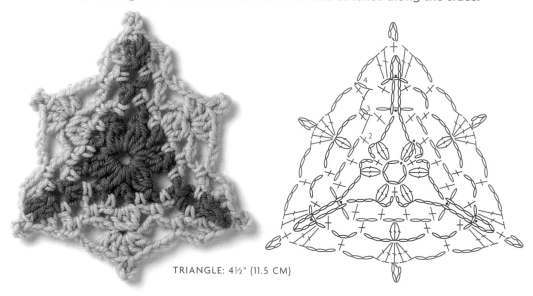

TRIANGLE: 4½" (11.5 CM)

Corner Chain Ch 13, slip st in 6th ch from hook, ch 3, skip 3 ch, slip st in next ch, ch 3 — *3 open loops made.*

Dc2tog *(double crochet 2 together)* Yarn over, insert hook into indicated stitch or space and pull up a loop, yarn over, pull through 2 loops, yarn over, insert hook into same stitch and pull up a loop, yarn over and pull through 2 loops, yarn over and pull through all 3 loops on hook.

Dc3tog *(double crochet 3 together)* Yarn over, insert hook into indicated stitch or space and pull up a loop, yarn over, pull through 2 loops on hook, (yarn over, insert hook into same stitch and pull up a loop, yarn over and pull through 2 loops) two times, yarn over and pull through all 4 loops on hook.

Tight Picot-4 Ch 4, insert hook from top to bottom through top and side edge of st just made and pull a loop through to slip st.

Ch 6, join with slip st to form ring.

Rnd 1 Ch 2, working into ring, dc2tog, make Corner Chain, (dc3tog, ch 3, sc, ch 3, dc3tog, make Corner Chain) two times, dc3tog, ch 3, sc, ch 3, join with slip st to top of first cluster. Fasten off.

Rnd 2 Standing sc in ch-3 space after any Corner Chain, *ch 2, sc in next ch-3 space, ch 2, sc in lower open loop of Corner Chain, holding Corner Chain to the front, ch 3, sc on other side of lower open loop**, ch 2, sc in next ch-3 space; rep from * around, ending last rep at **, join with hdc in first sc.

Rnd 3 Ch 1, sc in space formed by joining hdc, *ch 3, dc3tog in next space, ch 3, sc in next space, ch 3, sc in middle open loop of Corner Chain, holding Corner Chain to the front, ch 3, sc on other side of middle open loop**, ch 3, skip space behind Corner Chain, sc in next space; rep from * around, ending last rep at **, join with dc in first sc.

Rnd 4 Ch 1, sc in space formed by joining dc, *ch 3, (3 dc, Tight Picot-4, 2 dc) in next cluster, ch 3, skip 1 space, sc in next space, ch 3, 2 dc in next space, sc in top open loop of Corner Chain, Tight Picot-4, 2 dc in same Rnd-3 space, ch 3**, sc in next space; rep from * around, ending last rep at **, join with slip st to first sc. Fasten off.

picots in plural

81

Rnds 1 and 2 A ▮ **Rnd 3** B ▮

This six-pointed motif forms the basis for the motif used in the Snowy Shaped Shawl on page 226.

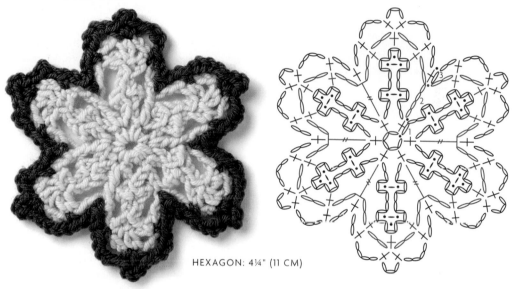

HEXAGON: 4¼" (11 CM)

Picot-3 Ch 3, slip st in 3rd ch from hook.

Triple Picot-3 (Ch 3, slip st in 3rd ch from hook) three times, slip st in base of first picot.

Ch 5, join with slip st to form ring.

Rnd 1 Ch 1, *sc in ring, ch 2, Picot-3, ch 2, Triple Picot-3, ch 2, Picot-3, slip st in base of corresponding picot on opposite side of leg, ch 2; rep from * five more times, join with slip st to first sc — 6 legs.

Rnd 2 Ch 6 (counts as tr and ch 2), *skip 1 picot, (sc in next picot, ch 2) three times, skip 1 picot**, tr in next sc, ch 2; rep from * around, ending last rep at **, join with slip st in 4th ch of ch-6.

Rnd 3 Ch 1, sc in same st, *ch 2, sc in next sc, ch 4, (sc, ch 3, sc) in next sc, ch 4, sc in next sc, ch 2**, sc in next tr; rep from *, ending last rep at **, join with slip st to first sc. Fasten off.

[**PICOTS IN PLURAL**]

In this motif family, picot-encrusted legs radiate to the edges, and once again what happens around those spokes defines the shape of the motif. For the connections, you have lots of picots and little spaces available for joining, plus several straight-ish, solid edges.

Rnd 1 A ▪   **Rnds 2 and 3** B ▫

This large and elegant motif is easier to make than it looks because each spoke and each point is identical. Use it as either an octagon or a circle.

OCTAGON OR CIRCLE: 6¼" (16 CM)

Picot-3 Ch 3, slip st in 3rd ch from hook.

Triple Picot-3 (Ch 3, slip st in 3rd ch from hook) three times, slip st in base of first picot.

___

Ch 4, join with slip st to form ring.

Rnd 1 Ch 1, *sc in ring, ch 2, (Picot-3, ch 2) two times, Triple Picot-3, ch 2, (Picot-3, slip st in base of corresponding picot on opposite side of leg, ch 2) two times; rep from * seven more times, join with slip st to first sc — 8 legs. Fasten off.

Rnd 2 Standing sc in center picot of any Triple Picot-3, ch 3, sc in same picot, *ch 3, skip 1 picot, dc in next ch-2 space between picots, ch 2, skip next 4 ch-2 spaces, dc in next ch-2 space, ch 3, skip 1 picot**, (sc, ch 3, sc) in next picot; rep from * around, ending last rep at **, join with slip st to first sc.

Rnd 3 Ch 5 (counts as dc and ch 2), *(dc, ch 2) two times in next space, dc in next sc, ch 2, dc in next space, ch 2, skip next space, dc in next space, ch 2**, dc in next sc, ch 2; rep from * around, ending last rep at **, join with slip st to 3rd ch of ch-5. Fasten off.

Alternating long and short picoted legs help establish the corners and sides of this square.

SQUARE: 4½" (11.5 CM)

Partial dc *(partial double crochet)* Yarn over, insert hook into stitch or space indicated and pull up a loop, yarn over and pull through 2 loops on hook.

Picot-3 Ch 3, slip st in 3rd ch from hook.

Triple Picot-3 (Ch 3, slip st in 3rd ch from hook) three times, slip st in base of first picot.

Ch 6, join with slip st to form ring.

Rnd 1 Ch 1, *sc in ring, ch 2, (Picot-3, ch 2) two times, Triple Picot-3, ch 2, (Picot-3, slip st in base of corresponding picot on opposite side of leg, ch 2) two times, sc in ring, ch 2, Picot-3, ch 2, Triple Picot-3, ch 2, Picot-3, slip st in base of corresponding picot on opposite side of leg, ch 2; rep from * three more times, join with slip st to first sc — *4 long legs and 4 short legs made.* Fasten off.

Rnd 2 Standing sc in center picot of Triple Picot-3 on any long leg, *(ch 2, sc in next picot) two times, ch 2, (insert hook in next picot and pull up a loop) two times, yarn over and pull through all 3 loops on hook to sc2tog, ch 2, sc in next picot, ch 2, (sc, ch 2, sc) in next picot, ch 2, sc in next picot, ch 2, sc2tog over next 2 picots, (ch 2, sc in next picot) two times, ch 2**, (sc, ch 2, sc) in next picot; rep from * around, ending last rep at **, sc in next picot, join with hdc to first sc.

Rnd 3 (Sc, ch 3, sc) in space formed by joining hdc, *ch 4, skip 1 sc, Partial dc in next sc, skip next 3 spaces, Partial dc in next sc, yarn over and pull through all 3 loops to dc2tog, ch 3, skip 1 space, sc in next space, ch 3, skip 1 sc, Partial dc in next sc, skip 2 sc, Partial dc in next sc, yarn over and pull through all 3 loops to dc2tog, ch 4, skip 1 space**, (sc, ch 3, sc) in next space; rep from * around, ending last rep at **, join with slip st to first sc, slip st in next space.

Rnd 4 Ch 1, (sc, ch 1, sc) in same space, *3 sc in next space, insert hook in same space and pull up a loop, insert hook in next space and pull up a loop, yarn over and pull through all 3 loops to sc2tog, 2 sc in same space, sc in next sc, 2 sc in next space, sc2tog over same and next space, 3 sc in same space**, (sc, ch 1, sc) in next space; rep from * around, ending last rep at **, join with slip st to first sc. Fasten off.

These four starry shapes were joined at their points, with a filler motif to bring them together, both structurally and visually. Where the filler motif meets two connected motifs, try working the connecting slip stitch over the existing join. Expanded, wouldn't this arrangement make a lovely shawl?

MOTIF #2   MOTIF #1

FILLER
MOTIF

MOTIF #3   MOTIF #4

FILLER MOTIF

Ch 4, join with slip st to form ring.

Rnd 1 Ch 1, *sc in ring, (ch 2, Picot-3) two times, ch 1, slip-st join between two motifs, ch 1, slip st in same st as last picot, ch 3, slip st in 3rd ch from hook, slip st in same st as last picot — *joining Triple Picot-3 made*, ch 2, Picot-3, slip st in base of corresponding picot on opposite side of leg, ch 2, sc in ring, ch 6, joining Triple Picot-3 in center ch-2 space of motif, slip st in bump on wrong side of each of next 6 ch; rep from * around, join with slip st to first sc. Fasten off.

FEATURES:

- JAYGo
- Filler motif
- Partial motif
- Slip-stitch join
- Connection in adjoining spaces
- Connection over existing join

Puff-stitch clusters take the place of picots on the legs of this square.

Dc2tog *(double crochet 2 together)* Yarn over, insert hook into indicated stitch or space and pull up a loop, yarn over, pull through 2 loops, yarn over, insert hook into same stitch and pull up a loop, yarn over and pull through 2 loops, yarn over and pull through all 3 loops on hook.

Dc3tog *(double crochet 3 together)* Yarn over, insert hook into indicated stitch or space and pull up a loop, yarn over, pull through 2 loops on hook, (yarn over, insert hook into same stitch and pull up a loop, yarn over and pull through 2 loops) two times, yarn over and pull through all 4 loops on hook.

Hdc-sctog *(half-double crochet–single crochet together)* Yarn over, insert hook into same space and pull up a loop, insert hook into next space and pull up a loop, yarn over and pull through all 4 loops on hook.

Partial dc *(partial double crochet)* Yarn over, insert hook into stitch or space indicated and pull up a loop, yarn over and pull through 2 loops on hook.

Puff Cluster Ch 4, (yarn over, insert hook into 4th ch from hook and pull up a loop) two times, yarn over and pull through all 5 loops on hook.

Sc2tog *(single crochet 2 stitches together)* (Insert hook into next st and pull up a loop) two times, yarn over and pull through all 3 loops on hook.

Sc-hdctog *(single crochet–half-double crochet together)* Insert hook into same space and pull up a loop, yarn over, insert hook into next space and pull up a loop, yarn over and pull through all 4 loops on hook.

Tr2tog *(treble crochet 2 together)* (Yarn over) two times, insert hook into indicated stitch or space and pull up a loop, (yarn over, pull through 2 loops) two times, (yarn over) two times, insert hook into same stitch or space and pull up a loop, (yarn over, pull through 2 loops) two times, yarn over and pull through all 3 loops on hook.

Ch 4, join with slip st to form ring.

Rnd 1 Ch 1, *sc in ring, ch 2, Puff Cluster, ch 2, (Puff Cluster) three times, slip st in base of 3rd cluster from hook, ch 2, Puff Cluster, slip st in base of opposite cluster, ch 2; rep from * three more times, join with slip st to first sc — 4 legs. Fasten off.

Rnd 2 Standing sc in ch-3 space of cluster at tip of any leg, ch 1, sc in same space, *ch 3, sc in ch-3 space of next cluster, ch 3, sc in next ch-2 space between clusters, ch 3, sc in ch-3 space of next cluster, ch 1, sc in ch-3 space of next cluster, ch 3, sc in next ch-2 space between clusters, ch 3, sc in ch-3 space of next cluster, ch 3**, (sc, ch 1, sc) in ch-3 space of next cluster; rep from * around, ending last rep at **, join with slip st to first sc, slip st in next space.

SQUARE: 4½" (11.5 CM)

Rnd 3 Ch 1, (sc, ch 1, sc) in same space, *ch 4, hdc in next sc, ch 2, Partial dc in next ch-3 space and in next sc, yarn over and pull through all 3 loops on hook to dc2tog, ch 3, dc3tog over next 3 spaces, ch 3, dc2tog over next sc and next ch-3 space, ch 2, hdc in next sc, ch 4, skip next ch-3 space**, (sc, ch 1, sc) in next ch-1 space; rep from * around, ending last rep at **, join with slip st to first sc, slip st in next space.

Rnd 4 Ch 1, (sc, ch 1, sc) in same space, *3 sc in next space, sc2tog over same and next space, sc in same space, sc-hdctog, dc in same space, tr2tog over same and next space, dc in same space, hdc-sctog, sc in same space, sc2tog over same and next spaces, 3 sc in same space**, (sc, ch 1, sc) in next space; rep from * around, ending last rep at **, join with slip st to first sc. Fasten off.

Here's another take on six picoted legs. How many variations can you invent?

HEXAGON: 6½" (16.5 CM)

Picot-3 Ch 3, slip st in 3rd ch from hook.

Standing dtr Beginning with a slip knot on hook, (yarn over) three times, insert hook into stitch or space indicated, pull up a loop (5 loops on hook), (yarn over and pull through 2 loops on hook) four times.

Triple Picot-3 (Ch 3, slip st in 3rd ch from hook) three times, slip st in base of first picot.

Ch 4, join with slip st to form ring.

Rnd 1 Ch 1, *sc in ring, ch 2, (Picot-3, ch 2) two times, Triple Picot-3, ch 2, (Picot-3, slip st in base of corresponding picot on opposite side of leg, ch 2) two times; rep from * five more times, join with slip st to first sc — 6 legs. Fasten off.

Rnd 2 Standing dtr in any sc from Rnd 1, *skip (ch 2, 1 Picot-3), tr in next ch-2 space between picots, skip 1 picot, dc in next ch-2 space between picots, ch 3, skip 1 picot, [dc, (ch 1, dc) two times] in next picot, ch 3, skip 1 picot, dc in next ch-2 space between picots, skip 1 picot, tr in next ch-2 space between picots, skip (1 picot, ch 2), dtr in next sc; rep from * around, omitting last dtr, join with slip st in top of first dtr.

Rnd 3 Ch 3 (counts as dc), *hdc in next tr, sc in next dc, 3 sc in next space, sc in next dc and space, (sc, ch 3, sc) in next dc, sc in next space and dc, 3 sc in next ch-3 space, sc in next dc, hdc in next tr, dc in next dtr; rep from * around, omitting last dc, join with slip st to top of ch-3. Fasten off.

Start with three picot legs, frame them with another color, then add a more-or-less free-floating picot swag. Now we're really getting somewhere!

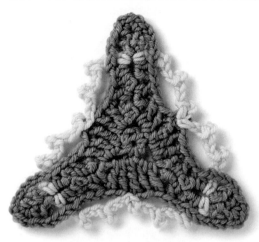

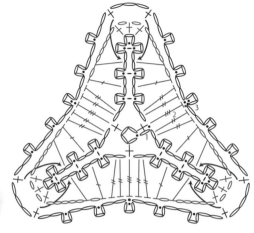

TRIANGLE: 4" (10 CM)

Picot-3 Ch 3, slip st in 3rd ch from hook.

Standing dtr Beginning with a slip knot on hook, (yarn over) three times, insert hook into stitch or space indicated, pull up a loop (5 loops on hook), (yarn over and pull through 2 loops on hook) four times.

Tight Picot-3 Ch 3, insert hook from top to bottom through top and side edge of sc just made and pull a loop through to form slip st.

Triple Picot-3 (Ch 3, slip st in 3rd ch from hook) three times, slip st in base of first picot.

Ch 4, join with slip st to form ring.

Rnd 1 Ch 1, *sc in ring, ch 2, (Picot-3, ch 2) two times, Triple Picot-3, ch 2, (Picot-3, slip st in base of corresponding picot on opposite side of leg, ch 2) two times; rep from * two more times, join with slip st to first sc — 3 legs. Fasten off.

Rnd 2 Standing dtr in any sc from Rnd 1, *2 tr in next ch-2 space, skip 1 picot, dc in next ch-2 space between picots, ch 1, skip 1 picot, hdc in next ch-2 space between picots, ch 5, skip 1 picot, [sc, (ch 1, sc) two times] in next picot, ch 5, skip 1 picot, hdc in next ch-2 space between picots, ch 1, skip 1 picot, dc in next ch-2 space between picots, 2 tr in next ch-2 space, dtr in next sc; rep from * around, omitting last dtr, join with slip st in top of first dtr. Fasten off.

Rnd 3 Slip st in same dtr, *Tight Picot-3, (ch 2, Picot-3) two times, ch 2; working behind Rnd-2 sts, sc in Rnd-1 ch-2 space at base of Triple Picot-3, ch 3, working behind Triple Picot-3, sc in next Rnd-1 ch-2 space at base of Triple Picot-3, ch 2, (Picot-3, ch 2) two times, slip st in next dtr; rep from * around. Fasten off.

Wrong side

connect

Here's another set of shapes that are connected before the final round. The six three-sided shapes create an almost circular fabric when presented alone; filler motifs might be appropriate for a larger fabric with additional motifs.

To make the connections, on Round 2 work (ch 2, slip st in adjacent ch-5 space of previous motif, ch 2) in place of the ch-5 loops as needed. You may choose to stitch and connect all the motifs through Round 2, then add Round 3 to all of them after they have been connected. It's your choice!

FEATURES:

- JAYGo
- Connection on next-to-last round
- Slip-stitch join
- Connection in adjoining spaces

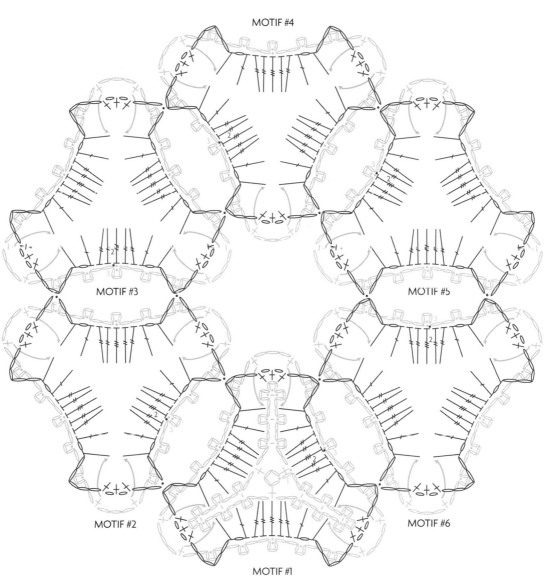

MOTIF #4

MOTIF #3

MOTIF #5

MOTIF #2

MOTIF #6

MOTIF #1

Here's a slightly fancier square, nicely framed with single crochet and picoted corners.

SQUARE: 4" (10 CM)

Partial dtr *(partial double treble)* (Yarn over) three times, insert hook into stitch or space indicated and pull up a loop, (yarn over and pull through 2 loops on hook) three times.

Partial tr *(partial treble)* (Yarn over) twice, insert hook into stitch or space indicated and pull up a loop, (yarn over and pull through 2 loops on hook) two times.

Picot-3 Ch 3, slip st in 3rd ch from hook.

Sc3tog *(single crochet 3 stitches together)* (Insert hook into next st and pull up a loop) three times, yarn over and pull through all 4 loops on hook.

Tight Picot-3 Ch 3, insert hook from top to bottom through top and side edge of sc just made and pull a loop through to form slip st.

Triple Picot-3 (Ch 3, slip st in 3rd ch from hook) three times, slip st in base of first picot.

Ch 6, join with slip st to form ring.

Rnd 1 Ch 1, *sc in ring, ch 2, (Picot-3, ch 2) two times, Triple Picot-3, ch 2, (Picot-3, slip st in base of corresponding picot in opposite side of leg, ch 2) two times, sc in ring, ch 2, Picot-3, ch 2, Triple Picot-3, ch 2, Picot-3, slip st in corresponding picot in opposite side of leg, ch 2; rep from * three more times, join with slip st to first sc — 4 long legs and 4 short legs. Fasten off.

Rnd 2 Standing sc in center picot of Triple Picot-3 on any long leg, 2 sc in same picot, *ch 3, dc in next ch-2 space between picots, Partial tr in next ch-2 space between picots, Partial dtr in next sc, skip 1 ch-2 space, Partial tr in next ch-2 space between picots, yarn over and pull through all 4 loops on hook, ch 3, skip 1 picot, sc in next picot, ch 3, Partial tr in next ch-2 space between picots, Partial dtr in next sc, skip 1 ch-2 space, Partial tr in next ch-2 space between picots, yarn over and pull through all 4 loops on hook, dc in next space, ch 3, skip 1 picot**, 3 sc in next picot; rep from * around, ending last rep at **, join with slip st to first sc.

Rnd 3 Ch 1, sc in same st, *(sc, Tight Picot-3, sc) in next sc, sc in next sc, 3 sc in next 2 spaces, ch 3, 3 sc in next 2 spaces, sc in next sc; rep from * around, omitting last sc, join with slip st to first sc. Fasten off.

[**TIP**] If this motif is going to be joined to others, try using a plain ch-3 in place of the corner Tight Picot-3s.

wheels and shells

88

Rnds 1 and 2 A ■   **Rnd 3 B** ■   **Rnds 4 and 5 C** ■

Here the first two rounds create the inner circles of the square. Round 3 is the center circle, while Rounds 4 and 5 create the "frame." Omit Round 5 for a squarer square.

SQUARE: 5" (12.5 CM)

Dc3tog *(double crochet 3 together)* Yarn over, insert hook into indicated stitch or space and pull up a loop, yarn over, pull through 2 loops on hook, (yarn over, insert hook into same stitch and pull up a loop, yarn over and pull through 2 loops) two times, yarn over and pull through all 4 loops on hook.

Ch 48, join with slip st to first ch, being careful not to twist chain.

Rnd 1 Ch 1, sc in first ch, *skip 2 ch, 7 dc in next ch — *shell made*, skip 2 ch, sc in next ch, skip 2 ch, 9 dc in next ch — *corner shell made*, skip 2 ch, sc in next ch; rep from * around, omitting last sc; do not join. Turn.

Rnd 2 *Rnd 2 is worked on the other side of the beginning chain.* Slip st over join from end of starting chain, *(dc, dc3tog, dc) in base of corner shell, slip st over next sc in Rnd 1, shell in ch at base of shell**, slip st over next sc in Rnd 1; rep from * around, ending last rep at **, slip st over beginning slip st. Fasten off.

Rnd 3 Begin with sliding loop. Ch 3 (counts as dc), 2 dc in ring, flat join to center dc of any

Rnd-2 shell, (4 dc in ring, flat join to center dc of next Rnd-2 shell) three times, dc in ring, join with slip st to top of ch-3. Fasten off.

Rnd 4 *Rnd 4 is worked around outside of Rnd 1.* Standing sc in 4th dc of any shell, *ch 3, dc under two strands formed by base of Rnd-2 slip st, ch 3, skip 3 dc, sc in next dc, ch 3, skip 1 dc, sc in next dc, ch 3, skip 3 dc, dc under two strands formed by base of Rnd-2 slip st, ch 3, skip 3 dc, sc in next dc; rep from * around, omitting last sc, join with slip st to first sc.

Rnd 5 *7 dc in next dc, slip st in next sc, 7 dc in corner ch-space, slip st in next sc, 7 dc in next dc, slip st in next sc; rep from * around, working last slip st in first slip st. Fasten off.

This sample features only Rounds 1–3 of Motif 88. The motifs are joined on the very first round, with a flat join at the peaks of the center shells and at adjacent stitches of the corner shells. Flat joins mimic the appearance of the joining points on all of the circles.

[WHEELS AND SHELLS]

Strong shell and circular elements combined with post stitches create these Catherine-wheel motifs. Some of these tend to be dense and heavy, so be sure to use a fiber-and-hook combination that allows for a pleasing, not-too-stiff fabric. Connecting these motifs at the peak of the shells is the obvious choice, but leaving off the final round to create straighter sides is another option.

MOTIF #2

MOTIF #1

MOTIF #4

MOTIF #3

MOTIF #1

Work Rounds 1–3 of Motif 88.

MOTIF #2

Ch 48, join with slip st to first ch, being careful not to twist chain.

Rnd 1 Ch 1, sc in first ch, *skip 2 ch, 7 dc in next ch — *shell made*, skip 2 ch, sc in next ch, skip 2 ch, 9 dc in next ch — *corner shell made*, skip 2 ch, sc in next ch; rep from * once more, skip 2 ch, make shell, skip 2 ch, sc in next ch, skip 2 ch, 7 dc in next ch, flat join to 3rd dc of any corner shell of adjoining motif, 2 dc in same ch of current motif, skip 2 ch, sc in next ch, skip 2 ch, 4 dc in next ch, flat join to 4th dc of next shell on adjoining motif, 3 dc in same ch of current motif, skip 2 ch, sc in next ch, 3 dc in next ch, flat join to 7th dc of next corner shell of adjoining motif, 6 dc in same ch of current motif, skip 2 ch; do not join. Turn.

Rnds 2 and 3 Work as for Rnds 2 and 3 of Motif 88.

Continue to add additional motifs in this manner, joining each motif to previous motifs at corner shells and at center of side shells.

FEATURES:
- JAYGo
- **Connection on first round**
- **Flat join**
- **Connection in adjoining stitches**

Put tall stitches into one place, and they fan out into shell-shaped groups. Put a large shell on top of a large cluster, and you get a circle. That's how the next several motifs begin. This square is the motif used in the Summer Baby Blanket on page 238.

SQUARE: 5½" (14 CM)

BPsc *(back post single crochet)* Yarn over, insert hook from back to front to back around post of stitch indicated and pull up a loop, yarn over and pull through 2 loops on hook.

BPtr *(back post treble crochet)* (Yarn over) two times, insert hook from back to front to back around post of stitch indicated and pull up a loop (yarn over and pull through 2 loops on hook) three times.

Partial tr *(partial treble)* (Yarn over) twice, insert hook into stitch or space indicated and pull up a loop, (yarn over and pull through 2 loops on hook) two times.

Standing BPsc Place slip knot on hook, insert hook from back to front to back around post of stitch indicated and pull up a loop, yarn over and pull through 2 loops on hook.

Standing BPtr Place slip knot on hook, (yarn over) two times, insert hook from back to front to back around post of stitch indicated and pull up a loop (yarn over and pull through 2 loops on hook) three times.

Note: When instructed to work into a cluster, work into the ch-1 st at the top of the cluster throughout.

Ch 5, join with slip st to form ring.

Rnd 1 *Ch 3, 3 Partial tr in ring, yarn over and pull through 4 loops on hook, ch 1 to close, ch 3, slip st in ring; rep from * three more times — 4 clusters.

Rnd 2 Skip next ch-3 space, *10 tr in top of next cluster — *corner shell made*, slip st into ring over Rnd-1 slip st; rep from * three more times. Fasten off.

Rnd 3 Standing BPtr around the post of any slip st between corner shells, *ch 2, skip 2 tr, BPsc around next tr, ch 1, skip 1 tr, BPsc around next tr, ch 3, BPsc around next tr, ch 1, skip 1 tr, BPsc around next tr**, ch 2, skip 2 tr, BPtr around next slip st; rep from * around, ending last rep at **, join with dc to first tr.

Rnd 4 *7 tr in next tr, skip 1 space, sc in next space, 9 tr in corner space, sc in next space; rep from * around, join with slip st to first tr. Fasten off.

Rnd 5 Standing BPsc in 8th tr of any 9-tr shell, ch 1, *BPtr around next sc, ch 2, skip 2 tr, BPsc around next tr, ch 1, skip 1 tr, BPsc around next tr, ch 2, skip 2 tr, BPtr around next sc, (ch 1, skip 1 tr, BPsc around next tr) two times, ch 3, skip 1 tr **, (BPsc around next tr, ch 1, skip 1 tr) two times, rep from * around, ending last rep at **, BPsc around next tr, skip 1 tr, join with sc to first sc.

Rnd 6 Ch 1, sc in space formed by joining sc, *(7 tr in next tr, skip 1 space, sc in next space) two times, 9 tr in corner space, sc in next space; rep from * around, omitting last sc, join with slip st to first sc. Fasten off.

90

Rnds 1, 2, 5, and 6 A ■   **Rnds 3 and 4** B ▨

Take the shell idea and combine it with post stitches, and you've introduced an angular element not evident on the previous square. Some call this Bavarian crochet, but whatever you call it, it's fascinating! See connection on page 204.

BPslip st *(back post slip stitch)* Insert hook from back to front to back around post of stitch indicated and pull up a loop and pull through st and loop on hook.

Partial BPtr *(partial back post treble)* (Yarn over) two times, insert hook back to front to back around post of designated stitch and pull up a loop, (yarn over and pull through 2 loops on hook) two times.

Partial tr *(partial treble)* (Yarn over) twice, insert hook into stitch or space indicated and pull up a loop, (yarn over and pull through 2 loops on hook) two times.

Standing BPslip st *(standing back post slip stitch)* Place slip knot on hook, insert hook from back to front to back around post of stitch indicated and pull up a loop and pull through st and loop on hook.

SQUARE: 5½" (14 CM)

Note: When instructed to work into a cluster, work into the ch-1 st at the top of the cluster throughout. To work a BPtr around a slip stitch, insert hook from back to front to back around the vertical portion of the slip stitch as it comes up from the center ring.

Ch 5, join with slip st to form ring.

Rnd 1 *Ch 3, 3 Partial tr in ring, yarn over and pull through 4 loops on hook, ch 1 to close, ch 3, slip st in ring; rep from * three more times — 4 clusters.

continued on next page

WHEELS AND SHELLS

Rnd 2 *Skip next ch-3 space, 10 tr in top of next cluster — *corner shell made*, slip st into ring over Rnd-1 slip st; rep from * three more times. Fasten off.

Rnd 3 Standing BPslip st around 8th tr of any corner shell, *ch 3; Partial BPtr around same st, Partial BPtr around next 2 tr, Partial BPtr around next slip st, Partial BPtr around next 3 tr of next corner shell, yarn over and pull through all 8 loops on hook, ch 1 to close — *valley cluster made*; ch 3, BPslip st around next tr, ch 3; Partial BPtr around same st, Partial BPtr around next 3 tr, yarn over and pull through 5 loops on hook, ch 1 to close — *corner cluster made*; ch 3, BPslip st around next tr; rep from * around.

Rnd 4 Skip next ch-3 space, *6 tr in next valley cluster — *shell made*, BPslip st around 4th tr from Rnd-2 corner shell, 10 tr in next corner cluster — *corner shell made*, BPslip st around 8th tr from Rnd-2 corner shell; rep from * around. Fasten off.

Rnd 5 BPsc in 8th tr of any corner group, ch 1, *BPtr in next sc, ch 2, skip 2 tr, BPsc in next tr, ch 1, skip 1 tr, BPsc in next tr, ch 2, skip 2 tr, BPtr in next sc, (ch 1, skip 1 tr, BPsc in next tr) two times, ch 3, skip 1 tr**, (BPsc in next tr, ch 1, skip 1 tr) two times; rep from * around, ending last rep at **, BPsc in next tr, skip 1 tr, join with sc to first sc.

Rnd 6 *6 tr in next valley cluster — *shell made*, BPslip st around 4th tr from Rnd-4 shell, shell in next valley cluster, BPslip st around 4th tr from Rnd-4 corner shell, corner shell in next corner cluster, BPslip st around 8th tr from Rnd-4 corner shell; rep from * around. Fasten off.

[**TIP**]

Working the BPslip st around the post of the stitch two rounds below on Rounds 4 and 6 creates a float of color at the point of the squares. If you prefer not to have this, work the slip stitch around the post of the stitch one round below.

Gentle scallops soften the lines of this shape, making it barely recognizable as a triangle.

BPsc *(back post single crochet)* See page 200

BPtr *(back post treble crochet)* See page 200

Partial tr *(partial treble)* See page 200

Standing BPtr *(standing back post treble)*
Place slip knot on hook, (yarn over) two times, insert hook from back to front to back around post of stitch indicated and pull up a loop (yarn over and pull through 2 loops on hook) three times.

Note: When instructed to work into a cluster, work into the ch-1 st at the top of the cluster throughout.

Ch 5, join with slip st to form ring.

TRIANGLE: 5½" (14 CM)

Rnd 1 *Ch 3, 4 Partial tr in ring, yarn over and pull through 5 loops on hook, ch 1 to close, ch 3, slip st in ring; rep from * two more times — 3 clusters.

Rnd 2 *Skip next ch-3 space, (3 dtr, 5 tr, 3 dtr) in top of next cluster — *corner shell made*, slip st into ring over Rnd-1 slip st; rep from * three more times. Fasten off.

Rnd 3 Standing BPtr around any slip st between corner shells, *ch 3, skip 2 dtr, BPsc around next dtr, ch 1, skip 1 tr, BPsc around next tr, ch 5, skip 1 tr, BPsc around next tr, ch 1, skip 1 tr, BPsc around next dtr**, ch 3, skip 2 dtr, BPtr around next slip st; rep from * around, ending last rep at **, join with dc in first tr.

Rnd 4 *7 tr in next tr, skip 1 space, sc in next space, 11 tr in corner ch-5 space, sc in next space; rep from * around, join with slip st to first tr. Fasten off.

Rnd 5 Standing BPtr in first sc of any side, *ch 2, skip 1 tr, (BPsc around next tr, ch 1, skip 1 tr) three times, ch 1, BPtr around next sc, skip 2 tr, BPsc around next tr, ch 1, skip 1 tr, BPsc around next tr, ch 3, skip 1 tr, BPsc around next tr, ch 1, skip 1 tr, BPsc around next tr, skip 2 tr**, ch 2, BPtr around next sc; rep from * around, ending last rep at **, join with dc in first tr.

Rnd 6 *9 tr in next tr, skip 1 sc, sc in next sc, skip 1 sc, 9 tr in next tr, skip 1 space, sc in next space, 9 tr in corner space, sc in next space; rep from * around, join with slip st to first tr. Fasten off.

connect

Motif 89

This sample connects the motifs on Round 5, omitting Round 6 to create straighter sides. After the motifs have all been connected, a border is added, mimicking the "missing" Round 6. If you like, you could use this 2×2 arrangement as a motif (with the border serving as the final round), then connect it to other mega-motifs.

Each connection is made with the final ch-1 at the top of valley clusters and corner clusters. Make the clusters up to the point of the final ch-1, then insert the hook into the top of adjacent cluster, yarn over and pull through cluster and through loop on hook to join, as follows:

Make Motif #1 through Rnd 5 and fasten off.

Make Motif #2 through Rnd 4.

Rnd 5 (Joining Rnd) Join with BPslip st around 8th tr of any 9-tr shell, *(ch 3, make valley cluster, ch 3, BPslip st around next tr) two times, ch 3**, make corner cluster, ch 3, BPslip st around next tr; rep from * once more, then repeat from * to ** once; make corner cluster omitting final ch-1, slip-stitch join in top of

any corner cluster from Motif #1 — *corner cluster join made*, ch 3, BPslip st around next tr, (ch 3, make valley cluster omitting final ch-1, slip-st join in top of next adjacent valley cluster on previous square — *valley cluster join made*, ch 3, BPslip st around next tr) two times, ch 3, make corner cluster join, ch 3, join with slip st to first slip st. Fasten off.

Join Motifs #3 and #4 in this manner, joining center corner clusters around previous joins.

BORDER

Round 6 of the motif has been expanded and adapted to become a complementary border, as follows:

Standing sc in first slip st of any side, *(shell in next valley cluster, sc in next slip st) two times, (2 dtr, 4 tr, 2 dtr) in next corner join — *large shell made*, sc in next slip st, (shell in next valley cluster, sc in next slip st) two times, corner shell in next corner cluster, sc in next slip st; rep from * around, omitting last sc, join with slip st to first sc. Fasten off.

FEATURES:

- JAYGo
- Adaption of last round
- Slip-stitch join
- Connection in adjoining stitches
- Complementary border round

MOTIF #1   BORDER

MOTIF #2

MOTIF #3   MOTIF #4

Post stitches on the second round of this hexagon evoke a three-dimensional flower. Try a series of these around the bottom of a little girl's dress.

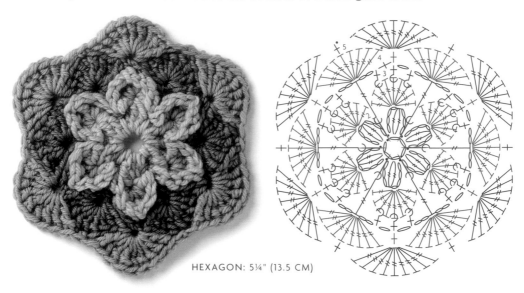

HEXAGON: 5¼" (13.5 CM)

BPsc *(back post single crochet)* Yarn over, insert hook from back to front to back around post of stitch indicated and pull up a loop, yarn over and pull through 2 loops on hook.

BPtr *(back post treble crochet)* (Yarn over) two times, insert hook from back to front to back around post of stitch indicated and pull up a loop (yarn over and pull through 2 loops on hook) three times.

Partial tr *(partial treble)* (Yarn over) twice, insert hook into stitch or space indicated and pull up a loop, (yarn over and pull through 2 loops on hook) two times.

Standing BPsc Place slip knot on hook, insert hook from back to front to back around post of stitch indicated and pull up a loop, yarn over and pull through 2 loops on hook.

Note: When instructed to work into a cluster, work into the ch-1 st at the top of the cluster throughout.

Ch 6, join with slip st to form ring.

Rnd 1 *Ch 3, 2 Partial tr in ring, yarn over and pull through 3 loops on hook, ch 1 to close, ch 3, slip st in ring; rep from * five more times — 6 clusters.

Rnd 2 *Skip next ch-3 space, 9 tr in top of next cluster — *corner shell made*, slip st into ring over Rnd-1 slip st; rep from * around. Fasten off.

Rnd 3 Standing BPsc around 7th tr of any corner shell, *ch 2, skip 2 tr, BPtr around next

slip st, ch 2, skip 2 tr, BPsc around next tr**, (ch 1, skip 1 tr, BPsc around next tr) two times; rep from * around, ending last rep at **, ch 2, skip 2 tr, BPsc around next tr, ch 1, skip 1 tr, BPsc around next tr, join with sc in first sc.

Rnd 4 *9 tr in next tr, skip 1 sc, sc in next sc; rep from * around, join with slip st to first tr. Fasten off.

Rnd 5 Standing sc in center tr of any 9-tr group, *9 tr in next sc, sc in center tr of next 9-tr group; rep from * around, omitting last sc, join with slip st to first sc. Fasten off.

Here, the three-dimensionality moves outward from the flower's center.

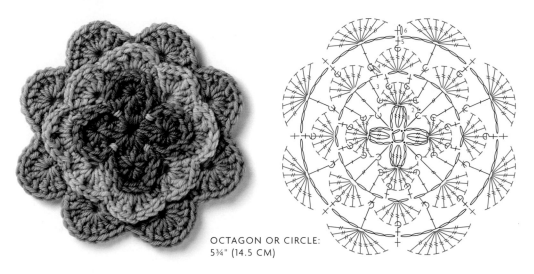

OCTAGON OR CIRCLE:
5¾" (14.5 CM)

BPdc *(back post double crochet)* Yarn over, insert hook from back to front to back around post of stitch indicated and pull up a loop, (yarn over and pull through 2 loops on hook) two times.

BPsc *(back post single crochet)* Insert hook from back to front to back around post of stitch indicated and pull up a loop, yarn over and pull through 2 loops on hook.

BPtr *(back post treble crochet)* (Yarn over) two times, insert hook from back to front to back around post of stitch indicated and pull up a loop (yarn over and pull through 2 loops on hook) three times.

Partial tr *(partial treble)* (Yarn over) twice, insert hook into stitch or space indicated and pull up a loop, (yarn over and pull through 2 loops on hook) two times.

Standing BPsc Place slip knot on hook, insert hook from back to front to back around post of stitch indicated and pull up a loop, yarn over and pull through 2 loops on hook.

Ch 5, join with slip st to form ring.

Rnd 1 *Ch 3, 3 Partial tr in ring, yarn over and pull through 4 loops on hook, ch 1 to close, ch 3, slip st in ring; rep from * three more times — 4 clusters.

Rnd 2 *Skip next ch-3 space, 10 tr in top of next cluster — *corner shell made*, slip st into ring over Rnd-1 slip st; rep from * three more times. Fasten off.

Rnd 3 Standing BPdc around 9th tr of any corner shell, *ch 1, BPtr around next slip st, ch 1, skip 1 tr, BPdc around next tr, ch 1, skip 1 tr, BPsc around next tr, ch 2, skip 2 tr, BPsc around next tr**, ch 1, skip 1 tr, BPdc around

next tr; rep from * around, ending last rep at **, join with sc to first dc.

Rnd 4 Ch 1, sc in space formed by joining sc, *7 tr in next tr, skip 1 space, sc in next space, 7 tr in corner ch-2 space, sc in next space; rep from * around, omitting last sc. Fasten off.

Rnd 5 Standing BPsc in center tr of any 7-tr group, *ch 3, BPdc in next sc, ch 3, BPsc in center tr of next 7-tr group; rep from * around, omitting last BPsc, join with slip st to first sc.

Rnd 6 Ch 1, sc in same st, *9 tr in next dc, sc in next sc; rep from * around, omitting last sc, join with slip st in first sc. Fasten off.

WHEELS AND SHELLS

94

Rnd 1 and Border Rnd 3 A ■ ■	**Rnd 2** B ■ ■ ■ ■ ■
Border Rnds 1 and 2 and Filler C ■	

This motif and the next two consist of smaller motifs that are first joined to each other, creating a mini garden of blooms that can be varied in any number of ways. Use the small motif by itself as a Quick & Easy option. The filler in the middle of the flowers in this square may seem a bit tricky to work; omit it if you don't care about a large center hole. See pages 212–213 for a connection.

SQUARE: 5" (12.5 CM)

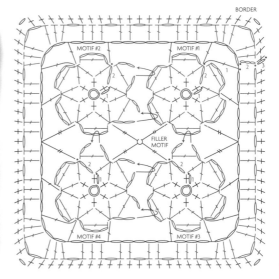

[INNER CONNECTIVITY]

Connecting shapes doesn't have to happen between motifs. You can connect shapes within motifs as well. These shapes show how smaller, independent motifs can be merged to create a larger whole. At this point, perhaps you have worked through all of the connected samples, and have your own ideas of ways to create inner-connected shapes. Work with as many smaller connected units as you choose, then use the techniques you have learned to find the best methods for your unique design.

Dc2tog *(double crochet 2 together)* Yarn over, insert hook into indicated stitch or space and pull up a loop, yarn over, pull through 2 loops, yarn over, insert hook into next stitch and pull up a loop, yarn over and pull through 2 loops, yarn over and pull through all 3 loops on hook.

Partial tr *(partial treble)* (Yarn over) twice, insert hook into stitch or space indicated and pull up a loop, (yarn over and pull through 2 loops on hook) two times.

Standing Partial tr *(standing partial treble)* Starting with a slip knot on hook, (yarn over) twice, insert hook into stitch or space indicated and pull up a loop, (yarn over and pull through 2 loops on hook) two times.

Tr2tog *(treble crochet 2 together)* (Yarn over) two times, insert hook into indicated stitch or space and pull up a loop, (yarn over, pull through 2 loops) two times, (yarn over) two times, insert hook into next stitch or space and pull up a loop, (yarn over, pull through 2 loops) two times, yarn over and pull through all 3 loops on hook.

FLOWERS

Begin with sliding loop.

Rnd 1 Ch 1, 6 sc in ring, join with slip st to first sc — 6 sc.

Rnd 2 Ch 2, dc in next sc (counts as dc2tog), ch 4, dc in 4th ch from hook — *petal made*; *dc2tog over same and next sc, make petal; rep from * around, join with slip st to first st. Fasten off.

Make three more flowers, joining petals to adjacent petals of previous motif(s) on Rnd 2 (according to diagram), as follows: ch 2, flat join in ch-4 space of previous petal, ch 2, dc in 4th ch from hook to complete petal.

FILLER MOTIF

Standing Partial tr in any free cluster in the opening between four small flowers, Partial tr in each of next 3 free clusters, yarn over and pull through all 5 loops on hook. Fasten off.

BORDER

Rnd 1 Referring to diagram for beginning of rnd, (standing dc, ch 3, dc) in first cluster, *ch 3, dc in next cluster, ch 5; working around next motif, dc in next cluster, ch 3, (dc, ch 3, dc) in next cluster, ch 3, dc in next cluster, ch 3, tr2tog over next cluster and over next cluster on next motif; ch 3, dc in next cluster, ch 3**, (dc, ch 3, dc) in next cluster; rep from * to ** once more; join with slip st to first dc, slip st in next space.

Rnd 2 Ch 3 (counts as dc), (2 dc, ch 2, 3 dc) in same space, *ch 1, 3 dc in next space, ch 1, (2 dc, ch 1) two times in next space, 3 dc in next space, ch 1, (3 dc, ch 2, 3 dc) in corner space, ch 1, 3 dc in next space, ch 1, (2 dc, ch 1) in next 2 spaces, 3 dc in next space, ch 1**, (3 dc, ch 2, 3 dc) in corner space; rep from * to ** once more; join with slip st to top of ch-3.

Rnd 3 Ch 1, sc in each dc and ch-1 space around, placing (sc, ch 1, sc) in each corner space. Fasten off.

Flower One each in A, B, and C ■ ▢ ■   **Border** D ▢

You can adapt this method of adding a border to any number of joined flowers. Here's a three-flower version of Motif 94, with a border that creates a rounded triangular shape.

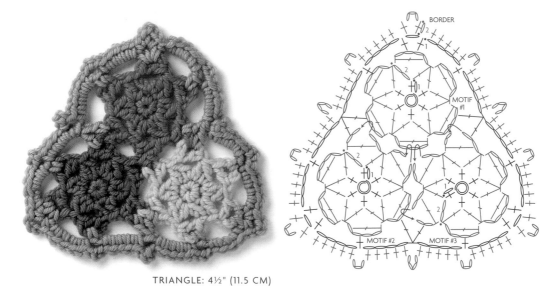

TRIANGLE: 4½" (11.5 CM)

Dc2tog *(double crochet 2 together)* Yarn over, insert hook into indicated stitch or space and pull up a loop, yarn over, pull through 2 loops, yarn over, insert hook into next stitch and pull up a loop, yarn over and pull through 2 loops, yarn over and pull through all 3 loops on hook.

FLOWERS
Begin with sliding loop.

Rnd 1 Ch 1, 6 sc in ring, join with slip st to first sc — 6 sc.

Rnd 2 Ch 2, dc in next sc (counts as dc2tog), ch 4, dc in 4th ch from hook — *petal made*; *dc2tog over same and next sc, make petal; rep from * around, join with slip st to first st. Fasten off.

Make two more motifs, joining petals to adjacent petals of previous motif(s) on Rnd 2 (according to diagram) as follows: ch 2, flat join to ch-space of previous petal, ch 2, dc in 4th ch from hook to complete petal.

BORDER
Rnd 1 Standing sc in ch-space of corner petal of any Flower, ch 1, sc in same space, *ch 4, sc in next petal-space, ch 4, dc2tog over next 2 petal-spaces, ch 4, sc in next petal-space, ch 4**, (sc, ch 1, sc) in next petal; rep from * around, ending last rep at **, join with slip st to first sc, slip st in next space.

Rnd 2 Ch 1, (sc, ch 3, sc) in same space, *5 sc in next space, ch 3, 5 sc in next space, ch 4, 5 sc in next space, ch 3, 5 sc in next space**, (sc, ch 3, sc) in next space; rep from * around, ending last rep at **, join with slip st to first sc. Fasten off.

A central small motif is surrounded by other identical motifs and then framed with a final round to create a large, rounded hexagon. Omit the framing round for a more organic look.

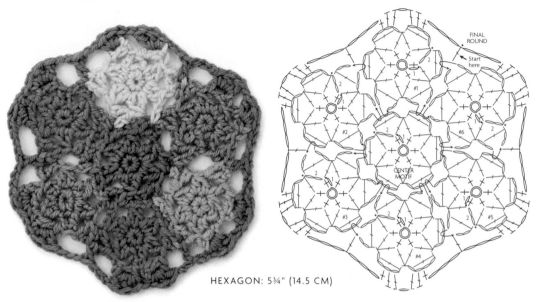

HEXAGON: 5¾" (14.5 CM)

Dc2tog *(double crochet 2 together)* Yarn over, insert hook into indicated stitch or space and pull up a loop, yarn over, pull through 2 loops, yarn over, insert hook into next stitch and pull up a loop, yarn over and pull through 2 loops, yarn over and pull through all 3 loops on hook.

CENTER MOTIF

Begin with sliding loop.

Rnd 1 Ch 1, 6 sc in ring, join with slip st to first sc — 6 sc.

Rnd 2 Ch 2, dc in next sc, ch 4, dc in 4th ch from hook — *petal made*; *dc2tog over same and next sc, make petal; rep from * around, join with slip st to first st. Fasten off.

FIRST OUTER MOTIF

Begin with sliding loop.

Rnd 1 Ch 1, 6 sc in ring, join with slip st to first sc — 6 sc.

Rnd 2 Ch 2, dc in next sc (counts as dc2tog), ch 4, dc in 4th ch from hook — *petal made*; *dc2tog over same and next sc, make petal; rep from * once more, dc2tog over same and next sc, ch 2, flat join to ch-space of any petal of Center Motif, ch 2, dc in 4th ch from hook — *petal join made*, dc2tog over same and next sc, petal join to next petal of Center Motif, dc2tog over same and next sc, make petal, join with slip st to top of first st. Fasten off.

MIDDLE OUTER MOTIFS

Begin with sliding loop.

Rnd 1 Ch 1, 6 sc in ring, join with slip st to first sc — 6 sc.

continued on next page

Rnd 2 Ch 2, dc in next sc (counts as dc2tog), make petal, *dc2tog over same and next sc, make petal; rep from * once more, dc2tog over same and next sc, petal join to next petal of Center Motif, dc2tog over same and next sc, petal join to next petal of Center Motif (previous motif was joined in this same space), dc2tog over same and next sc, petal join in next free petal of previous motif, join with slip st to top of first st. Fasten off.

FINAL OUTER MOTIF
Begin with sliding loop.

Rnd 1 Ch 1, 6 sc in ring, join with slip st to first sc — 6 sc.

Rnd 2 Ch 2, dc in next sc (counts as dc2tog), (make petal, dc2tog over same and next sc), two times, petal join to last petal of Outer Motif #1, dc2tog over same and next sc, petal join to next petal of Center Motif (Outer Motif #1 was joined in this same space), dc2tog over same and next sc, petal join to next petal of Center Motif (previous motif was joined in this same space), dc2tog over same and next sc, petal join in next free petal of previous motif, join with slip st to top of first st. Fasten off.

FINAL ROUND
Standing dc in side of any flat join between outer motifs, *ch 3, (sc, 2 dc) in ch-space of next petal, ch 1, (2 dc, sc) in ch-space of next petal, ch 3, dc in side of next flat join; rep from * around, omitting last dc, join with slip st to first dc. Fasten off.

Expand Motif 94 to create a larger motif, then add a frame around the whole thing. This example is four flowers wide by two flowers tall, but it would work equally well as a 4×4, or any other arrangement. After the flowers are connected and the filler motifs added, make the frame around the entire piece. The final round can be connected to other straight edges with any seaming or JAYGo method. For variation, use multiple colors for the smaller flowers, with the filler the same color as the border.

Work a total of 8 flowers as for Motif 94, connecting as you go on Rnd 2 and creating a rectangle four flowers wide by two flowers high. Work three Filler Motifs as for Motif 94.

BORDER
Rnd 1 Referring to diagram for beginning of round, (standing dc, ch 3, dc) in first cluster, *[ch 3, dc in next cluster, ch 5; working around next motif, dc in next cluster] three times, ch 3, (dc, ch 3, dc) in next cluster, ch 3, dc in next cluster, ch 3, tr2tog over next cluster and over next cluster on next motif; ch 3, dc in next cluster, ch 3**, (dc, ch 3, dc) in next cluster; rep from * to ** once more; join with slip st to first dc, slip st in next space.

Rnd 2 Ch 3 (counts as dc), (2 dc, ch 2, 3 dc) in same space, *ch 1, 3 dc in next space, ch 1, [(2 dc, ch 1) two times in next space, 3 dc in next space, ch 1] three times, (3 dc, ch 2, 3 dc) in corner space, ch 1, 3 dc in next space, ch 1, (2 dc, ch 1) in next 2 spaces, 3 dc in next space, ch 1**, (3 dc, ch 2, 3 dc) in corner space; rep from * to ** once more; join with slip st to top of ch-3.

Rnd 3 Ch 1, sc in each dc and ch-1 space around, placing (sc, ch 1, sc) in each corner space. Fasten off.

Motif 94   **Rnds 1 and 2** A ■ ■

Filler and Border Rnd 3 B ■

Border Rnds 1 and 2 C ■ ■

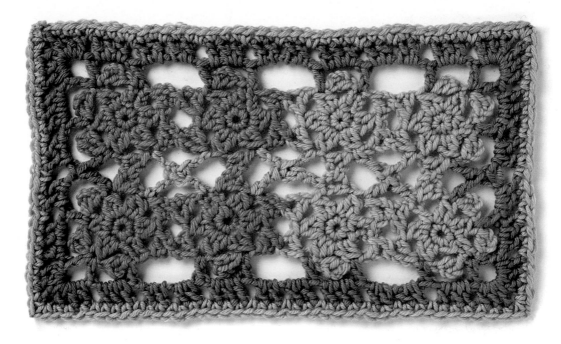

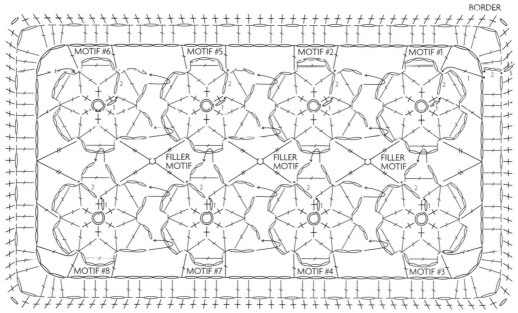

FEATURES:

- (Internal) JAYGo
- Flat join
- Filler motifs
- Connection in adjoining spaces

INNER CONNECTIVITY

Let's start with a single ring, then work the main motif around the inset ring to create an almost free-floating piece. The final round connects to both the main motif and the inset ring.

HEXAGON: 4¾" (12 CM)

NOTE: REFER TO TEXT FOR CLARIFICATION OF RND 2

MAIN MOTIF

INSET RING

Ch 16, join with slip st to form ring.

Rnd 1 Ch 3 (counts as dc), 29 dc in ring, join with slip st to top of ch-3 — 30 dc. Fasten off.

MAIN MOTIF

Begin with sliding loop.

Rnd 1 Ch 3 (counts as dc), 11 dc in ring, join with slip st to top of ch-3 — 12 dc.

Rnd 2 Place Inset Ring around Rnd 1; *working behind Inset Ring, ch 12, dc in 8th ch from hook — *open loop made*, working in front of Inset Ring, ch 4, skip 1 dc, slip st in next st from Rnd 1, ch 12, slip st in 8th ch from hook, working behind Inset Ring, ch 4, skip 1 dc, slip st in next st behind Inset Ring; rep from * around. Fasten off.

Rnd 3 Standing dc in any open loop, 12 dc in same loop, sc in next dc of Inset Ring, *13 dc in next open loop, skip 4 dc on Inset Ring, sc in next dc of Inset Ring; rep from * around, join with slip st to top of first dc. Fasten off.

Here's another motif with an inset ring, this time with a ruffled edge and a rounded shape.

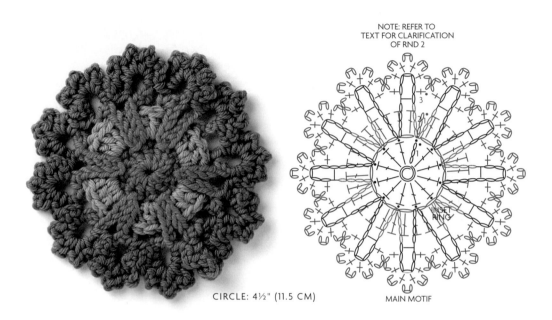

NOTE: REFER TO
TEXT FOR CLARIFICATION
OF RND 2

INSET
RING

CIRCLE: 4½" (11.5 CM)

MAIN MOTIF

INSET RING

Ch 16, join with slip st to form ring.

Rnd 1 Ch 3 (counts as dc), 29 dc in ring, join with slip st to top of ch-3 — 30 dc. Fasten off.

MAIN MOTIF

Begin with sliding loop.

Rnd 1 Ch 3 (counts as dc), 11 dc in ring, join with slip st to top of ch-3 — 12 dc.

Rnd 2 Place Inset Ring around Rnd 1; *working behind Inset Ring, ch 10, hdc in 6th ch from hook — *open loop made*, working in front of Inset Ring, ch 4, slip st in next st from Rnd 1, ch 10, hdc in 6th ch from hook, working behind Inset Ring, ch 4, slip st in next st from Rnd 1; rep from * around. Fasten off.

Rnd 3 Standing sc in any open loop, *(ch 3, sc in same loop) five times in same loop, sc in next open loop; rep from * around, omitting last sc, join with slip st to first sc. Fasten off.

Interconnected rings create the focal point for this three-dimensional triangle. You need three locking stitch markers or scraps of waste yarn to make this motif.

RING 1

Ch 13, join with slip st to form ring.

Rnd 1 Ch 3 (counts as dc), 29 dc in ring, join with slip st to top of ch-3 — 30 dc. Fasten off.

RING 2

Ch 13, insert chain tail from front to back through center of Ring 1, join with slip st to form ring.

Rnd 1 Work as for Ring 1.

RING 3

Ch 14, insert chain tail from front to back through center of Rings 2 and 1, join with slip st to form ring.

Rnd 1 Work as for Ring 1.

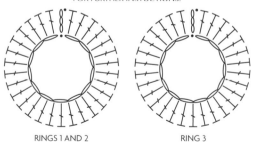

RINGS 1–3 ARE WORKED INTERTWINED WITH EACH OTHER. REFER TO TEXT FOR FURTHER INSTUCTIONS.

RINGS 1 AND 2   RING 3

OUTER TRIANGLE

Arrange circles so that each ch-3 beginning ch is hidden behind front ring. Instructions are written for right-handed crochet with left-handed directions in brackets.

Rnd 1 (Joining Rnd) Hold piece so that Ring 3 is on upper right [left], Ring 1 is on upper left [right], and Ring 2 is at center bottom. Place Marker A through the Ring-1 and Ring-3 sts that overlap each other; counting counterclockwise [clockwise] on Ring 1, place Marker B through the 12th st from Marker A and through the adjacent Ring-2 dc; continuing on Ring 2, place Marker C through the 12th st from Marker B and through the adjacent Ring-3 dc that is 12 sts clockwise [counterclockwise] from Marker A. You now have 36 dc: 3 marked pairs of sts (each counts as 1 st), 11 dcs between each pair of markers (see photo on page 219).

Begin round with standing dc through both Marker A sts; continuing on Ring 1 only, (ch 1, skip 1 dc, dc in next dc) two times, ch 1, skip 1 dc, (tr, ch 3, tr) in next dc, (ch 1, skip 1 dc, dc in next dc) two times, ch 1, skip 1 dc, dc through both Marker B sts; continuing on Ring 2 only, (ch 1, skip 1 dc, dc in next dc) two times, ch 1, skip 1 dc, (tr, ch 3, tr) in next dc, (ch 1, skip 1 dc, dc in next dc) two times, ch 1, skip 1 dc, dc through both Marker C sts; continuing on Ring 3 only, (ch 1, skip 1 dc, dc in next dc) two times, ch 1, skip 1 dc, (tr, ch 3, tr) in next dc, (ch 1, skip 1 dc, dc in next dc) two times, ch 1, skip 1 dc, join with slip st to first dc.

Rnd 2 Ch 3 (counts as dc), *(dc in next space, dc in next st) three times, (dc, 2 tr, ch 1, 2 tr, dc) in next space, dc in next tr, (dc in next space, dc in next dc) three times; rep from * around, omitting last dc, join with slip st to top of ch-3. Fasten off.

TRIANGLE: 4½" (11.5 CM)

* = MARKER

IN RND 1, AT EACH MARKER,
WORK ONE DC INTO TWO CORRESPONDING DCS
SHOWN IN RED ON THE DIAGRAM.

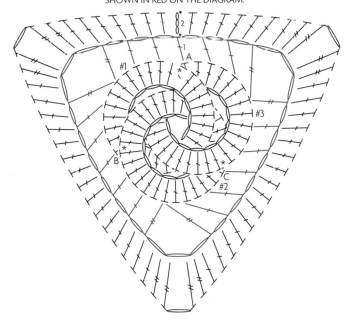

[**TIP**] This triangle would easily accept additional rounds of double crochet or other types of stitches. Just remember to increase at the corners to keep the piece flat.

You might expect three interconnected rings to be useful only in a triangle, but here the rings magically morph into a square thanks to a little sleight of hand (and varying stitch heights) on Round 1. You need three locking stitch markers or scraps of yarn to make this motif.

SQUARE: 4¼" (11 CM)

RING 1

Ch 13, join with slip st to form ring.

Rnd 1 Ch 3 (counts as dc), 29 dc in ring, join with slip st to top of ch-3 — 30 dc. Fasten off.

RING 2

Ch 13, insert chain tail from front to back through center of Ring 1, join with slip st to form ring.

Rnd 1 Work as for Ring 1.

RING 3

Ch 14, insert chain tail from front to back through center of Rings 2 and 1, join with slip st to form ring.

Rnd 1 Work as for Ring 1.

RINGS 1–3 ARE WORKED
INTERTWINED WITH EACH OTHER.
REFER TO TEXT
FOR FURTHER INSTUCTIONS.

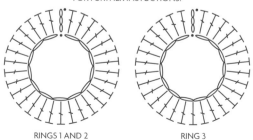

RINGS 1 AND 2   RING 3

OUTER SQUARE

Arrange rings so that each ch-3 beginning ch is hidden behind front ring. Instructions are written for right-handed crochet with left-handed directions in brackets.

Rnd 1 (Joining Rnd) Hold piece so that Ring 3 is on upper right [left], Ring 1 is on upper left [right], and Ring 2 is at center bottom. Place Marker A through the Ring-1 and Ring-3 sts that overlap each other; counting counterclockwise [clockwise] on Ring 1, place Marker B through the 12th st from Marker A st and through the adjacent Ring-2 dc; continuing on Ring 2, place Marker C through the 14th st from Marker B and through the adjacent Ring-3 dc that is 14 sts clockwise [counterclockwise] from Marker A. *You now have 40 dc*: 3 marked pairs of sts (each counts as 1 st), 11 dcs between Markers A and B, 13 dcs between Markers B and C, and 13 dcs between Markers C and A.

Begin round with standing tr through both Marker-A sts; continuing on Ring 1 only, (ch 1, skip 1 dc, dc in next dc) two times, ch 1, skip 1 dc, tr in next dc, ch 1, skip 1 dc, (tr, ch 3, tr) in next dc, ch 1, skip 1 dc, dc in next dc, ch 1, skip 1 dc, tr through both Marker-B sts; continuing on Ring 2 only, ch 1, skip 1 dc, dc in next

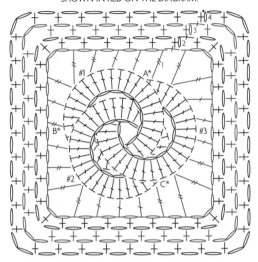

* = MARKER

IN RND 1, AT EACH MARKER,
WORK ONE TR INTO TWO CORRESPONDING DCS
SHOWN IN RED ON THE DIAGRAM.

dc, ch 1, skip 1 dc, tr in next dc, ch 1, skip 1 dc, (tr, ch 3, tr) in next dc, (ch 1, skip 1 dc, dc in next dc) three times, ch 1, skip 1 dc, tr through both Marker-C sts; continuing on Ring 3 only, ch 1, skip 1 dc, (tr, ch 3, tr) in next dc, ch 1, skip 1 dc, tr in next dc, (ch 1, skip 1 dc, dc in next dc) three times, ch 1, skip 1 dc, (tr, ch 3, tr) in next dc, skip 1 dc, join with sc to first st.

Rnd 2 Ch 1, sc in space formed by joining sc, *(ch 1, sc in next space) four times, (ch 1, sc) three times in corner space**, ch 1, sc in next space; rep from * around, ending last rep at **, join with sc to first sc.

Rnd 3 Ch 1, sc in space formed by joining sc, *(ch 1, sc in next space) six times, ch 3, sc in next space**, ch 1, sc in next space; rep from * around, ending last rep at **, join with sc to first sc.

Rnd 4 Ch 1, sc in space formed by joining sc, *(ch 1, sc in next space) six times, ch 1, (sc, ch 2, sc) in corner space, ch 1, sc in next space; rep from * around, omitting last sc, join with slip st to first sc. Fasten off.

Inset Square A ■ **Rnds 1 and 2** B ■ **Rnd 3** C ■

This unusual four-sided shape is worked around a nearly free-floating double crochet square.

SQUARE: 4" (10 CM)

WORK RND 1 OF INSET SQUARE INTO BUMP ON WS OF CHAIN

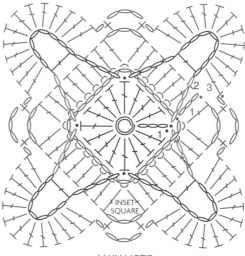

MAIN MOTIF

INSET SQUARE

Ch 28, join with slip st to first sc.

Rnd 1 Working in back bump of each ch, ch 3 (counts as dc), dc in next 5 ch, (dc, ch 3, dc) in next ch, *dc in next 6 ch, (dc, ch 3, dc) in next ch; rep from * around, join with slip st to top of ch-3. Fasten off.

MAIN MOTIF

Begin with sliding loop.

Rnd 1 Ch 3 (counts as dc), 15 dc in ring, join with slip st to top of ch-3 — 16 dc.

Rnd 2 Place Inset Square around Rnd 1; *working behind Inset Square, ch 12, dc in 8th ch from hook — *open loop made*; working in front of Inset Square, ch 4, skip 3 dc, slip st in next dc from Rnd 1, ch 12, dc in 8th ch from hook; working behind Inset Square, ch 4, skip 3 dc, slip st in next st behind Inset Square; rep from * once more. Fasten off.

Rnd 3 Standing dc in any open loop, *12 dc in same loop, ch 1, (sc, ch 3, sc) in next corner space of Inset Square, ch 1, dc in next open loop; rep from * around, omitting last dc, join with slip st to first dc. Fasten off.

PART III

PATTERNS

Linen Place Mat

Linen's centuries-old appeal is due to its absorbant and hard-wearing qualities, and the beautiful way it takes dye. This elegant placemat has a built-in coaster — a different motif from the others that make up the mat. The Petal Motifs are a variation of Motif 42 (page 120), while the Coaster Motif is based on Motif 46 (page 127). All the motifs are worked using a join-as-you-go (JAYGo) method (see page 35).

Dc3tog (double crochet 3 together) Yarn over, insert hook into indicated stitch or space and pull up a loop, yarn over, pull through 2 loops on hook, (yarn over, insert hook into same stitch and pull up a loop, yarn over and pull through 2 loops) two times, yarn over and pull through all 4 loops on hook.

Dtr3tog (double treble 3 together) (Yarn over) three times, insert hook into indicated stitch or space and pull up a loop, (yarn over and pull through 2 loops on hook) three times, [(yarn over) three times, insert hook into same stitch or space and pull up a

loop, (yarn over and pull through 2 loops on hook) three times] two times, yarn over and pull through 4 loops on hook.

Partial tr (partial treble) (Yarn over) twice, insert hook into stitch or space indicated and pull up a loop, (yarn over and pull through 2 loops on hook) two times.

Tr2tog (treble crochet 2 together) (Yarn over) two times, insert hook into indicated stitch or space and pull up a loop, (yarn over, pull through 2 loops) two times, (yarn over) two times, insert hook into same stitch or

space and pull up a loop, (yarn over, pull through 2 loops) two times, yarn over and pull through all 3 loops on hook.

Tr3tog (treble crochet 3 together) (Yarn over) two times, insert hook into indicated stitch or space and pull up a loop, (yarn over, pull through 2 loops) two times, [(yarn over) two times, insert hook into same stitch or space and pull up a loop, (yarn over, pull through 2 loops) two times] two times, yarn over and pull through all 4 loops on hook.

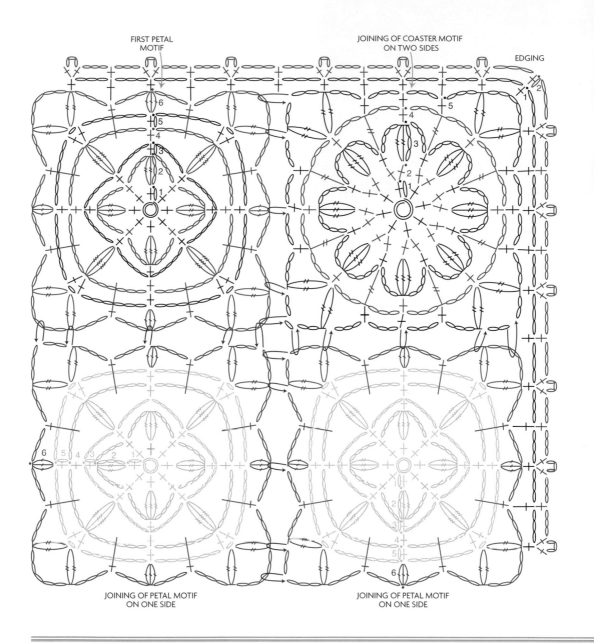

FIRST PETAL MOTIF

JOINING OF COASTER MOTIF ON TWO SIDES

EDGING

JOINING OF PETAL MOTIF ON ONE SIDE

JOINING OF PETAL MOTIF ON ONE SIDE

Finished Measurements

13½" high × 18" wide (34 cm × 46 cm)

Yarn

Euroflax Linen, 100% wet-spun linen, 270 yds/3.5 oz (246 m/100g), 1 skein each #18 natural (A), #65 goldenrod (B), and #43 pewter (C) (1 skein of each color makes four placemats, taking care with color changes. See note under Coaster Motif.)

Hook

G/6 (4.0 mm) *or size you need to obtain correct gauge*

Gauge

Petal Motif Rounds 1–6 = 4½" (11.5 cm) side-to-side before washing; Petal Motif Rounds 1–6 = 4" (10 cm) side-to-side after washing

Note: Linen may change gauge significantly after washing. Take gauge both before and after washing your swatch.

Rnd 5 Ch 1, sc in same st, *ch 6, (sc, ch 1, sc) in next cluster, ch 6, sc in next sc; rep from * around, omitting last sc, join with slip st to first sc. Fasten off.

Rnd 6 With C, beginning with slip knot on hook, dc3tog in first st, *ch 3, sc in Rnd-4 ch-space over 2 chains, ch 3, (tr2tog, ch 5, tr2tog) in next space, ch 3, sc in Rnd-4 ch-space over 2 chains, ch 3**, dc3tog in next sc; rep from * around, ending last rep at **, join with slip st join to first sc. Fasten off.

Petal Motif

With A, begin with sliding loop.

Rnd 1 Ch 1, 8 sc in ring, join with slip st to first sc — 8 sc.

Rnd 2 Ch 3 (counts as Partial tr), tr2tog in same st — *beginning cluster made*, *ch 4, sc in next sc, ch 4**, tr3tog in next sc; rep from * around, ending last rep at **, join with slip st to beginning cluster.

Rnd 3 Ch 1, sc in same st, *ch 5, sc in next sc, ch 5, sc in next cluster; rep from * around, omitting last sc, join with slip st to first sc. Fasten off.

Rnd 4 With B, standing sc in first sc, *ch 6, dtr3tog in next sc, ch 6, sc in next sc; rep from * around, omitting last sc, join with slip st to first sc.

Coaster Motif

Note: If making four placemats, work two beginning with color A and two beginning with color B.

With A (B), begin with a sliding loop.

Rnd 1 Ch 1, 8 sc in ring, join with slip st to first sc — 8 sc. Fasten off.

Rnd 2 With B (A), 2 sc in each sc around, join with slip st to first sc.

Rnd 3 Ch 3 (counts as Partial tr), tr2tog in same st — *beginning cluster made*, *ch 4, sc in next sc, ch 4**, tr3tog in next sc; rep from * around, ending last rep at **, join with slip st to beginning cluster. Fasten off.

Rnd 4 With A (B), standing sc in top of any cluster, *ch 3, tr in next sc, ch 3, sc in top of next cluster; rep from * around, omitting last sc, join with slip st to first sc. Fasten off.

Rnd 5 With C, standing sc in any tr, *ch 3, sc in next sc, ch 3, sc in next tr, ch 3, (tr2tog, ch 5, tr2tog) in next sc, ch 3, sc in next tr, rep from * around, omitting last sc, join with invisible join to first sc. Fasten off.

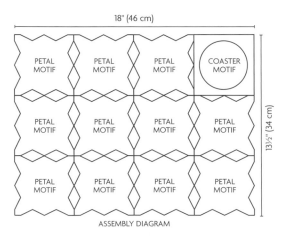

18" (46 cm)

13½" (34 cm)

PETAL MOTIF	PETAL MOTIF	PETAL MOTIF	COASTER MOTIF
PETAL MOTIF	PETAL MOTIF	PETAL MOTIF	PETAL MOTIF
PETAL MOTIF	PETAL MOTIF	PETAL MOTIF	PETAL MOTIF

ASSEMBLY DIAGRAM

Placemat

Work one Petal Motif.

JOINING THE MOTIFS

Referring to the assembly diagram for arrangement of motifs, make and join 10 additional Petal Motifs and one Coaster Motif, joining each motif to previous motifs on the final round, as follows:

Join one Petal Motif to another Petal Motif at ch-5 corners, tr2tog clusters, dc3tog clusters.

Join one Petal Motif to three Petal Motifs at ch-5 corners, tr2tog clusters, dc3tog clusters, and where four motifs join at a corner, work corner chain of fourth motif as follows: Ch 2, flat join to corner space of first motif, ch 1, skipping corner space of motif diagonally across from current motif, flat join to corner space of next motif, ch 2.

Join Coaster Motif to three Petal Motifs at ch-5 corners, tr2tog clusters, and at center of each side (sc-to-dc2tog cluster).

Edging

Rnd 1 With C and RS facing, standing sc in outside corner ch-5 space of Coaster Motif, ch 3, sc in next cluster, (ch 3, sc in next sc) three times, ch 3, sc in next cluster, [ch 3, sc in join between current motif and next motif, (ch 3, sc in next cluster, ch 3, sc in next sc) two times, ch 3, sc in next cluster] three times, ch 3, sc in corner ch-5 space; continue in this manner around remaining sides, ending with sc in join between last Petal Motif and Coaster Motif; sc in next cluster, (ch 3, sc in next sc) three times, ch 3, sc in next cluster, ch 3, join with slip st to first sc.

Rnd 2 Ch 1, sc in same sc, *ch 3, (sc, ch 3, sc) in next sc, ch 3, sc in next sc; rep from * around, omitting last sc, join with slip st to first sc. Fasten off.

Weave in ends. Wash and block.

Snowy Shaped Shawl

Finished Measurements
Approximately 33" (84 cm)
wide at widest point
and 20" (51 cm) long at
center back

Yarn
Karabella Lace Mohair,
61% superkid mohair/
8% wool/31% polyamide,
540 yds/1.75 oz
(500 m/50g), 1 skein
#3225 light mint

Hook
F/5 (3.75 mm) *or size you
need to obtain correct
gauge*

Gauge
1 motif = 3¼" (8.5 cm)
diameter, point-to-point

Lacy hexagons in an asymmetrical pattern may evoke snow showers on a winter's day, but this shawl would be perfect worn over a summer dress or on a wedding day. One skein of yarn is all it takes to make this lovely shawl, which uses Motif 81 (page 185).

Large Motif
Ch 4, join with slip st to form ring.

Rnd 1 Ch 1, *sc in ring, ch 2, Picot-3, ch 2, Triple Picot-3, ch 2, Picot-3, slip st in base of opposite picot, ch 2; rep from * five more times, join with slip st to first sc.

Rnd 2 Ch 6 (counts as tr and ch 2), *skip 1 picot, (sc in next picot, ch 2) three times, skip 1 picot, tr in next sc, ch 2; rep from * around, omitting last tr, join with slip st in 4th ch of ch-6. Fasten off.

Small Motif
Work as for Large Motif through Rnd 1 only. Fasten off.

Picot-3 Ch 3, slip st in 3rd ch from hook.

Triple Picot-3 (Ch 3, slip st in 3rd ch from hook) three times, slip st in base of first picot.

Notes: Mohair yarn can be difficult to rip out. Take care to stitch accurately, although there should be plenty of yarn available for one or two motifs to be cut and discarded. The optional neck band stabilizes the edge of the shawl and allows it to hang better.*

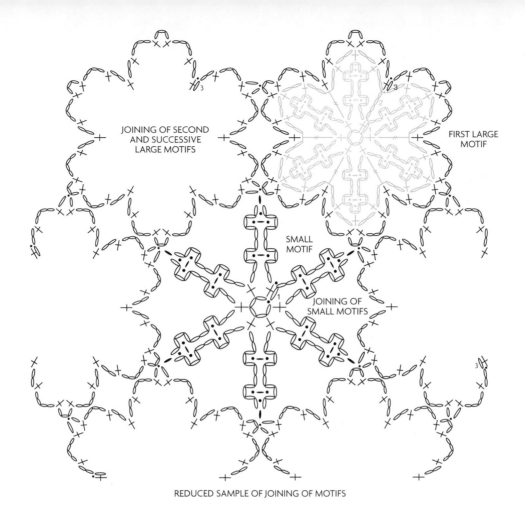

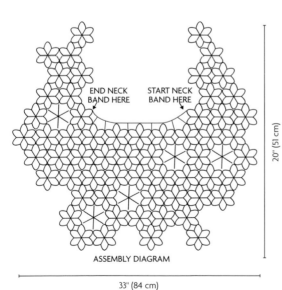

JOINING OF SECOND AND SUCCESSIVE LARGE MOTIFS

FIRST LARGE MOTIF

SMALL MOTIF

JOINING OF SMALL MOTIFS

REDUCED SAMPLE OF JOINING OF MOTIFS

END NECK BAND HERE

START NECK BAND HERE

20" (51 cm)

ASSEMBLY DIAGRAM

33" (84 cm)

= LARGE MOTIF

= SMALL MOTIF

= NECK BAND

Shawl

Referring to assembly diagram, make 60 Large Motifs, joining each motif to previous motifs with a slip-st join on Rnd 2. Make 5 Small Motifs, joining to previous motifs with a slip-st join at the center of the Triple Picot-3.

MAKING THE NECK EDGE

With RS facing, join yarn with sc at tip of motif indicated. Working around neck edge, (ch 7, tr in next join between motifs) two times, (ch 7, sc in next tip of motif, ch 7, dc in next join) two times, ch 7, sc in next tip of motif, (ch 7, tr in next join) two times, ch 7, sc in next tip of motif. Fasten off.

FINISHING

Weave in ends. Block.

Reversible Camp Rug

Use this cozy reversible rug by the bed for a warm wake-up for your tootsies, or stitch it in a machine-washable yarn for a pet bed or bath mat. You'll probably want to use a rug pad underneath to prevent slipping. Make the rug any size you like: one ball of each color makes three squares. This uses a variation of Motif 33 (page 101).

Finished
Measurements
Approximately 18¾" × 28" (47.5 cm × 71 cm)

Yarn
Cascade Yarns Lana Grande, 100% Peruvian wool, 87 yds/3.5 oz (79 m/100g), 1 skein each #6050 dark brown (A) and #6056 tan (B)

Hook
N/15 (10 mm) *or size you need to obtain correct gauge*

Gauge
Rnds 1 and 2 = approximately 4¼" (11 cm)

Other Supplies
Tapestry needle

Note: Right side and wrong side are designated below for clarity. But since the rug is reversible, both sides are really right sides.

Square

With A, begin with sliding loop.

Rnd 1 (RS) Ch 3 (counts as dc), 15 dc in ring, join with slip st to top of ch-3 — 16 dc.

Rnd 2 (RS) Ch 4 (counts as dc and ch 1), skip 1 dc, (dc, ch 3, dc) in next dc, ch 1, skip 1 dc, *dc in next dc, ch 1, skip 1 dc, (dc, ch 3, dc) in next dc, ch 1, skip 1 dc; rep from * around, join with slip st to 3rd ch of ch-4; drop loop from hook, turn.

Rnd 3 (WS) With B, (standing sc, ch 3, sc) in any ch-3 corner space, ch 1, *keeping Rnd-2 sts to the back, (tr in next skipped dc from Rnd 1, ch 1) two times**, (sc, ch 3, sc) in next

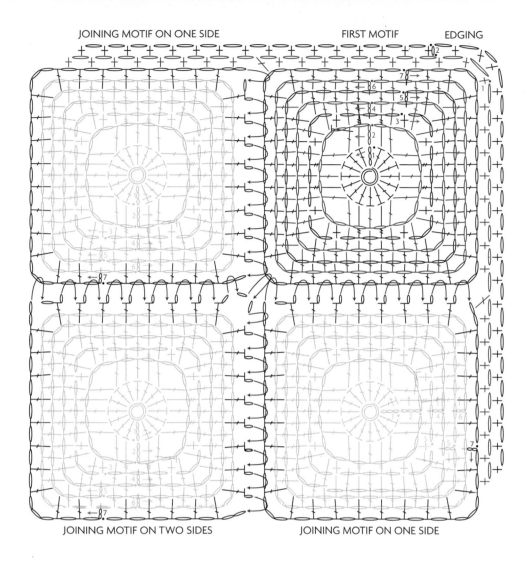

JOINING MOTIF ON ONE SIDE   FIRST MOTIF   EDGING

JOINING MOTIF ON TWO SIDES   JOINING MOTIF ON ONE SIDE

ch-3 space, ch 1; rep from * around, ending last rep at **, join with slip st to first sc; drop loop from hook, turn.

Rnd 4 (RS) *Rnd 4 is worked into Rnd-2 sts over Rnd-3 chs unless otherwise stated.* Place dropped loop from Rnd 2 onto hook, insert hook into Rnd-3 space and ch 1 to slip st over Rnd-3 ch, ch 3 (counts as dc and ch 1); dc in next dc,* ch 1; keeping Rnd-3 space to the back, (dc, ch 3, dc) in next ch-3 space between Rnd-3 scs**; working over Rnd-3 chs, (ch 1, dc in next dc) three times; rep from * around, ending last rep at **, ch 1, dc in next dc, ch 1, join with slip st to 3rd ch of ch 4; drop loop from hook, turn.

Rnd 5 (WS) *Rnd 5 is worked into Rnd-3 sts over Rnd-4 chs unless otherwise stated.* Place dropped loop from Rnd 3 onto hook, insert hook into Rnd-4 space and ch 1 to slip st around Rnd-4 ch, ch 3 (counts as dc and ch 1); *(dc, ch 3, dc) in next space (through both layers), ch 1, dc in next sc, (ch 1, dc in next tr) two times, ch 1**; dc in next sc, ch 1; rep from * around, ending last rep at **, join with slip st to 3rd ch of ch-4; drop loop from hook, turn.

Rnd 6 (RS) *Rnd 6 is worked into Rnd-4 sts over Rnd-5 chs unless otherwise stated.* Place dropped loop from Rnd 4 onto hook, slip st over Rnd-5 chain, ch 3 (counts as dc and ch 1), *(dc in next dc, ch 1) two times; keeping Rnd-5 ch to the back, (dc, ch 3, dc) in next ch-3 space between Rnd-5 dcs**; (ch 1, dc in next dc) three times, ch 1; rep from * around, ending last rep at **, (ch 1, dc in next dc) two times, ch 1, join with slip st to 3rd ch of ch-4. Fasten off A. Turn.

Rnd 7 (WS) *Rnd 7 is worked into Rnd-5 sts over Rnd-6 chs unless otherwise stated.* Place dropped loop from Rnd 5 onto hook, insert hook into Rnd-6 space and slip st around Rnd-6 ch, ch 3 (counts as dc and ch 1), dc in next dc, ch 1, *(dc, ch 3, dc) in next space through both layers, ch 1**, working over Rnd-6 chs, (dc in next dc, ch 1) six times; rep from * around, ending last rep at **, (dc in next dc, ch 1) four times, join with slip st to 3rd ch of ch 4. Fasten off B.

Rug

Make one square. Make a second square through Rnd 6. Join to previous square as follows:

Rnd 7 *Rnd 7 is worked into Rnd-5 sts over Rnd-3 chs unless otherwise stated.* Place Rnd-5 loop onto hook, insert hook into Rnd-6 space and slip st around Rnd-6 ch, ch 3, dc in next dc, ch 1, *(dc, ch 3, dc) in next space through both layers, ch 1**, working over Rnd-6 chs, (dc in next dc, ch 1) six times; rep from * once, (dc, ch 2, flat join to corner of previous motif, ch 1, dc) in next space through both layers, (ch 1, flat join in next space of previous motif, dc in next dc) six times, ch 1, flat join in next space of previous

3	2	1
6	5	4

18¾" (47.5 cm)

28" (71 cm)

motif, (dc, ch 1, flat join to corner of previous motif, ch 2, dc) in next space through both layers, ch 1, (dc in next dc, ch 1) four times, join with slip st to 3rd ch of ch-4. Fasten off B.

Referring to diagram, join four more squares to form a large rectangle. At interior corners where a fourth square meets three previous squares, work corners as follows:

Dc in next space through both layers, ch 1, flat join in next space of previous motif, ch 1, flat join in corner space of square diagonally-opposite, ch 1, flat join in corner space of next square, dc in same space of current square through both layers.

EDGING

Rnd 1 With A, (standing sc, ch 1, sc) in corner space of Square 1, ch 1, *[(sc in next space, ch 1) eight times, sc in same space, ch 1, sc in next space, ch 1] two times, (sc in next space, ch 1) seven times, (sc, ch 1) two times in corner space, (sc in next space, ch 1) eight times, sc in same space, ch 1, sc in next space, ch 1, (sc in next space, ch 1) seven times**, (sc, ch 1) two times in corner space; rep from * to ** once more, join with slip st to first sc. Fasten off A.

Rnd 2 With B, standing sc in any ch-space along one side, ch 1, *(sc, ch 1) in each space to corner space, (sc, ch 1) two times in corner space; rep from *, ending (sc, ch 1) in each space to end of round, join with slip st to first sc. Fasten off B. Weave in ends.

Mary Frances Pincushions

These sweet pieces can be stuffed and used as pincushions or filled with fragrant potpourri and used as sachets. A final joining round connects the two pieces, so be sure to complete the lining and stuff it before going too far! Variations of Motifs 33 (page 101) and 34 (page 102) are shown here, but almost any motif with a coordinating lining would be suitable. Instructions are given for the variation of Motif 34.

Circle Pincushion

Make two circles as follows.

Begin with sliding loop.

Rnd 1 (RS) With A, ch 3 (counts as dc), 11 dc in ring, join with slip st to top of ch-3 — 12 dc.

Rnd 2 (RS) Ch 6 (counts as dc and ch 3), skip 1 dc, *dc in next dc, ch 3, skip 1 dc; rep from * around, join with slip st to 3rd ch of ch-4; drop loop from hook, turn.

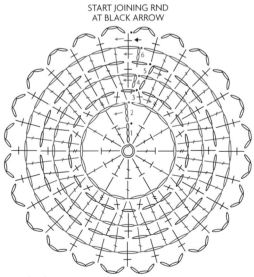

START JOINING RND
AT BLACK ARROW

CIRCLE PINCUSHION

REFER TO THE TEXT FOR PLACEMENT
OF STITCHES IN FRONT OF,
BEHIND, OR OVER EXISTING STITCHES

Finished Measurements
Approximately 3½"
(9 cm) in diameter

Yarn
Universal Yarn Nazli
Gelin Garden 3 crochet
thread, 100% Peruvian
cotton, 136 yds/1.75 oz
(125 m/50 g), 1 ball each
#1 white (A) and #11
medium blue (B) makes
at least two pincushions.

Hook
E/4 (3.5 mm) or size
you need to obtain
correct gauge

Gauge
Rnds 1–6 of circle =
approximately 3¼"
(8.5 cm)

Other Supplies
Small amount of fabric
for lining, needle and
thread to match lining
fabric, small amount
of fiberfill stuffing
for pincushion and/or
potpourri for sachet

V-st (Dc, ch 1, dc) in 1 stitch.

Rnd 3 (WS) With B, standing sc in any ch-3 space, ch 1, *keeping Rnd-2 sts to the back, tr in next skipped dc from Rnd 1, ch 1, sc in same space, ch 1**, sc in next space, ch 1; rep from * around, ending last rep at **, join with slip st to first sc; drop loop from hook, turn.

Rnd 4 (RS) *Rnd 4 is worked into Rnd-2 sts over Rnd-3 chs unless otherwise stated.* Place dropped loop from Rnd 2 onto hook, insert hook into Rnd-3 space and ch 1 to slip st over Rnd-3 ch, ch 3 (counts as dc and ch 1); dc in same st, ch 1, *keeping Rnd-3 space to the back, dc in next ch-3 space in Rnd 2 after next sc in Rnd-3, ch 1, dc in same ch-3 space in Rnd 2 after next tr in Rnd 3, ch 1**; working over Rnd-3 ch, V-st in next dc, ch 1; rep from * around, ending last rep at **, join with slip st to 3rd ch of ch-4, drop loop from hook, turn.

Rnd 5 (WS) *Rnd 5 is worked into Rnd-3 sts over Rnd-4 chs unless otherwise stated.* Place dropped loop from Rnd 3 onto hook, ch 1, insert hook into Rnd-4 space and ch 1 to slip st over Rnd-4 ch, ch 2 (counts as dc and ch 1), *sc in next tr in Rnd-3, ch 1, dc in next sc, ch 1, sc in next ch-1 space, ch 1**, dc in next sc, ch 1; rep from * around, ending last rep at **, join with slip st to 3rd ch of ch-4, drop loop from hook, turn.

Rnd 6 (RS) *Rnd 6 is worked into Rnd-4 sts over Rnd-5 chs unless otherwise stated.* Place dropped loop from Rnd 4 onto hook, ch 1 to slip st over Rnd-5 ch, ch 3 (counts as dc and ch 1), *dc in next dc, ch 1; rep from * around, join with slip st to 3rd ch of ch-4. Fasten off.

LINING THE CIRCLES

Cut two fabric circles ½" (13 mm) larger than crocheted circles. Holding WS of fabric together, stitch around circle with a ½" (13 mm) seam allowance and leaving a 1" (2.5 cm) opening for stuffing. Turn lining right side out and stuff firmly with fiberfill, or fill with potpourri for sachet. Stitch lining closed.

FINISHING

Hold Circle 1 and Circle 2 with WS together.

Joining Rnd (RS) *Joining Rnd is worked into both circles, into Rnd-5 sts over Rnd-6 chs unless otherwise stated.* With B, standing sc in any pair of Rnd-5 scs (that is, into any sc on both Circle 1 and Circle 2), *ch 3, sc in next pair of dcs**, ch 3, sc in next pair of scs; rep from * around, inserting lining before completing round and ending last rep at **, join with slip st to first slip st. Fasten off. Weave in ends.

Square Pincushion

Make two squares as follows.

Begin with sliding loop.

Rnd 1 (RS) With A, ch 3 (counts as dc), 15 dc in ring, join with slip st to top of ch-3 — 16 dc.

Rnd 2 (RS) Ch 4 (counts as dc and ch 1), skip 1 dc, (dc, ch 3, dc) in next dc, ch 1, skip 1 dc, *dc in next dc, ch 1, skip 1 dc, (dc, ch 3, dc) in next dc, ch 1, skip 1 dc; rep from * around, join with slip st to 3rd ch of ch-4; drop loop from hook, turn.

Rnd 3 (WS) With B, (standing sc, ch 3, sc) in any ch-3 corner space, ch 1, *keeping Rnd-2 sts to the back, (tr in next skipped dc from Rnd 1, ch 1) two times**, (sc, ch 3, sc) in next ch-3 space, ch 1; rep from * around, ending last rep at **, join with slip st to first sc; drop loop from hook and place on holder, turn.

Rnd 4 (RS) *Rnd 4 is worked into Rnd-2 sts over Rnd-3 chs unless otherwise stated.* Place dropped loop from Rnd 2 onto hook, insert hook into Rnd-3 ch-space and ch 1 to slip st over Rnd-3 ch, ch 3 (counts as dc and ch 1); *dc in next dc, ch 1; keeping Rnd-3 ch-space to the back, (dc, ch 3, dc) in next ch-3 space between Rnd-3 scs**; working over Rnd-3 chs, (ch 1, dc in next dc) two times, ch 1; rep from * around, ending last rep at **, ch 1, dc in next dc, ch 1, join with slip st to 3rd ch of ch-4; drop loop from hook, turn.

Rnd 5 (WS) *Rnd 5 is worked into Rnd-3 sts over Rnd-4 chs unless otherwise stated.* Place dropped loop from Rnd 3 onto hook, insert hook into Rnd-4 ch-space and ch 1 to slip st around Rnd-4 ch, ch 3, *(dc, ch 3, dc) in next ch-spaces (through both layers), ch 1, dc in next sc, (ch 1, dc in next dc) two times, ch 1**, dc in next sc, ch 1; rep from * around, ending last rep at **, join with slip st to 3rd ch of ch-4. Fasten off. Turn.

Rnd 6 (RS) *Rnd 6 is worked into Rnd-4 sts over Rnd-5 chs unless otherwise stated.* Place dropped loop from Rnd 4 onto hook, insert hook into Rnd-5 space and ch 1 to slip

st over Rnd-5 ch, ch 3 (counts as dc and ch 1), *(dc in next dc, ch 1) two times, (dc, ch 3, dc) in next ch-space**, (ch 1, dc in next dc) three times, ch 1; rep from * around, ending last rep at **, (ch 1, dc in next dc) two times, ch 1, join with slip st to 3rd ch of ch-4. Fasten off.

FINISHING

Make Lining same as for Circle Pincushion, using square motif as a template. Hold Square 1 and Square 2 with WS together.

Joining Rnd (RS) *Joining Rnd is worked into both squares, into Rnd-5 sts over Rnd-6 chs unless otherwise stated.* With B, (standing dc, ch 3, dc) in any Rnd-5 corner ch-spaces [that is, into corner spaces of Square 1 and Square 2, working over Rnd-6 chs] *(ch 3, sc in next pair of dcs) six times**, ch 3, (dc, ch 3, dc) in next corner space; rep from * around, inserting lining before completing round and ending last rep at **, join with slip st to first slip st. Fasten off. Weave in ends.

START JOINING RND
AT BLACK ARROW

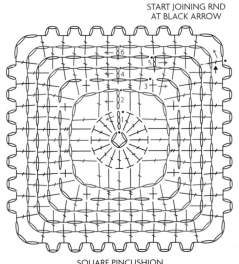

SQUARE PINCUSHION

REFER TO THE TEXT FOR PLACEMENT
OF STITCHES IN FRONT OF,
BEHIND, OR OVER EXISTING STITCHES

Layered Motif Afghan

Layered hexagons in cool blues and greens may remind you of flowers and leaves floating on a calm pond. Once you get the hang of the basic layered motif — a variation of Motif 30 (page 96) — they are a breeze to stitch. A final continuous round around each motif joins the individual pieces, making this a best-of-both-worlds project: maximum portability plus easy joining and finishing.

Overlay Hexagon Motif

Using A, B, or C for Rnds 1–4, begin with sliding loop.

Rnd 1 (RS) Ch 3 (counts as dc), 11 dc in ring, join with slip st in top of ch-3 — 12 dc.

Rnd 2 Ch 5 (counts as dc and ch 2), dc in same st, ch 1, skip 1 dc, *(dc, ch 2, dc) in next dc, ch 1, skip 1 dc; rep from * around, join with slip st to 3rd ch of ch-5.

Rnd 3 Ch 4 (counts as dc and ch 1), *(dc, ch 2, dc) in next space**, ch 1, (dc in next dc, ch 1) two times; rep from * around, ending last rep at **, ch 1, dc in next dc, ch 1, join with slip st to 3rd ch of ch-4.

Rnd 4 Ch 4 (counts as dc and ch 1), dc in next dc, ch 1, *(dc, ch 3, dc) in next space**, (ch 1, dc in next dc) four times, ch 1; rep from * around, ending last rep at **, (ch 1, dc in next dc) two times, ch 1, join with invisible join to 3rd ch of ch-4. Fasten off.

Rnd 5 (WS) *Rnd 5 is worked into Rnd-1 sts.* Turn motif over so that WS of Rnd 1 is facing. With MC, beg with slip knot on hook, tr in any skipped dc of Rnd 1, ch 2, tr in same st, ch 1, * (tr, ch 2, tr) in next skipped dc, ch 1; rep from * around, join with slip st to first tr.

Finished Measurements
Approximately 44" × 60"
(112 cm × 152 cm)

Yarn
Plymouth Galway, 100% wool, 210 yds/3.5 oz, (192 m/100 g), 8 skeins #116 teal (MC); 2 skeins each #89 purple (A) and #127 green (B); 1 skein #111 turquoise (C)

Hook
Size I/9 (5.5 mm) *or size you need to obtain correct gauge*

Gauge
Rounds 1–8 = 6" (15 cm) side-to-side, after blocking (but the gauge is not crucial in this project)

Other Supplies
Locking stitch markers or coilless safety pins, tapestry needle

Notes: Motifs are stitched separately then joined with a final, continuous joining round around all motifs.

MC is the background color; colors A, B, and C are the overlay colors.

The overlay is secured to the background on Round 7.

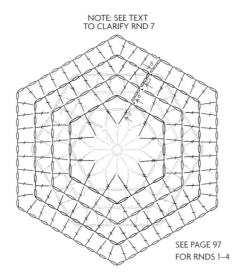

NOTE: SEE TEXT
TO CLARIFY RND 7

SEE PAGE 97
FOR RNDS 1–4

Rnd 6 Ch 4 (counts as dc and ch 1), *(dc, ch 2, dc) in next ch-2 space, ch 1**, (dc in next tr, ch 1) two times; rep from * around, ending last rep at **, dc in next tr, ch 1, join with slip st to 3rd ch of ch-4.

Rnd 7 Ch 4 (counts as dc and ch 1), dc in next dc, *ch 1, (dc, ch 2, dc) in next space and in corresponding Rnd-4 space together**, (ch 1, dc in next dc) four times; rep from * around, ending last rep at **, (ch 1, dc in next dc) two times, ch 1, join with slip st to 3rd ch of ch-4.

Rnd 8 Ch 4 (counts as dc and ch 1), (dc in next dc, ch 1) two times, *(dc, ch 2, dc) in next space**, (ch 1, dc in next dc) six times, ch 1; rep from * around, ending last rep at **, (ch 1, dc in next dc) three times, ch 1, join with invisible join to 3rd ch of ch-4. Fasten off.

Afghan

Work 18 motifs each in A and B; work 14 motifs in C.

Note: Use locking stitch markers, coilless safety pins, or waste yarn to hold several motifs together while working the Joining Round.

JOINING THE MOTIFS

Refer to the assembly diagram (page 237) for arrangement of colors and order of assembly. The numbers inside the hexagons indicate the order in which they are first joined to previous motifs. The letters refer to the color of the overlay.

Joining Rnd, Top Tier Referring to assembly diagram, with RS facing and MC, beg at the upper right-hand corner of Motif #1, standing dc in corner space of first motif, [ch 1, (dc in next dc, ch 1) to corner; (dc, ch 2, dc) in corner space] two times, ch 1, (dc in next dc, ch 1) to corner; dc in corner space, ch 2, dc in corner space of next motif, ch 1, flat join to adjacent space of previous motif, (dc in next dc, ch 1, flat join to adjacent space of previous motif) to corner, (dc, ch 1, flat join to corner space of previous motif, ch 1, dc) in corner space; continue working in this manner until the first six motifs have been joined to connect the top-tier motifs. Continue working around the remaining edges of Motif #6 to beginning corner, end *dc in beginning corner space, ch 1, flat join in ch-2 space between motifs, ch 1, dc in adjacent corner space of next motif, ch 1, (dc in next dc, ch 1) to corner, (dc, ch 2, dc) in corner, ch 1, (dc in next dc, ch 1) to corner; rep from * across lower edge of top tier motifs, ending with dc in bottom corner space of Motif #1 and leaving remaining two sides of Motif #1 unfinished.

Joining Rnd, Second Tier Ch 2, dc in any corner space of Motif #7, ch 1, flat join to adjacent ch-1 space of previous motif, (dc in next dc, ch 1, flat join to adjacent space of previous motif) to corner, (dc, ch 1, flat join to corner space of previous motif, ch 1, dc) in corner space of current motif, ch 1, (dc in next dc, ch 1, flat join to adjacent space) to corner, (dc, ch 1, flat join to adjacent corner space, ch 1, dc) in corner space, ch 1, (dc in next dc, ch 1) to corner, dc in corner space, ch 2, dc in any corner space of Motif #8, ch 1, flat join to adjacent ch-space of previous motif, dc in next dc; continue in this manner to connect second-tier motifs to each other and to first-tier motifs.

Working in this manner, join all motifs according to diagram, ending by working along the lower edge and up the side edge of afghan, join with slip st to first dc.

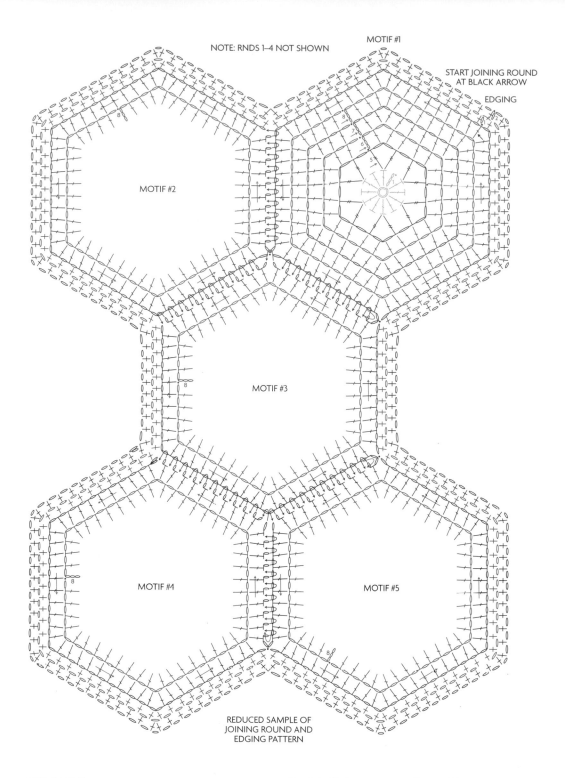

NOTE: RNDS 1–4 NOT SHOWN

MOTIF #1

START JOINING ROUND AT BLACK ARROW

EDGING

MOTIF #2

MOTIF #3

MOTIF #4

MOTIF #5

REDUCED SAMPLE OF JOINING ROUND AND EDGING PATTERN

EDGING

Rnd 1 Ch 1, (sc, ch 1) in each space around, placing (sc, ch 1) two times in each exterior corner space and omitting the ch-1 between the scs at interior corner spaces; ending with sc in last space, join with sc to first sc.

Rnd 2 Ch 1, sc in space formed by joining sc, ch 1, (sc, ch 1) in each space around, placing (sc, ch 1) two times in each exterior corner space and working (sc2tog, ch 1) in 2 ch-spaces at each interior corner, join with slip st to first sc. Fasten off. Weave in ends.

MOTIF #6 A

MOTIF #5 B

MOTIF #4 C

MOTIF #3 A

MOTIF #2 B

MOTIF #1 C

MOTIF #11 A

MOTIF #10 B

MOTIF #9 C

MOTIF #8 A

MOTIF #7 B

MOTIF #17 A

MOTIF #16 B

MOTIF #15 C

MOTIF #14 A

MOTIF #13 B

MOTIF #12 C

MOTIF #22 A

MOTIF #21 B

MOTIF #20 C

MOTIF #19 A

MOTIF #18 B

MOTIF #28 A

MOTIF #27 B

MOTIF #26 C

MOTIF #25 A

MOTIF #24 B

MOTIF #23 C

MOTIF #33 A

MOTIF #32 B

MOTIF #31 C

MOTIF #30 A

MOTIF #29 B

MOTIF #39 A

MOTIF #38 B

MOTIF #37 C

MOTIF #36 A

MOTIF #35 B

MOTIF #34 C

MOTIF #44 A

MOTIF #43 B

MOTIF #42 C

MOTIF #41 A

MOTIF #40 B

MOTIF #50 A

MOTIF #49 B

MOTIF #48 C

MOTIF #47 A

MOTIF #46 B

MOTIF #45 C

60" (152 cm)

ASSEMBLY DIAGRAM

44" (112 cm)

Sc2tog (single crochet 2 stitches together) (Insert hook into next st and pull up a loop) two times, yarn over and pull through all 3 loops on hook.

Summer Baby Blanket

This bright, lightweight blanket is just the thing to welcome a summer baby! Or join the motifs into a large rectangle for a shawl for Mom. It is made with Motif 89 (page 200).

Square Motif

With A, B, C, D, or E, ch 5, join with slip st to form ring.

Rnd 1 *Ch 3, 3 Partial tr in ring, yarn over and pull through 4 loops on hook, ch 1 to close, ch 3, slip st in ring; rep from * three more times — 4 clusters.

Rnd 2 Skip next ch-3 space, *10 tr in top of next cluster — *corner shell made*, slip st into ring over Rnd-1 slip st; rep from * three more times. Fasten off.

Rnd 3 Join MC with BPtr around any slip st between corner shells, *ch 2, skip 2 tr, BPsc around next tr, ch 1, skip 1 tr, BPsc around next tr, ch 3, BPsc around next tr, ch 1, skip 1 tr, BPsc around next tr**, ch 2, skip 2 tr, BPtr around next slip st; rep from * around, ending last rep at **, join with dc to first tr.

Rnd 4 *7 tr in next tr, skip 1 space, sc in next space, 9 tr in corner space, sc in next space; rep from * around, join with slip st to first tr. Fasten off.

Rnd 5 Join MC with BPsc in 8th tr of any 9-tr shell, ch 1, * BPtr around next sc, ch 2, skip 2 tr, BPsc around next tr, ch 1, skip 1 tr, BPsc around next tr, ch 2, skip 2 tr, BPtr around next sc, (ch 1, skip 1 tr, BPsc around next tr) two times, ch 3, skip 1 tr**, (BPsc around next tr, ch 1, skip 1 tr) two times; rep from * around, ending last rep at **, BPsc around next tr, skip 1 tr, join with sc to first sc.

Finished Measurements
30" (76 cm) square

Yarn
Lion Brand Collection Cotton Bamboo, 52% cotton/48% rayon from bamboo, 245 yds/3.5 oz (224 m/100g), 4 balls #98 Magnolia (MC), 1 ball each #107 Hyacinth (A), #135 Persimmon (B), #139 Hibiscus (C), #170 Gardenia (D), and #174 Snapdragon (E)

Hook
Size G/6 (4.0 mm) *or size you need to obtain correct gauge*

Gauge
Rounds 1–7 = 6" (15 cm)

Note: Motifs are worked using a join-as-you-go (JAYGo) method (see page 35). Refer to assembly diagram for placement of motifs. When instructed to work into a cluster, work into the ch-1 st at the top of the cluster throughout. To work a BPtr around a slip stitch, insert hook from back to front to back around the vertical portion of the slip stitch as it comes up from the center ring.

For stitch definitions, see glossary (page 264).

Rnd 6 Ch 1, sc in space formed by joining sc, *(7 tr in next tr, skip 1 space, sc in next space) two times, 9 tr in corner space, sc in next space; rep from * around, omitting last sc, join with slip st to first sc. Fasten off.

Blanket

Referring to the assembly diagram for color arrangement of motifs, make and join 25 Square Motifs, joining each motif to previous motifs with flat joins (page 37) on the final round. Make joins after the center treble of each 7-treble shells and after the 3rd and 7th trebles of the corner 9-treble shells. Weave in ends.

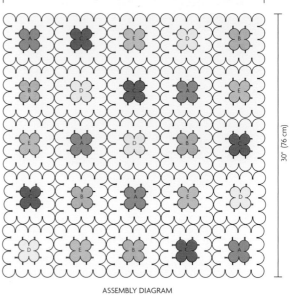

ASSEMBLY DIAGRAM

MOTIF #1

MOTIF #2

MOTIF #3

MOTIF #4

REDUCED SAMPLE OF JOINING MOTIFS

Pie Wedge Pillow

Because these triangles have slightly curved sides, it only takes five of them to create a circle, instead of the six you would expect. The curved sides also create a convex shape perfect for fitting over a round pillow form. Reverse the colors on one side of the pillow for a completely different look! This is Motif 72 (page 167).

Triangle Motif

Begin with a sliding loop.

Rnd 1 Ch 6 (counts as dc and ch-3), sc in 3rd ch from hook, 3 dc around the post of ch-3, tr in ring, *dc in ring, ch 3, sc in 3rd ch from hook, 3 dc around the post of dc, tr in ring; rep from * once more, join with slip st to 3rd ch of ch-6. Fasten off.

Rnd 2 Join with slip st in any ch-3 corner space, *ch 3, 3 dc in same space, skip 1 sc, dc in next 3 dc, 3 dc in next tr, slip st in next ch-3 corner space; rep from * around. Fasten off.

Rnd 3 Join with slip st in 3rd ch of any ch-3 corner, *ch 3, 2 dc in same st, dc in next 8 dc, 3 dc in next dc, slip st in 3rd ch of next ch-3; rep from * around. Fasten off.

Rnd 4 Join with slip st in 3rd ch of any ch-3 corner, *ch 3, 2 dc in same st, dc in next 12 dc, 3 dc in next dc, slip st in 3rd ch of next ch-3; rep from * around. Fasten off.

Rnd 5 Join with slip st in 3rd ch of any ch-3 corner, ch 3, dc in same st, *dc in next 16 dc, 3 tr in next dc, slip st in 3rd ch of next ch-3**, ch 3, 2 dc in same st; rep from * around, ending last rep at **.

Rnd 6 Ch 3, slip st in 3rd ch of next ch-3, ch 2, hdc in same st, *hdc in next dc, sc in next 14 dc, hdc in next 2 dc, dc in next 2 dc, (2 dc, tr) in next dc**, 3 hdc in 3rd ch of next ch-3 hdc in next dc; rep from * around, ending last rep at **, 2 hdc in base of beg ch 2, join with slip st to top of ch 2. Fasten off.

Finished Measurements
14" (35.5 cm) diameter

Yarn
Cascade 220 Superwash, 100% superwash wool, 220 yds/3.5 oz, (200 m/100g), 1 skein each #908 Magenta (A), #804 Amethyst (B), and #803 Royal Purple (C)

Hook
Size H/8 (5.0 mm) *or size you need to obtain correct gauge*

Gauge
Triangle motif = 4" (10 cm) tip-to-side

Other Supplies
14" (36 cm) round pillow form (sample used Poly-fil Soft Touch Brand by Fairfield)

Note: Motifs are worked separately, then joined with a single crochet seam. If desired, cover pillow form with fabric in a solid color similar to yarn color to minimize show-through of pillow form.

Pillow

These directions are for a pillow featuring differently colored sides.

Note: Stretching the crocheted fabric over a pillow form may stretch the stitches somewhat. If necessary, use yarn tails to sew the gap between the beginning and end of Rounds 5 and 6.

FIRST SIDE

Make five Triangle Motifs, using the following color sequence:

> Rnds 1 and 4 C ■
> Rnds 2, 5, and 6 A ■
> Rnd 3 B ■

Holding pieces with wrong sides together, and referring to photo for arrangement of triangles, single crochet through both loops of adjacent edge stitches to create a single crochet join (see page 37). Join all five pieces in this manner. Weave in ends.

SECOND SIDE

Make five Triangle Motifs, using the following color sequence:

> Rnds 1 and 4 A ■
> Rnd 2 B ■
> Rnds 3, 5, and 6 C ■

Join pieces and sew gaps as for first side.

Block both pieces. Each piece should measure about 13½" (34 cm) in diameter when blocked.

FINISHING

Joining Rnd Holding sides with wrong sides together and second side facing, with A, sc through both loops of adjacent edge sts around, inserting pillow form before completing seam and adjusting stitch count to result in a multiple of 3 sts; join with slip st to first st. Fasten off.

EDGING

Rnd 1 With second side facing, join B with slip st in any sc, *ch 4, 3 tr in same st, skip 2 sc, slip st in next st; rep from * around, join with slip st in first st. Fasten off. Turn.

Rnd 2 *Rnd 2 is worked into the Joining Rnd, with Rnd 1 held in back.* With first side facing, join C with slip st in any skipped sc, *ch 4, 3 tr in same st, skip 2 sc, slip st in next st; rep from * around, join with slip st in first st. Fasten off.

Weave in ends.

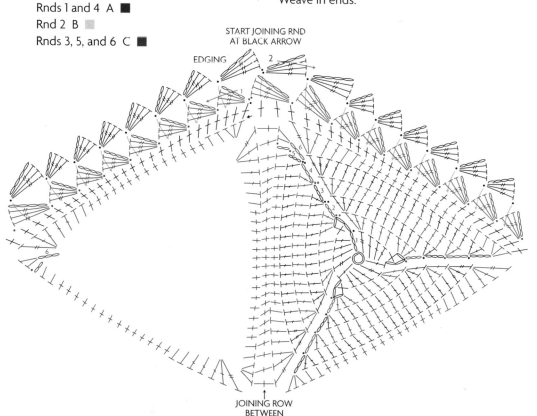

START JOINING RND
AT BLACK ARROW

EDGING

JOINING ROW
BETWEEN
TRIANGLES

Flower Garland

Try an unexpected connection method! In this garland, individual tiny flowers are threaded onto monofilament thread and held in place with square knots. These flowers are a portion of Motif 59 (page 146), but you can use any motif at all. As a matter of fact, this is an excellent technique to let your imagination run wild — use geometric shapes, 3-D motifs, anything you can think of to string together as a mobile, wall hanging, or garland.

Flower 1 (make 16)

With A, ch 5, join with slip st to form ring.

Rnd 1 Ch 3 (counts as dc), 17 dc in ring — 18 dc. Fasten off.

Rnd 2 Join B with slip st in any st, *(ch 3, 2 tr) in same st, Picot-3, (2 tr, ch 3, slip st) in next st, ch 1, skip 1 dc**, slip st in next dc; rep from * around, ending at **, join with slip st in first dc — 6 petals. Fasten off. Weave in ends.

Flower 2 (make 7)

Substitute a Beaded Picot-3 for the regular Picot-3 to have a bead at the tips of the petals.

With A, begin with sliding loop.

Rnd 1 Ch 1, 9 sc in ring, join with slip st in back loop of first sc — 9 sc.

Rnd 2 Ch 3 (counts as dc), FLdc in same st, 2 FLdc in each sc around — 18 dc. Fasten off.

Rnd 3 Join B with slip st in any st, *(ch 3, 2 tr) in same st, Picot-3, (2 tr, ch 3, slip st) in next st, ch 1, skip 1 dc**, slip st in next dc; rep from * around, ending at **, join with slip st in first dc — 6 petals. Fasten off.

Rnd 4 *Rnd 4 sts are worked into the front loops of Rnd-1 sts.* With C, standing sc in front loop of any Rnd-1 sc, ch 3, * FLsc in next sc, ch 3; rep from * around, join with slip st to first sc. Fasten off.

Weave in ends.

Finished Measurements
Individual flowers are about 1.5" (3.5 cm) in diameter. Piece shown is 9 ft (2.7 m) long, but garland may be made any length desired.

Yarn
Universal Yarn Nazli Gelin Garden 10 crochet thread, 100% Peruvian cotton, 308 yds/1.75 oz (282 m/ 50 g), a few yards each in colors of your choice (shown in #5 pink, #12 purple, #14 apple green, #21 blue, #22 lavender, #23 turquoise, #26 yellow, #27 orange)

Hook
Size 0 (1.75 mm) steel hook *or size you need to obtain correct gauge*

FLOWER #1

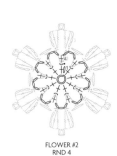

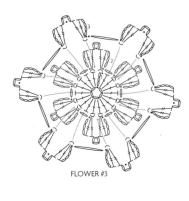

FLOWER #3

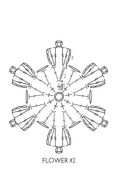

FLOWER #2

FLOWER #2
RND 4

Flower 3 (make 7)

With A, ch 5, join with slip st to form ring.

Rnd 1 Ch 3 (counts as dc), 17 dc in ring —
18 dc. Fasten off.

Rnd 2 *Rnd 2 is worked in front loop only
of Rnd-1 sts.* Join B with slip st in front loop
of any st, *(ch 3, 2 FLtr) in same st, Picot-3,
(2 FLtr, ch 3, slip st) in front loop of next st,
ch 1, skip 1 dc**, slip st in front loop of next
dc; rep from * around, ending at **, join
with slip st in first dc — 6 petals. Fasten off.

Rnd 3 *Rnd 3 is worked in back loop only
of Rnd-1 sts.* Join B with slip st in back loop
of any st *(see note below)*, *(ch 4, 2 BLdtr)
in same st, Picot-3, (2 BLdtr, ch 4, slip st) in
back loop of next st, ch 1, skip 1 dc**, slip st
in back loop of next dc; rep from * around,
ending at **, join with slip st in first dc —
6 petals. Fasten off. Weave in ends.

*Note: When working last round of Flower 3, vary
beginning of round to begin in first, second, or third
stitch.*

Gauge
Rounds 1–3 = 1⅞" (4.75 cm) tip-
to-tip (Gauge is not crucial in this
pattern.)

Other Supplies
Clear 8-pound fishing line or other
clear filament, size 8 seed beads

*Notes: Garland is made with
three flower patterns, using the
color combinations and embellishments of your choice to make
each flower unique.*

*Color A is the color of the flower
center; Color B is the petal color;
Color C is an accent color.*

*Add beads to petals as desired by
working Beaded Picot-3 in place
of Picot-3.*

*Flowers are joined with fishing
line, clear monofilament thread,
or a crochet thread. Use a square
knot to hold the flowers in place.*

FLOWER GARLAND

Embellishments

Some embellishments can be added after you've made the basic flower.

Surface chain around Rnd-1 dcs or scs
Holding C on wrong side of fabric, *insert hook from front to back between two dcs, yarn over, and pull up a loop through fabric and through loop on hook; rep from * around, working between dc posts, ending by cutting C and pulling yarn to right side. Thread tail through tapestry needle, then insert tapestry needle around both "legs" of first surface chain, then from front to back through same place where yarn comes to right side. Weave in ends.

Center accent With C, begin with sliding loop. Ch 1, (sc in ring, ch 3) six times, join with invisible join (tapestry needle join, page 16) to first sc. Fasten off. Use tails to sew accent to center of Basic Flower.

Joining the Flowers

Cut filament to desired length plus 24" (61 cm), plus 1" (2.5 cm) for each flower to be joined. Thread end of filament through tip of one flower; pull flower toward center of base; tie in place with a single overhand knot. Working from center of base outward, repeat for remaining flowers. Before joining last two flowers, trim base to desired length plus 4" (10 cm). Tie remaining flowers onto ends of base and trim ends.

Beaded Picot-3 Ch 1, push bead up to hook, ch 2, slip st in 3rd ch from hook.

BLdtr (back loop double treble crochet) Work 1 double treble crochet into the back loop only.

FLdc (front loop double crochet) Work 1 double crochet into the front loop only.

FLsc (front loop single crochet) Work 1 single crochet into the front loop only.

FLtr (front loop treble crochet) Work 1 treble crochet into the front loop only.

FLdtr (front loop double treble crochet) Work 1 double treble crochet into the front loop only.

Picot-3 Ch 3, slip st in 3rd ch from hook.

Surface chain Holding yarn on wrong side of fabric, insert hook from front to back into next st and pull up a loop through fabric and through loop on hook.

Poet Vest

Long color changes in the yarn combine with simple JAYGo squares to create this unique vest. The stitching is easy-peasy, but read through all the instructions before beginning to gain a better understanding of the overall construction. If you like, omit the button and button loop and use a lovely shawl pin to close the front.

Motif

Begin with a sliding loop.

Rnd 1 Ch 3 (counts as dc), 15 dc in ring, join with slip st to top of ch-3 — 16 dc.

Rnd 2 Ch 3 (counts as dc), dc in next 2 dc, *ch 5, skip 1 dc**, dc in next 3 dc; rep from * around, ending last rep at **, join with slip st to top of ch-3.

Rnd 3 Ch 3 (counts as dc), dc in next 2 dc, *ch 2, (dc, ch 5, dc) in next ch-space, ch 2**, dc in next 3 dc; rep from * around, ending last rep at **, join with slip st to top of ch-3. Fasten off.

Half Motif

Begin with sliding loop.

Row 1 Ch 3 (counts as dc), 10 dc in ring, turn — 11 dc.

Row 2 Ch 3 (counts as dc), dc in next 2 dc, *ch 5, skip 1 dc, dc in next 3 dc; rep from * once more, turn.

Row 3 Ch 3 (counts as dc), dc in next 2 dc, *ch 2, (dc, ch 5, dc) in next ch-space, ch 2, dc in next 3 dc; rep from * once more. Fasten off.

Making the Vest

BACK

Make one square (Motif #1). Make a second square through Rnd 2, then join to Motif #1 as follows:

Sizes
Women's Small (Medium, Large, X-Large, XX-Large); sample shown in size Medium

Finished Bust: 34 (38¼, 42½, 46¾, 51)"/86 (97, 108, 119, 130) cm

Finished Length: 22¼ (22¼, 23½, 25½, 26½)"/ 57 (57, 60, 65, 67) cm

Yarn
Wisdom Yarns Poems Sock, 75% superwash wool/25% nylon, 3.5 oz (100 g)/459 yds (420 m), 3 (3, 4, 4, 5) balls #955 Tropical Sunset

Hook
D/3 (3.25 mm) hook *or size you need to obtain correct gauge*

Gauge
Rounds 1–3 = 2⅛" (5.5 cm), blocked

Other Supplies
One 1" (2.5 cm) button

Rnd 3 Ch 3 (counts as dc), dc in next 2 dc, *ch 2, (dc, ch 5, dc) in next ch-space, ch 2, dc in next 3 dc, rep from * once more, ch 2, dc in next ch-space, ch 3; joining to Motif #1, flat join in first corner space, ch 2, dc in same space, ch 1, flat join in adjacent space, ch 2, dc in next 2 dcs, flat join to adjacent dc, dc in next dc, ch 1, flat join, ch 1, dc in next ch-space, ch 2, flat join, ch 3, dc in same space, ch 2, join with slip st to top of ch-3.

Referring to assembly diagram for your size (pages 249–250), continue in this manner to join additional squares in a column as indicated. Beginning again at lower edge of garment, join next square to Motif #1 as follows:

Rnd 3 Ch 3 (counts as dc), dc in next 2 dc, *ch 2, (dc, ch 5, dc) in next ch-space, ch 2, dc in next 3 dc, rep from * once more, ch 2, dc in next ch-space, ch 3, flat join in 2nd corner space of previous motif, ch 2, dc in same space, ch 1, flat join in adjacent space, ch 2, dc in next 2 dcs, flat join to adjacent dc, dc in next dc, ch 1, flat join in adjacent space, ch 1, dc in next ch-space, ch 2, flat join in adjacent corner space, ch 3, dc in same space, ch 2, join with slip st to top of ch-3. Fasten off.

Join next motif to two previous motifs as follows:

Rnd 3 Ch 3 (counts as dc), dc in next 2 dc, ch 2, (dc, ch 5, dc) in next ch-space, ch 2, dc in next 3 dc, ch 2, dc in next ch-space, ch 3; joining to last complete motif worked, flat

join in first corner space, ch 2, dc in same space, ch 1, flat join to next adjacent space, dc in next 2 dcs, flat join to adjacent dc, dc in next dc, ch 1, flat join to next adjacent space, ch 1, dc in next ch-space, ch 2, flat join to adjacent corner space, ch 1; joining to Motif #2, flat join in corner ch-space, ch 2, dc in same ch-space of current motif, ch 1, flat join to adjacent space, ch 1, dc in next 2 dc, flat join, dc in next dc, ch 1, flat join, ch 1, dc in next space, ch 2, flat join to adjacent corner space, ch 3, dc in same ch-space, ch 2, join with slip st to top of ch-3. Fasten off.

Referring to assembly diagram for your size, continue in this manner to join motifs in order, working from the lower edge of the body, until you reach the end of the first ball of yarn, ending with a complete motif. (Do not change yarns in the middle of a motif.)

Notes: The vest body is worked in columns from the lower edge upward, beginning at the right underarm or right back. There are no seams. Motifs are joined as you work the final round of each square, creating a single fabric. Left front shoulders are joined to left back shoulders and right front shoulders are joined to right back shoulders as you work.

The assembly diagrams show the order in which the motifs are worked and joined; refer to the one for your size frequently.

Motifs are joined to previous ones at corner ch-5 spaces, ch-2 spaces, and the center dc of each 3-dc group along the edge. Half motifs (if applicable) are joined at corner ch-5 spaces, ch-2 spaces, the center dc of the 3-dc group

along the long edge, and in the first and last 2 dc along each short edge.

Instructions are given so that the color sequence in the garment remains as close to the way it appears in the yarn as possible. Read Starting a New Ball (page 248) for a better understanding of color changes.

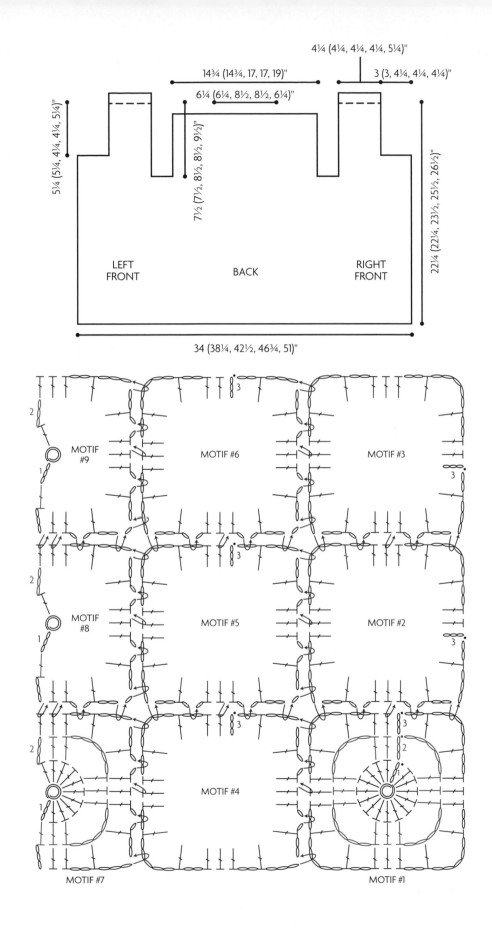

4¼ (4¼, 4¼, 4¼, 5¼)"

14¾ (14¾, 17, 17, 19)"

3 (3, 4¼, 4¼, 4¼)"

6¼ (6¼, 8½, 8½, 6¼)"

5¼ (5¼, 4¼, 4¼, 5¼)"

7½ (7½, 8½, 8½, 9½)"

22¼ (22¼, 23½, 25½, 26½)"

LEFT
FRONT

BACK

RIGHT
FRONT

34 (38¼, 42½, 46¾, 51)"

2

MOTIF
#9

1

MOTIF #6

MOTIF #3

3

3

2

MOTIF
#8

1

MOTIF #5

MOTIF #2

3

3

2

MOTIF #4

1

3

2

1

MOTIF #7

MOTIF #1

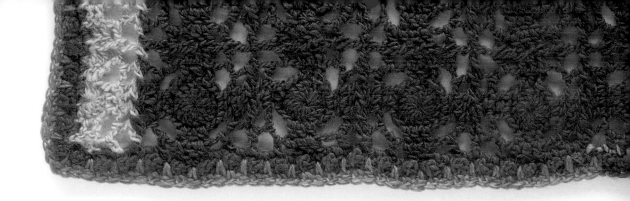

Starting a New Ball

Note: Before continuing, read this entire section.

Begin hand-winding a center-pull ball (see page 20) with the new yarn. As you are winding and you come to a section of yarn that is the same color as the last square worked on the vest, break the yarn. Set aside the hand-wound ball, and resume working the vest with the main ball of yarn. Note that some of the squares may be very similar colors; work in good light to make a good comparison of colors. If you use all of this ball of yarn, repeat with the hand-wound ball to make another color match.

Knots in the yarn or the inability to color-match on the last ball of yarn may require a shift in the color sequence. Make these transitions at the beginning of a vertical column if possible, but don't worry too much if that is not possible. One or two color shifts will not be noticeable in the overall garment.

SHOULDER JOINS AND LEFT FRONT

Continue working joined motifs as necessary to complete all squares through Motif #87 (94, 112, 139, 152). Join next square to previous square and to Motif #70 (70, 88, 104, 116). Continue working Left Front through Motif 98 (105, 123, 151, 165). Join next motif to two previous squares and to Motif #60 (60, 77, 92, 104).

For XX-Large only: Work through Motif #176, then work two Half Motifs (177 and 178). Join next Half Motif to two previous squares and to half of Motif #92.

Continue working Left Front as shown in the assembly diagram through the Left Front edge.

RIGHT FRONT

The first series of motifs for the Right Front is worked independently of the Back and Left Front.

Work motifs or half motifs #116–153 (123–167, 143–189, 173–224, 200–266) as indicated on diagram, joining the next series of motifs to previous Right Front motifs, working Right Front, and joining shoulders as indicated on assembly diagram.

WORKING THE FINAL SERIES OF SQUARES

The final strip of squares joins the Right Front to the Back. Join Motif #154 (168, 190, 225, 267) to Motif #1 and Motif 143 (161, 183, 217, 259). Work remaining motifs according to the assembly diagram, joining each to the Back, the previous motif, and the Right Front.

Sc3tog (single crochet 3 stitches together) (Insert hook into next st and pull up a loop) three times, yarn over and pull through all 4 loops on hook.

Spike dc Yarn over, insert hook into stitch or space indicated, yarn over, pull up a loop to level of current round, (yarn over and pull though 2 loops on hook) two times.

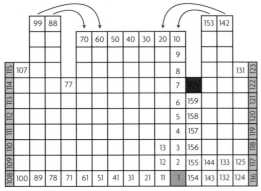

ASSEMBLY DIAGRAM
SIZE SMALL

ASSEMBLY DIAGRAM
SIZE MEDIUM

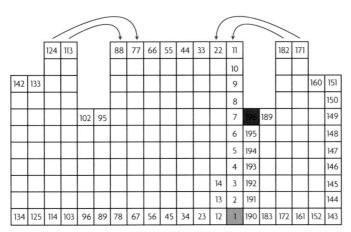

ASSEMBLY DIAGRAM
SIZE LARGE

= MOTIF #1

= LAST MOTIF

= HALF SQUARE

= INDICATES SQUARES JOINED TO CREATE SHOULDER SEAMS

ASSEMBLY DIAGRAM
SIZE X-LARGE

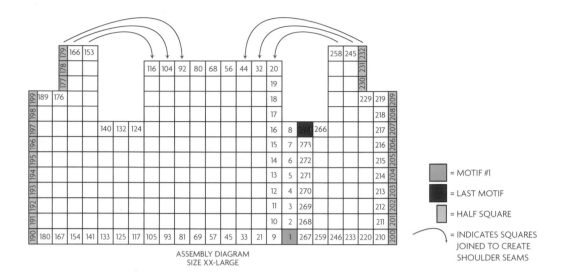

ASSEMBLY DIAGRAM
SIZE XX-LARGE

= MOTIF #1

= LAST MOTIF

= HALF SQUARE

= INDICATES SQUARES JOINED TO CREATE SHOULDER SEAMS

Finishing

Block body.

Note: Read all instructions before proceeding.

BODY EDGING

With RS facing, join yarn at lower edge of left underarm.

Rnd 1 Ch 1, sc evenly around, using the following guidelines: Place 1 sc in each dc; place 2 sc in each ch-space; place 2 sc in side of each row-end dc on Half Squares (where applicable); place 1 hdc in each center hole of Half Squares (where applicable); place extra scs in upper and lower front corners as necessary to allow edge to lie flat; join with slip st to first sc.

Rnd 2 Ch 1, sc in same space, *insert hook into next st and pull up a loop, (yarn over and pull through 1 loop) three times, yarn over and pull through both loops on hook, skip 1 st, sc in next st; rep from * around, omitting last sc, join with slip st to first st. *In order to allow edging to lie flat at corners and to end at the end of a repeat, omit skipped sts as necessary at corners of Left and Right Fronts and skip additional sts as necessary at interior corners. Edging may be slightly rippled along straight edges at this point.*

Rnd 3 Ch 1, *Spike dc in st below next sc, sc in next st; rep from * around, placing 3 sts in each corner of Left and Right Fronts, and working sc3tog at interior corners, join with slip st to first st. Fasten off.

EDGING THE ARMHOLE

Work as for Body Edging around each armhole opening.

WORKING THE BUTTON LOOP

With RS facing, join yarn on Right Front edge 5 sts below corner stitch. Ch 1, sc in same st and in next st; *do not turn;* sc in left side of sc just made (the stitch just created has a vertical left leg); rep from * until loop is long enough to reach around button, slightly stretched; sc in same st and in next st on Right Front edge. Fasten off.

Sew button opposite button loop. Weave in ends. Block.

Lacy Skirt

Colorful stretchy yarn combines with 4" (10 cm) medallions (Motif 15, page 68) to create this easy-to-stitch skirt. The continuous-motif method creates a seamless circular tube that can be customized for any size and length. If you prefer multiple colors, stitch individual motifs (see page 256) and use a join-as-you-go method. Wear it over a pair of leggings or yoga pants, or sew in a stretchy lining.

Foundation Chain Motif

Ch 16 for foundation chain, slip st in 4th ch from hook to form ring.

Rnd 1 Ch 2, skip 2 foundation ch, Crossover slip st in next foundation ch, ch 2, *dc2tog in ring, ch 2; rep from * four more times, join with slip st to top of first cluster — 6 clusters.

Rnd 2 Slip st in next 2 foundation ch, Crossover slip st in next foundation ch (counts as dc), dc in same st, ch 1, *3 dc in next cluster, ch 1; rep from * around, ending dc in first st, join with slip st to top of first dc — six 3-dc shells.

Finished Length
4 tiers: approximately
17" (43 cm)

5 tiers: approximately 20" (51 cm)

6 tiers: approximately 23" (58.5 cm)

Finished Hip Measurements
36 (40, 44, 48, 52)"/
91 (102, 112, 122, 132) cm

Yarn
Kollage Luscious, 63% cotton/
37% nylon elastic, 185 yds/2 oz
(169 m/55 g), 5 (5, 6, 6, 7) balls
#6715 Apricot

Hook
G/6 (4.0 mm) or size you need to obtain correct gauge

Gauge
Rounds 1–4 = 4" (10 cm)

Other Supplies
Tapestry needle

Notes: Skirt is constructed as one entire seamless piece with a variation of the basic motif that uses foundation chains to work connected motifs. The fabric is worked back and forth until all motifs have been started, then joined into a tube as the final motifs are completed. The waist-band is added last. Refer to the stitching diagram (pages 254–255) for detailed instructions.

Beginning with the lower left-hand motif (lower right-hand for lefties), work a series of joined partial motifs for the first tier. Complete the first-tier motifs as you work back across the top of the tier to the first motif, adding extensions at the corners for subsequent tiers. Work a portion of the last round of the first motif, then move on to begin the second tier, joining each motif to the first tier and to previous motifs as indicated.

Rnd 3 Slip st in next 2 foundation ch, Crossover slip st in next foundation ch (counts as dc), 2 dc in same st, ch 3, 5 dc in center of next 3-dc shell, ch 3; rep from * around, ending 2 dc in first st, join with slip st to top of first dc — six 5-dc shells.

Note: Working Rnd 4 varies depending on its position; see specific instructions below.

Lower Tier

Work Foundation Chain Motif through Rnd 3.

Rnd 4, first motif Slip st in next 2 foundation ch, Crossover slip st in next foundation ch (counts as dc), 2 dc in same st, [ch 3, (sc, ch 3, sc) in next space, ch 3, 5 dc in center of next 5-dc shell] two times, ch 3, (sc, ch 3, sc) in next space, ch 3, 3 dc in center of next 5-dc shell. *Rnd 4 remains incomplete.*

Ch 1 for connecting st between motifs.

SUBSEQUENT MOTIFS

Work 7 (8, 9, 10, 11) additional Foundation Chain Motifs in this manner with a ch-1 connection between each. Work one more foundation chain through Rnd 3 — 9 (10, 11, 12, 13) partial motifs in lower tier.

COMPLETING THE LOWER TIER

Rnd 4 Slip st in next 2 foundation ch, Crossover slip st in next foundation ch (counts as dc), 2 dc in same st, [[(ch 3, sc) two times in next space, ch 3, 5 dc in center of next 5-dc shell] three times, [ch 3, extended corner in next space, ch 3, 5 dc in center of next 5-dc shell] two times, ch 3, extended corner in next space, ch 3, 2 dc in first st, slip st in top of first dc, slip st in ch-1 st between motifs.

Rnd 4, next motif 2 dc in same st as partial 5-dc shell, ch 3, sc in next space, ch 4, slip st in adjoining ch-9 loop of previous motif, ch 4, sc in same space — *extended corner join made*, ch 3, 5 dc in center of next 5-dc shell, ch 3, extended corner in next space ch 3, 5 dc in center of next 5-dc shell, ch 3, extended corner in next space, ch 3, 2 dc in first st, slip st in top of first dc, slip st in ch-1 st between motifs.

Continue in this manner to work across top of lower tier, joining each motif to previous motifs at extended corners, to last motif (first motif of tier).

Rnd 4, last motif 2 dc in same st as partial 5-dc shell, ch 3, extended corner join, ch 3, 5 dc in center of next 5-dc shell, ch 3, extended corner in next space, ch 3, 3 dc in center of next 5-dc shell. *Rnd 4 remains incomplete on this motif.*

Ch 1 for connecting st between motifs.

Second Tier

Work Foundation Chain Motif through Rnd 3.

Rnd 4 Slip st in next 2 foundation ch, Crossover slip st in next foundation ch (counts as dc), 2 dc in same st, ch 3, extended corner join, ch 3, 3 dc in center of next 5-dc shell. *Rnd 4 remains incomplete.*

Ch 1 for connecting st between motifs.

Crossover slip st Insert hook into stitch indicated, pass foundation chain over working yarn, yarn over and pull through all loops on hook to complete slip st.

Dc2tog (double crochet 2 together) Yarn over, insert hook into indicated stitch or space and pull up a loop, yarn over, pull through 2 loops, yarn over, insert hook into same stitch and pull up a loop, yarn over and pull through 2 loops, yarn over and pull through all 3 loops on hook.

Extended corner (Sc, ch 9, sc) in ch-space.

NEXT MOTIF

Work Foundation Chain Motif through Rnd 3.

Rnd 4 Slip st in next 2 foundation ch, Cross-over slip st in next foundation ch (counts as dc), 2 dc in same st, [ch 3, extended corner join around slip st of adjacent corner-joins, ch 3, 2 dc in center of next 5-dc shell, flat join in center st of adjacent shell, 3 dc in center of same 5-dc shell—*shell join made*, ch 3, extended corner join around slip st of adjacent corner-joins, ch 3, shell join, ch 3, extended corner join in adjacent ch-9 loop, ch 3, 3 dc in center of next 5-dc shell. *Rnd 4 remains incomplete.*

Ch 1 for connecting st between motifs.

SUBSEQUENT MOTIFS

Work 7 (8, 9, 10, 11) additional motifs in this manner, joining at extended corners and adjacent shells. Complete the second tier by completing Rnd 4 on all motifs, joining at extended corners and adjacent shells, and leaving first motif of tier incomplete to begin the next tier.

Additional Tiers

Referring to diagram, work additional tiers as needed for desired length, ending before completing Rnd 4 of top tier.

Completing the Top Tier and Joining the Skirt

Continue Rnd 4 as before on all top-tier motifs to first motif of tier, but omit the extended corner at the center top of each motif and work a (sc, ch 3, sc) corner instead.

Rnd 4, final motif, top tier 2 dc in same st as partial 5-dc shell, ch 3, extended corner join in adjacent ch-9 loop of previous motif, ch 3, 5 dc in center of next shell, ch 3, (sc, ch 3, sc) in next space, 5 dc in center of next shell, ch 3; extended corner join in adjacent ch-9 loop of *last* motif of same tier to form a tube, ch 3, shell join, ch 3, extended corner

join around slip st of adjacent corner joins. *For even number of tiers only:* Ch 3, shell join, ch 3, extended corner in next space. *For all sizes:* Ch 3, 2 dc in first st, slip st in connecting ch.

Continue in this manner to complete Rnd 4 of the first motif of each tier, joining each with extended corner joins and shell joins to close the tube; end 2 dc in first st of first motif, slip st in top of first dc. Fasten off.

Making the Waistband

Rnd 1 With RS facing, standing sc in any center ch-3 space on side of any motif on top tier, ch 2, *sc in next ch-space, ch 2, sc in center dc of next shell, ch 2, dc in slip st of next corner joins, ch 2, sc in center dc of next shell, ch 2**, (sc in next ch-space, ch 2) two times; rep from * around, ending last rep at **, sc in next ch-space, ch 2, join with slip st to top of first sc — 54 (60, 66, 72, 78) ch-2 spaces.

Rnd 2 Ch 2 (counts as hdc), hdc in each sc and 2 hdc in each ch-2 space around, join with slip st to top of ch-2 — 162 (180, 198, 216, 234) hdc.

Rnd 3 Ch 1, sc in same st, *sc in next 3 sc, hdc in next 3 hdc, dc in next 5 hdc, hdc in next 3 hdc, sc in next 4 hdc; rep from * around, omitting last sc, join with slip st to first sc — 9 (10, 11, 12, 13) 5-dc sections.

Rnd 4 Ch 1, sc in same st, sc in next 2 sts, ch 1, skip 1 st, *sc in next 3 sts, ch 1, skip 1 st; rep from * around ending sc in last 2 (0, 2, 0, 2) sts, join with slip st to first sc — 40 (45, 49, 54, 58) ch-1 spaces.

Rnd 5 Ch 1, sc in same st, ch 1, skip 1 sc, *sc in next st or space, ch 1, skip 1 st or space; rep from * around, ending sc in last 0 (1, 1, 0, 0) st, join with slip st to first sc. Fasten off.

Weave in ends. Block skirt.

= SHADED AREA REPRESENTS
LAST MOTIF OF EACH TIER

WAISTBAND

REDUCED SAMPLE OF CONTINUOUS JOINING OF MOTIFS
FOR AN ODD NUMBER OF TIERS

MOTIF #3

MOTIF #3

MOTIF #3

MOTIF #1

START
HERE

MOTIF #1

MOTIF #1

MOTIF #2

MOTIF #2

MOTIF #2

MOTIF #3

MOTIF #3

MOTIF #3

LOWER
TIER

SECOND
TIER

TOP
TIER

WAISTBAND

TOP TIER

THIRD TIER

MOTIF #3

SECOND TIER

MOTIF #3

LOWER TIER

MOTIF #3

MOTIF #2

MOTIF #2

MOTIF #2

MOTIF #1

MOTIF #1

MOTIF #1

MOTIF #3

MOTIF #3

MOTIF #3

START HERE

REDUCED SAMPLE OF CONTINUOUS JOINING OF MOTIFS FOR AN EVEN NUMBER OF TIERS

= SHADED AREA REPRESENTS LAST MOTIF OF EACH TIER

	1	2	3	4	5	6	7	8	9	10	11	12	13
TOP TIER	1	2	3	4	5	6	7	8	9	10	11	12	13
FIFTH TIER	1	2	3	4	5	6	7	8	9	10	11	12	13
FOURTH TIER	1	2	3	4	5	6	7	8	9	10	11	12	13
THIRD TIER	1	2	3	4	5	6	7	8	9	10	11	12	13
SECOND TIER	1	2	3	4	5	6	7	8	9	10	11	12	13
LOWER TIER	1	2	3	4	5	6	7	8	9	10	11	12	13

S   M   L   XL   XXL

ASSEMBLY DIAGRAM

LACY SKIRT

Tie

Ch 4, join with slip st to form a ring.

Ch 2, dc in ring (counts as dc2tog), ch 1, (dc2tog in ring, ch 2) five times, join with slip st to top of first cluster, chain a length equal to the circumference of the waistband, plus 6" (15 cm) to serve as waist tie and founda-tion chain for end of tie. Slip st in 4th ch from hook to form ring; ch 2, skip 1 foundation ch, Crossover slip st in next foundation ch, ch 2, (dc2tog in ring, ch 2) five times, join with slip st to top of first cluster — 6 clusters. Fasten off. Weave in ends.

Thread tie through waistband eyelets.

CHAIN LENGTH OF
WAISTBAND PLUS 6" (15 cm)

SECOND END

FIRST END

TIE

Basic Motif

These instructions are for the basic motif used in the skirt. If you choose to work individual motifs, rather than using the continuous-join method, use this basic motif (a variation of Motif 15), working extended corners in place of (sc, ch 3, sc) on the final rounds as needed to allow for connections between motifs.

Begin with sliding loop.

Rnd 1 Ch 2, dc in ring (counts as dc2tog), ch 2, *dc2tog in ring, ch 2; rep from * 4 more times, join with slip st to top of first cluster — 6 clusters.

Rnd 2 Ch 3 (counts as dc), dc in same st, ch 1, *3 dc in next cluster, ch 1; rep from * around, ending dc in first st, join with slip st to top of ch-3 — six 3-dc shells.

Rnd 3 Ch 3 (counts as dc), 2 dc in same st, ch 3, *5 dc in center of next 3-dc shell, ch 3; rep from * around, ending 2 dc in first st, join with slip st to top of ch-3 — six 5-dc shells.

Rnd 4 Ch 3 (counts as dc), 2 dc in same st, *ch 3, (sc, ch 3, sc) in next space, ch 3**, 5 dc in center of next 5-dc shell; rep from * around, ending last rep at **, 2 dc in first st, join with slip st to top of ch-3 — six 5-dc shells. Fasten off.

INDEPENDENT MOTIF

Cottage Lamp Shade

Use any motifs you like to make your own cotton lampshade that's perfect for the bedside at a beach cottage. Upcycle an old lampshade or buy an inexpensive one to deconstruct. What follows is less a pattern than a tutorial on how to craft a custom shade using your favorite motifs. Use multiple colors and threads to your heart's delight. It's a free-form/Irish crochet/modern/retro/DIY joy!

Preparing the Template

Examine the lampshade or lampshade frame to become familiar with its construction. It may be made as a single piece, with struts connecting the upper and lower rims, or it may be made of upper and lower rings, with the shade itself separating the rings. The sample shade consists of two pieces: the upper ring, including the portion that sits on the lamp, and the lower ring. The two pieces of the frame are connected by a cloth-covered plastic shade, which is attached to the frame with cloth tape.

Preserving the shape of the shade itself, carefully remove the shade from the frame. Use scissors if necessary, but try to minimize any damage to the shade. In the sample, this was easily accomplished by peeling the tape off the upper and lower frames, separating

Finished Measurements
Shade shown: 5" (12.7 cm) top diameter × 10" (25.4 cm) bottom diameter × 7" (17.7 cm) high (sample used a Target Room Essentials Mix-and-Match small lampshade, style 074-08-0237)

Yarn
Aunt Lydia's Crochet Thread Classic 10, 100% mercerized cotton, 400 yds (366 m), 1 or 2 balls #0001 white

Hook
Size 1.0–1.5 mm steel hook, or size you are most comfortable using to create firm but not tight motifs

Gauge
Gauge is not crucial in this project.

Other Supplies
Lampshade frame of any size; scissors; clean newsprint or other large piece of paper, or several pieces of 8½" × 11" (21.5 cm × 28 cm) paper taped together to use as a template; large flat surface that will accommodate pins, like a bulletin board, foam insulation board, cutting board, or similar surface; rustproof pins or tape; pencil; tapestry needle; small amount of waste yarn in a coordinating color; approximately ½ yd (46 cm) or more lightweight fabric (exact amount needed depends on size of shade); sewing needle and coordinating thread

the pieces and allowing the shade itself to come off in a single piece.

Place a large sheet of paper onto a flat surface. Place the old shade onto the paper and tape or pin it in place, if necessary. Using a pencil, trace around the shade. Remove the shade and set it aside. Cut out the paper template and place it on the flat surface. You will be using the template to help you form a fabric in the same shape as the original shade.

Making the Motifs

Using your choice of hook size and motif patterns, make a variety of motifs in pleasing shapes. Use different shapes, and feel free to work only a few rounds of a motif, or add your own variations to existing motifs to make them your own. Play with sizes, as well; you may want to use several large motifs interspersed with dainty ones, or you may prefer keeping the sizes relatively equal.

As you stitch, block the motifs and then place on the template and play with arranging them to fit. Leave ¼" (6 mm) or more between each motif. When the template is about half full, begin to pin the motifs straight onto the template surface, stretching each to its fullest extent.

Continue to stitch and pin additional motifs, arranging them as necessary to fill the template.

JOINING THE MOTIFS

Begin working a series of short chains between the motifs, connecting the chains to individual motifs at the corners, sides, and other locations as appropriate, and connecting the chains themselves to other chains to form a mesh. Use a variety of joining methods: flat join, slip-stitch join, and single crochet. Don't hesitate to use taller stitches like double and treble crochet to "reach down" to make a connection. Attempt to keep the motifs in their original positions as much as possible. Work in different directions: forward, backward, up, down, diagonally. Just try not to work in straight lines!

You'll have to unpin the motifs from the template surface as you work, and you may have several paths of chains going at once. Keep stretching the emerging fabric and checking it against the shape of the template as you work.

Once most of the motifs are joined in a flat fabric, pick it up and hold it up to the lampshade frame to test the fit. Make any adjustments necessary; you may have to

---

Notes: The instructions describe how the lampshade in the photograph was crafted. Use them as a guide when working on your own lampshade. Depending on the shape of your frame, the materials chosen, and your crafting skill, you may be able to improve upon the suggestions. You will certainly have to adapt them to fit your specific situation.

The overall method involves making a template from an existing lampshade, then stitching individual motifs to be arranged on the template. The motifs are then joined to each other using a free-form mesh of chains, single, double and treble crochet stitches, along with slip-stitch and other types of joins. The mesh serves to fill in the spaces between the motifs. Once the motif/mesh fabric is complete, it is crocheted onto the lamp shade frame.

If the lightbulb shows too brightly through the shade, either overlap additional motifs over existing motifs and sew them onto the mesh, add additional connected chains to form a tighter spider-web of mesh, or add a fabric lining (as shown).

rip out and redo some joins to create a well-fitting shade.

Place the shade back onto the template and work a chain evenly across the top edge to match the edge of the template, using single crochet and double crochet joins to motifs and to existing chains as necessary to form a smooth line; join the last stitch of the top chain to the beginning of the chain to form a circle. This top chain will be used to connect the shade to the frame.

Continue working a mesh toward the lower edge of the fabric, bringing each edge of the fabric into the appropriate shape. Finally, make a lower chain to match the lower edge of the template, working as for the top chain and joining the last stitch with a slip stitch. This chain will be connected to the lower frame.

Preparing the Frame

If necessary, clean the frame(s) of any dirt, rust, or glue.

Beginning with a slip knot on your hook, sc around the top edge of the frame, placing stitches close together so as to completely cover the frame; join with slip st to first st. Fasten off. Cover the lower frame in the same manner.

Attaching the Shade

Using waste yarn, loosely tie the top chain to the top frame in several locations.

The joining round will be worked over the existing stitches on the frame, not into them. Join the shade to the frame as follows:

With RS facing, beginning with slip knot on hook, sc over frame and into any chain-space on top chain — *spike sc made*, *ch 3, spike sc into top chain; rep from * around, working evenly around top chain, join with slip st to first sc. Fasten off. Remove waste yarn.

Attach the bottom of the shade in the same way.

Optional Fabric Lining

Use the template to cut a fabric lining, adding ½" (13 mm) seam allowance on ends and ¼" (6 mm) seam allowance on top and bottom edges. Fold under upper and lower edges ¼" (6 mm) and press. Fold under ¼" (6 mm) once more and press. Sew narrow hem on upper and lower edges.

Note that the lining will be slightly shorter than the template.

With RS together, sew ends of shade together, then turn under seam allowance and sew a narrow hem. Using sewing needle and thread, sew upper and lower edges of lining to single crochet stitches covering frame.

motif directory

LAYERED MESH

Motif 29
page 95

Motif 30
page 96

Motif 31
page 98

Motif 32
page 99

Motif 33
page 101

Motif 34
page 102

Motif 35
page 106

SC/DC

Motif 36
page 110

Motif 37
page 111

Motif 38
page 114

Motif 39
page 115

Motif 40
page 118

Motif 41
page 119

ALL CLUSTERED

Motif 42
page 120

Motif 43
page 122

Motif 44
page 123

Motif 45
page 126

Motif 46
page 127

Motif 47
page 128

Motif 48
page 129

TRIPLE PETALS

Motif 49
page 132

Motif 50
page 133

Motif 51
page 135

Motif 52
page 136

Motif 53
page 137

Motif 54
page 140

START WITH A FLOWER

Motif 55
page 141

Motif 56
page 142

Motif 57
page 143

Motif 58
page 144

Motif 59
page 146

Motif 60
page 147

Motif 61
page 148

Motif 62
page 149

3-D FUN

Motif 63
page 152

Motif 64
page 156

Motif 65
page 157

Motif 66
page 160

Motif 67
page 161

Motif 68
page 162

SWIRLS

Motif 69
page 164

Motif 70
page 165

Motif 71
page 166

Motif 72
page 167

Motif 73
page 170

Motif 74
page 171

RADIANTS

Motif 75
page 174

Motif 76
page 175

Motif 77
page 180

Motif 78
page 182

Motif 79
page 183

Motif 80
page 184

glossary

Beaded Picot-3 Ch 1, push bead up to hook, ch 2, slip st in 3rd ch from hook.

BLdc (back loop double crochet) Work 1 double crochet into the back loop only.

Block Stitch Sc in stitch or space indicated, ch 3, 3 dc in sc just made.

BLsc (back loop single crochet) Work 1 single crochet into the back loop only.

BLtr3tog (back loop treble 3 stitches together) Work tr3tog into the back loops only.

BPdc (back post double crochet) Yarn over, insert hook from back to front to back around post of stitch indicated and pull up a loop, (yarn over and pull through 2 loops on hook) two times.

BPdc2tog (back post double crochet 2 stitches together) (Yarn over, insert hook from back to front to back around post of next dc, yarn over and pull up a loop, yarn over and pull through 2 loops on hook) two times, yarn over and pull through all 3 loops on hook.

BPdtr (back post double treble) (Yarn over) three times, insert hook from back to front to back around post of stitch indicated and pull up a loop (yarn over and pull through 2 loops on hook) four times.

BPsc (back post single crochet) Insert hook from back to front to back around post of stitch indicated and pull up a loop, yarn over and pull through 2 loops on hook.

BPslip st (back post slip stitch) Insert hook from back to front to back around post of stitch indicated and pull up a loop through st and through loop on hook.

BPtr (back post treble crochet) (Yarn over) two times, insert hook from back to front to back around post of stitch indicated and pull up a loop (yarn over and pull through 2 loops on hook) three times.

Ch (chain stitch) Yarn over, pull yarn through stitch on hook.

Cluster any group of stitches that have been worked together, for example, dc5tog.

Crab Stitch (Reverse single crochet) Working from left to right for right-handers, or from right to left for left handers, and keeping hook pointed toward the left (right); insert hook into work, wrap yarn over hook and draw the yarn through work, wrap yarn around hook again and draw yarn through both loops on hook.

Crocodile Stitch Instructions are written for right-handed crochet with left-handed directions in brackets. Holding piece with first st to be worked to the right [left] at 3 o'clock [9 o'clock] position and working from right to left [left to right], starting with standing dc, work 5 dc around post of dc, ch 2; rotate piece 180° to 9 o'clock [3 o'clock] position, 5 dc around post of next dc.

Dc (double crochet) Yarn over, insert hook into stitch or space indicated, pull up a loop (3 loops on hook), (yarn over, pull yarn through 2 loops on hook) two times.

Dc2tog (double crochet 2 together) Yarn over, insert hook into indicated stitch or space and pull up a loop, yarn over, pull through 2 loops, yarn over, insert hook into stitch or space indicated and pull up a loop, yarn over and pull through 2 loops, yarn over and pull through all 3 loops on hook.

Dc3tog (double crochet 3 together) Yarn over, insert hook into indicated stitch or space and pull up a loop, yarn over, pull through 2 loops on hook, (yarn over, insert hook into same stitch and pull up a loop, yarn over and pull through 2 loops) two times, yarn over and pull through all 4 loops on hook.

Dtr (double treble) (Yarn over) three times, insert hook into stitch or space indicated and pull up a loop, (yarn over and pull through 2 loops on hook) four times.

Dtr3tog (double treble 3 together) (Yarn over) three times, insert hook into indicated stitch or space and pull up a loop, (yarn over and pull through 2 loops on hook) three times, [[(yarn over) three times, insert hook into stitch or space indicated and pull up a loop, (yarn over and pull through 2 loops on hook) three times] two times, yarn over and pull through 4 loops on hook.

Edc (extended double crochet) Yarn over, insert hook into stitch or space indicated and pull up a loop, yarn over and pull through 1 loop on hook, (yarn over and pull through 2 loops on hook) two times.

Esc (extended single crochet) Insert hook into stitch or space indicated and pull up a loop, yarn over and pull through 1 loop on hook, yarn over and pull through 2 loops on hook.

Flat join Drop loop from hook, insert hook from front to back in next joining point, return dropped loop to hook, pull the dropped loop through the stitch or space; continue working stitches of current motif. See page 37.

FLdc (front loop double crochet) Work 1 double crochet into the front loop only.

FLsc (front loop single crochet) Work 1 single crochet into the front loop only.

FLtr (front loop treble crochet) Work 1 treble crochet into the front loop only.

FLtr2tog (front loop treble 2 stitches together) Work tr2tog into the front loops only.

FLtr3tog (front loop treble 3 stitches together) Work tr3tog into the front loops only.

FPdc (front post double crochet) Yarn over, insert hook from front to back to front around post of stitch indicated and pull up a loop, (yarn over and pull through 2 loops on hook) two times.

FPtr (front post treble crochet) (Yarn over) two times, insert hook from front to back to front around post of stitch indicated and pull up a loop, (yarn over and pull through 2 loops on hook) three times.

Hdc (half double crochet) Yarn over, insert hook into stitch or space indicated and pull up a loop (3 loops on hook), yarn over and pull through all 3 loops on hook.

Joining point The stitch or space on a motif where it is joined to another motif.

Partial dc (partial double crochet) Yarn over, insert hook into stitch or space indicated and pull up a loop, yarn over and pull through 2 loops on hook.

Partial dtr (partial double treble) (Yarn over) three times, insert hook into stitch or space indicated and pull up a loop, (yarn over and pull through 2 loops on hook) three times.

Partial BPdtr (Yarn over) three times, insert hook from back to front to back around post of designated st and pull up a loop, (yarn over and pull through 2 loops on hook) three times.

Partial BPtr (Yarn over) two times, insert hook from back to front to back around post of designated stitch and pull up a loop, (yarn over and pull through 2 loops on hook) two times.

Partial FPdtr (partial front post double treble crochet) (Yarn over) three times, insert hook from front to back to front around post of designated st and pull up a loop, (yarn over and pull through 2 loops on hook) three times.

Partial tr (partial treble) (Yarn over) twice, insert hook into stitch or space indicated and pull up a loop, (yarn over and pull through 2 loops on hook) two times.

Picot-3 Ch 3, slip st in 3rd ch from hook.

Picot-4 Ch 4, slip st in 4th ch from hook.

Popcorn Make 5 dc in 1 stitch or space, drop loop from hook and insert hook from front to back through top of first stitch in the Popcorn, then into dropped loop, yarn over and pull through 2 loops on hook.

Puff Cluster Ch 4, (yarn over, insert hook into 4th ch from hook and pull up a loop) two times, yarn over and pull through all 5 loops on hook.

Rep Repeat.

Reverse sc (Reverse single crochet) See Crab Stitch.

Rnd Round.

RS Right side.

Sc (single crochet) Insert hook into stitch or space indicated and pull up a loop, yarn over and pull through two loops on hook.

Sc join Insert hook into next joining point, yarn over and pull up a loop, yarn over and pull through both loops on hook to complete sc.

Sc2tog (single crochet 2 stitches together) (Insert hook into next st and pull up a loop) two times, yarn over and pull through all 3 loops on hook.

Sc3tog (single crochet 3 stitches together) (Insert hook into next st and pull up a loop) three times, yarn over and pull through all 4 loops on hook.

Slip st (slip stitch) Insert hook into stitch or space indicated, yarn over and pull through both loops on hook.

Slip-st join Insert hook into next joining point, yarn over and pull through joining point and though loop on hook.

Spike sc Insert hook into stitch or space one or more rounds below next stitch and pull up a loop to level of current round, yarn over and pull through both loops on hook.

St(s) Stitch(es).

Standing st (slip st, sc, dc, tr, etc) Beginning with slip knot on hook, work the designated stitch.

Surface chain Holding yarn on wrong side of fabric, insert hook from front to back into next stitch and pull up a loop through fabric and through loop on hook.

Tight Picot-3 Ch 3, insert hook from top to bottom through top and side edge of stitch just made and pull a loop through to form slip stitch.

Tight Picot-4 Ch 4, insert hook from top to bottom through top and side edge of sc just made and pull a loop through to form slip st.

Tog Together.

Tr (treble crochet) (Yarn over) two times, insert hook into stitch or space indicated, pull up a loop (4 loops on hook), (yarn over and pull through 2 loops on hook) three times.

Tr2tog (treble crochet 2 together) (Yarn over) two times, insert hook into indicated stitch or space and pull up a loop, (yarn over, pull through 2 loops) two times, (yarn over) two times, insert hook into stitch or space indicated and pull up a loop, (yarn over, pull through 2 loops) two times, yarn over and pull through all 3 loops on hook.

Tr3tog (treble crochet 3 together) (Yarn over) two times, insert hook into indicated stitch or space and pull up a loop, (yarn over, pull through 2 loops) two times, [(yarn over) two times, insert hook into stitch or space indicated and pull up a loop, (yarn over, pull through 2 loops) two times] two times, yarn over and pull through all 4 loops on hook.

Triple Picot-3 (Ch 3, slip st in 3rd ch from hook) three times, slip stitch in base of first picot.

V-st (Dc, ch 1, dc) in 1 stitch *or* (dc, ch 2, dc) in 1 stitch.

WS Wrong side.

Yarn Sources

Cascade Yarns
www.cascadeyarn.com

Coats & Clark
800-648-1479
www.coatsandclark.com

Karabella Yarns, Inc.
800-550-0898
www.karabellayarns.com

Kollage Yarns
888-829-7758
www.kollageyarns.com

Lion Brand Yarn
800-258-9276
www.lionbrand.com

Louet North America
800-897-6444
www.louet.com

Plymouth Yarn Company, Inc.
215-788-0459
www.plymouthyarn.com

Shelridge Farm
866-291-1566
www.shelridge.com

Universal Yarn, Inc.
877-864-9276
www.universalyarn.com

acknowledgments

DESPITE THE AUTHOR'S NAME ON THE COVER, any book is a collaboration. Although it's impossible to give enough credit where it's due, let me try. Karen Manthey, tech editor and illustrator par excellence, has the patience of a saint and the even temper to match; I'm so fortunate she worked on this book. My eternal thanks to everyone at Storey who helped, including Pam Thompson, who took on the job of Author- and Manuscript-Wrangler and turned this into a real book; Carolyn Eckert, for her color sense and doing so much more than just fitting it all in; Gwen Steege, whose calm encouragement never flags; Alethea Morrison, Mars Vilaubi, and Mark Donne, for not laughing at me at the video shoot; Ilona Sherratt, for shepherding all the diagrams into the pages; Alee Marsh, who makes me feel like I'm the only author she has to promote; and the marketing and sales staff, for getting the book to an audience. Thanks to John Polak, for allowing us into his amazing studio, taking beautiful pictures, and maintaining his patience throughout; and Jo Chattman, for making the projects come to life in her stylish photographs.

Others are also responsible and due my thanks, including my friends Barbara Kreuter, whose many talents may be underappreciated by everyone but me, and Myra Wood, for sharing her expertise and making me look good; test stitchers Brenda Beck, Kristy Lucas, and Robyn Riley; Don and Buffy Taylor, whose beautiful Shelridge Farms DK-weight wool was used in all the sample motifs. The colors of this yarn made it oh-so-difficult for me to stop playing (er, stitching) long enough to write actual words.

Thanks also to Greg Pullen, who suggested "transversal" as a search term; and Roy Dotrice, George Guidell, John Rubenstein, Scott Brick, and the authors whose words they narrate. I couldn't stitch a book's worth of motifs without you.

And finally, trite-but-true, I couldn't do this without the complete support of my family. Bill, it's miraculous how you tolerate my deadlines with their requisite mess and single-mindedness, while working full-time and cheerfully keeping me fed. Thank you with all my heart. Meg, I'm so proud of the talented and skilled young woman you are! No one could ask for a better daughter and assistant. Charles, you keep me thinking and up-to-date on everything that matters.

index

Page references in *italic* indicate photos or illustrations.

The Edie Eckman Crochet Library

Edie Eckman has been the go-to crochet resource since she first wrote *The Crochet Answer Book*. If you don't already own Edie's complete crochet library, you're missing out on hundreds of motifs to play with and the tips, tricks, and techniques Edie loves to share with her readers!

The Crochet Answer Book
320 pages. Flexibind.
ISBN 978-1-58017-598-2.

No matter how experienced a crocheter you are, sticky questions arise with each new project. Here are all your questions, followed by reassuring answers to set every problem right. With advice on everything from counting stitches to blocking and joining, this handy little resource always comes through in a crisis.

Around the Corner Crochet Borders
320 pages. Paper.
ISBN 978-1-60342-538-4.

A crochet border is the perfect finishing touch on the edges of any fiber project. Creating one, however, often requires turning a corner and shaping the edging around a 90-degree angle. This is rarely simple, and most edging patterns don't include specific instructions for turning the corner. Edie Eckman comes to the rescue with this collection of 150 colorful crochet frames that do supply these instructions. Color photographs let you see the details up close. Easy, marvelous crochet borders are just around the corner!

Beyond the Square Crochet Motifs
208 pages. Hardcover with concealed wire-o.
ISBN 978-1-60342-039-6.

Crochet motifs can be circles, stars, triangles, hexagons, and much more. Here are 144 designs of every size and shape, guaranteed to keep you happy for years as you experiment with color combinations, different sizes, and endless uses for the finished motif.